NEWFOUNDLAND

St. John's

Cow Head

QUEBEC

Gaspé

Lac St-Jean

Charlottetown

P.E.I.

NEW
BRUNSWICK

Kapuskasing

Quebec

Fredericton

NOVA
SCOTIA

Montréal

MAINE

Halifax

Ottawa

Freeport

Port Joli

Sault Ste. Marie

VERMONT

NEW
HAMPSHIRE

Toronto

MICHIGAN

NEW YORK

MASSACHUSETTS

CONN.

R.I.

PENNSYLVANIA

TARIO

A D A

N

SCALE

0    100    200    300 mi

0   100  200  300  400  500 km

# THE CANADA TRIP

OTHER BOOKS BY CHARLES GORDON

*How to Be Not Too Bad*
*At the Cottage*
*The Governor General's Bunny Hop*

# THE CANADA TRIP

Charles Gordon

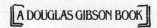
A DOUGLAS GIBSON BOOK

M&S

*For the Business Manager. Where next?*

**Canadian Cataloguing in Publication Data**

Gordon, Charles, 1940–
    The Canada trip

ISBN 0-7710-3389-3

1. Gordon, Charles, 1940–     – Journeys – Canada – Humour.
2. Canada – Description and travel – Humour.   I. Title.

PS8563.O8354C3   1997     917.104´648´0207     C97-930189-0
PR9199.3.G67C3   1997

Typesetting by M&S, Toronto
Maps by Tom Sankey
Printed and bound in Canada

"The Cranberry Tree" by Enid Delgatty Rutland, originally published in *Where the Highway Ends, Stories and Rhythms of Flin Flon* (Brian Kinsley, ed., Ottawa: Flintoba Enterprises, 1995), appears by kind permission of the publisher.
Excerpts from *Sarah Binks* by Paul Hiebert are taken from the New Canadian Library edition and appear courtesy of the Binks Family.

The publishers acknowledge the support of the Canada Council and the Ontario Arts Council for their publishing program.

A Douglas Gibson Book

McClelland & Stewart Inc.
*The Canadian Publishers*
481 University Avenue
Toronto, Ontario
M5G 2E9

1 2 3 4 5    01 00 99 98 97

# CONTENTS

# INTRODUCTION

---

## 15,539 Miles of Good Road

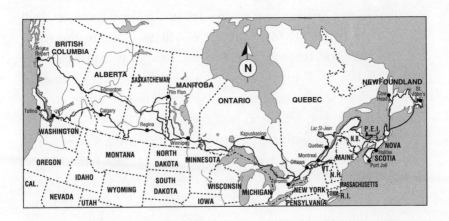

We are back from three months on the highways of Canada, driving 24,863 kilometres, which is 15,539 miles to you old-timers. We saw three moose, five whales, a bear, many chipmunks, many people taking photographs of chipmunks, two antelope, a caribou, six rabbits, a statue of a giant goose, a statue of a giant sheep, three coyotes, a deer, elk in the woods, elk in parking lots, a statue of a giant lobster, a seal, two baseball games, a big-horned sheep, two jazz festivals, a pretty bad hot-hamburger sandwich, two icebergs, three luxury hotels, eleven roadside motels, fourteen bed-and-breakfasts, four resorts, 127 highways, two oceans, two casinos, thirteen ferries, and a submarine.

We can tell you about the Château Lake Louise and the Prestige Motel. We studied the continental reach of poutine, the Persian and the Denver sandwich. We visited the homes of Anne of Green Gables, Margaret Laurence, Ralph Connor, Louis Riel, Paddle-to-the-Sea, Josiah Flintabbatey Flonatin, Husky the Muskie, and the Regina Manifesto. We saw hundreds of Germans and Japanese, dozens of Americans and Brits, and some Canadians. We visited nine provincial legislatures, six art galleries, and one public library. We saw enough of Canada to realize there are ten more books in the parts we missed.

You could write one of them. In five years, a great chunk of the population of Canada, the leading edge of the Baby Boomers, will take early retirement. Many of them will also take to the road. Those with good sense will take to the road in Canada. In some ways, this is a book for them – not a guidebook, but a record of how it feels to see the country. Maybe it will inspire others to start their own journeys. I want to read their books.

This one began with a little trip in the late winter, sort of a limbering-up exercise to get ready for the big one that would begin in June. The little trip took us from Ottawa to Toronto to North Hatley, Quebec and back to Ottawa. While we were doing it, we thought about the big trip to come. It was in North Hatley over a candlelight dinner at Manoir Hovey, that Nancy asked:

"What do you want me to do?"

We already knew that she was coming along; we had both arranged leaves from our respective jobs. Now we had to decide her role. I would be writing and trying to find huge Canadian insights and to spot moose beside the road. I would be trying to avoid colourful characters, figuring they've all been done in four-minute documentaries on the TV news. Would she, my wife of thirty-one years, get stuck with all the driving? Or when I was driving, would she have to write down all the witty things I said, if any? She was uneasy. We had driven long distances before – Ottawa to Kenora several times – but never anything like this.

"You could be the business manager," I said.

This didn't surprise her. It didn't take thirty-one years for Nancy to figure out that the smaller details of existence, such things as do we have any money and is there a place to stay tonight, are among the areas in which I don't excel. So she would take charge of those areas and I would try to find some other areas to excel in, such as ending sentences with prepositions.

"This could be good," I said. "In the book I could call you The Business Manager. You know how writers like to create characters and give them clever names."

"No," she said.

Oh well. Maybe I could come up with a clever name for myself. Norman Mailer used to do that. In *The Armies of the Night*, he was Aquarius. Dalton Camp, in a very fine book, *Points of Departure*, actually got away with calling himself The Varlet. But I couldn't think of anything offhand. In thirty-some years of daily journalism I had got out of the habit of even using "I." This was all going to take some getting used to. Maybe I could give the car a funny name.

The Eastern Townships is a good place to contemplate a drive across the country. It is a beautiful part of the world, of course, and, if not a microcosm of Canada, at least a place where many of the important elements interact. It is in Quebec, but the English are here, speaking their language. More and more of them speak French, however, and it is now a shock to hear a clerk in a store say to a customer: "I'm sorry, I don't speak French." I have heard that said in North Hatley and it probably wouldn't have been any shock at all twenty years ago.

One of the reasons the idea of travelling was so appealing is that we, like many Canadians, have huge gaps in our knowledge of the country and its geography. The extended Gordon family cottage at Lake of the Woods is largely to blame. Like many Canadians, we put all our vacation time into the cottage, time that might otherwise be spent getting to know the rest of the country.

Of course, even given the time, Canada is not an easy country
to get to know. Transcontinental train travel has all but disappeared.
Airlines make it cheaper to fly to London or Miami than to
Winnipeg or Halifax. The climate doesn't help matters. Desperate
to get someplace warm in the winter, many Canadians blow the
family travel budget on Florida or Phoenix or Hawaii, depending
upon which part of our country they inhabit. Many factors con-
spire to keep Canadians from knowing Canada.

They want to know it, though. This much was clear from our
friends' advance reactions to the trip. They were excited by the idea,
and had many recommendations. They wanted us to go places –
sometimes places they happened to like, often to their home towns,
the places they grew up. Always, they said: "How lucky you are!" It
was odd to hear that in this time of national grouchiness, this time
when Canadians are supposed to be so mad at Canada, so fed up, so
annoyed at all the talk about Canada. But in fact Canadians love the
land, love the places in it. They love to think about the places they
would go if they had the chance. If this book has a political side, it
is about the irony of a country so quarrelsome it threatens to break
apart, yet so loved by its inhabitants that they can think of nothing
they'd sooner do than travel it coast to coast.

We had to visit Gull Lake. We had to see Smooth Rock Falls.
The Saguenay was a must. A friend had a friend in Gimli. Another
friend knew of some strange doings on the outskirts of Lethbridge.
Someone in the Toyota service department knew of a restaurant in
Vancouver where Margaret Trudeau goes. There was a funny guy in
Quebec City. There was a road hardly anyone travels in northwest-
ern Newfoundland. There was an island in Nova Scotia. There was
a highway into southern B.C. that not enough people appreciated.

Then there were the places that had special meaning for us and
our families. My grandfather, who was both the minister Charles
W. Gordon and the novelist Ralph Connor, grew up in Glengarry
County near Ottawa. He preached in the Rockies, at Banff and
Canmore, then raised his family in Winnipeg, where Nancy's

mother was also born. My parents lived mostly in the United States and overseas when my sister, Alison, and I were growing up, but also in Edmonton. Nancy's father was raised on a dairy farm north of Belleville, Ontario, in Presbyterian, Tory, Orange Lodge country. He later moved to Fort William, now part of Thunder Bay, where Nancy and her sister, Mary, were brought up. We spent the first ten years of our marriage in Brandon, Manitoba, where I got my first newspaper job and Nancy taught at Brandon College. Our two children, both now grown and trying to make a living as actors, were born there.

There were those places. And then there were the places we had never seen. And the places we have passed along the highway and said, "We should drop in there some day, when we have the time." Now we had the time.

Certain assumptions went with us, the emotional baggage of the trip. We were not going to come away from this trip disliking Canada. I was born in the United States, a dual citizen in the days when you had to choose at twenty-one. I never regretted choosing Canada. Both of us have travelled outside the country. We always return thinking we live in the best country in the world, a place where the values are right, where things work — everything from the telephone system to the political system. It is relative, of course. Things could be better. But they could be a lot worse.

Another part of the emotional baggage was the feeling that the country has been analysed to death. I was not going out there to ask whither Canada. I might ask whither the Men's room or whither the ferry to Manitoulin Island, but that would be about it. I would try to avoid being journalistic. I was tired of that too, of arriving in a city and trying to be an expert on it for the next day's paper. It was a relief not to have to write "This town of 11,726 is of two minds today" and other staples of the trade.

This was a difficult habit to break. The temptation is to try to understand a place quickly, then analyse it and explain it. But you can't do it in a couple of days and the admission that you can't is liberating. I would write, and think, as a traveller, not a journalist. The object would be to describe what I saw, rather than to draw conclusions.

Looking at the maps and figuring out the time allotted – three months – it was easy to see that we would miss a lot. For a start, we would miss the Territories. We would spend hours in places where we should spend days, days in places where we should spend weeks. And when we got back people would say "How could you miss Red Deer?" "How could you miss Niagara-on-the-Lake?" "How could you go to B.C. and not see the Queen Charlottes?"

The only response is that no one can do it all and I want to read your book.

We tried not to over-plan. There were people we wanted to see and I wrote to them. We realized quickly that simply driving coast to coast, one-way, in the traditional manner, would leave too much unseen. Instead we would do a loop, driving east one way, back to Ottawa another. We would go west by what used to be called the Canadian Pacific route, when there was one: the north shore of Lake Superior, Kenora, Winnipeg, Regina, Calgary, Vancouver. We would come back what used to be called the Canadian National route, when there was one: Edmonton, Saskatoon, Cochrane, North Bay. And we would leave room to depart from the plan if the situation called for it.

The Trans-Canada Highway would not be avoided completely – in some parts of Canada it is the only way from Point A to Point B and in some parts of Canada it is also the prettiest – but we would take smaller highways wherever possible. Expressways would be avoided except where we felt the need to take one. There was nothing dogmatic about this route.

We had an expense advance and a rough budget, which would allow us to live more or less normally. We would stay in roadside motels, in bed-and-breakfasts. Occasionally we would break the bank and try a luxury hotel if we could convince ourselves that the book demanded it. If a friend or relative offered lodging, we would take it. We lacked the expertise, the experience, the equipment, and the inclination to camp.

These were the overall guidelines we had with us when we left Ottawa on June 3. We tried to avoid having deadlines but there were a couple of unavoidable ones: I wanted to write about base-ball and jazz in Montreal, so we had to be there at a time when the jazz festival was on and the Expos were in town. Our son, John, was doing a one-man show at the Toronto Fringe Festival, so we wanted to be in Toronto for that. And the trip had to be over in time to allow me to write before my leave of absence from the *Ottawa Citizen* was up. Other deadlines would emerge as we went on – the necessity of making reservations on certain ferries, the fact that a friend we wanted to see would be out of town except a week from Wednesday. That sort of thing. Otherwise, we would just drive along, stopping each night when we felt like it. As the summer wore on, we began sharing the road with more and more people and started to feel the need to phone ahead for accommodations. Later still, as we got away from the main tourist track, we were able to revert to the pleasurable adhockishness of the early part of the trip.

Two weeks into the trip, when we had reached St. John's, Newfoundland, my mother became desperately ill. We flew back to Ottawa, where she died, at eighty-five, four days after we returned. She had worked, in her professional life, in book pub-lishing in the United States, and had always been tickled that her two children, Alison and I, wound up as writers. Quite inadver-tently, she too had been a traveller, following my globe-trotting father, King Gordon, around, setting up households in places like Tokyo, Cairo, and Rome, often singlehandedly while my father's work with the United Nations took him elsewhere. It could not have been fun for her but she helped to make it fun for us. We put together a memorial service that I hope reflected her life and particularly her powerful sense of humour. After that, there was nothing to do but go back to St. John's, pick up the car and start moving again. Writing and travelling was a good way to honour her memory. Also the only way available. It was therapeutic to be able to do that. But there was an unreality about it that hit me weeks later as I drove down Carling Avenue on our way through Ottawa to the West. "I'll just drop in and tell her how the trip is going," I thought. Nancy had the same thought in Edmonton, when we saw the house where she lived in the sixties. "I'll drop a postcard to Ruth and tell her we saw it."

Books about trips across the country are nothing new, of course. People have walked and bicycled and canoed and flown and taken the last train and probably the first one too. Among the many books that have been done on the subject are two I looked at by people who drove. One was Edward McCourt, an English professor at the University of Saskatchewan and a prolific writer. His book, *The Road Across Canada*, published in 1965, was about a trip he and his wife took along the entire length of the Trans-Canada Highway, 5,000 miles, from St. John's to Victoria in 1963, just after the road had officially been opened in 1962. McCourt's book is insightful and funny and sometimes grumpy. The Trans-Canada may have been officially opened, but someone had neglected to pave the Newfoundland part of it. McCourt was also limited, as he was acutely aware, by the necessity of sticking to the Trans-Canada, which frequently takes the path of least resistance – in other words, the path away from the interesting landscapes, the mountains and the rivers, the small towns. *The Road Across Canada* is full of wistful references to the sights he could be seeing if only he could get off the highway. Occasionally, as in a side trip into Saskatchewan's Cypress Hills, he simply throws off the traces and bolts.

"To travel the Trans-Canada Highway for its full length," McCourt wrote, "is an exhilarating and exhausting experience best enjoyed, as most travel on the North American continent is, in the early spring or fall when the weather is temperate, the black flies and mosquitoes quiescent, and the traffic light."

The strangest book I encountered was by an Englishman, J. S. Gowland, who travelled across the country by himself in 1956. Somehow he managed to skip Newfoundland and Prince Edward Island, but he did go up the Alaska Highway to Alaska, the total distance covered being 12,500 miles. Gowland's book, called *Return to Canada*, was published in 1957 by the T. Werner Laurie company of London. In it, he described how he and his 1955 Austin A50 went right across the country on a total budget of three hundred dollars. He would have lasted about two days with us at that rate, but he seemed to be an extremely skilful freeloader, parking in farmyards, cadging meals, and somehow managing to get new tires and free servicing for his vehicle, which he called Judy.

Mr. Gowland, as he is called in his publisher's blurbs, had been, at some unspecified time before the Second World War, a forest ranger in the Rockies, and had written two previous books about that experience, in which he had changed the names of all the people and towns and even rivers. Thus Sikanaska, of *Sikanaska Trail*, was really Kananaskis, as he reveals, throwing caution to the winds. Mr. Gowland is pushing sixty when he undertakes his trip, but is fearless, quite content to set off over closed roads, pushing Judy through the mud.

He is also a student of the road, fond of making comparisons between driving in Canada and driving back home. "People do not wander across the road as they do in Britain; there are no bicycles, no children running in the road and, last but by no means least, there are *no dogs* hareing into the traffic. All of which make it much easier to concentrate on the business of driving and on the other traffic."

Despite having been written only forty years ago, there is a wonderfully archaic sound to Gowland's English, to his presumptions and to his style of life on the road. "I collected my mail in Cochrane," he writes at one point, "and left some laundry with a gentleman rejoicing in the name of Wong Lee, plus instructions to send it ahead to Calgary, Alberta."

We have progressed so far that we can no longer do such things. On the other hand, we no longer need to. Here is how far we have come: Four days before we were to leave Ottawa, a fax machine began phoning my house. Beginning in the early afternoon and continuing for a couple of hours, it would phone every three minutes. Someone had put a fax on the machine and set it to redial automatically and then left to do something. I don't have a fax machine. Every three minutes I would pick up the phone and hear beeps and whistles and hang up. I immediately thought of a friend with a fax and a history of inaccurate speed-dialling. I called him and he denied everything. Eventually the faxing stopped.

The next morning about 10:00 a.m., it began again. This time I did what any fourteen-year-old would have done the first time: I hit *69 to find out the number that had called me. A voice gave me the number, an unfamiliar one, and I dialled it. It turned out to be Ottawa City Hall that was faxing me. Before I could register my complaint, I had to listen to two or three minutes of a recorded voice telling me what buttons to press for what services. Finally, I found out I could get an operator by pressing 0. I did and explained my problem. A fax machine was bothering me, but the fax machine had the general city hall number. Was there any way of letting people know I wasn't a fax machine? The operator was nice but pessimistic (and not terribly surprised either). She said there were ten fax machines in the building. I left my name and number and she said she would try her best.

Two minutes later the fax phoned me again. This time I hit *69 and then 1, to be connected directly to the number that had called me. The recorded voice told me that the call could not be completed in this manner. It was time to get out of Ottawa.

On a sunny Monday we did, the words of Mr. Gowland ringing in my ears: "Canada's immensity can be thoroughly appreciated only by crossing its length and breadth, mile by mile, in a vehicle under your own control."

## Getting Quebec Over With

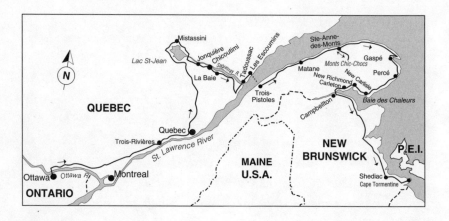

We cross the Quebec border at 11:00 a.m. on Monday morning, June 3, feeling momentous. To add to the momentousness, we have been to the bank to get those cards you put into the machine and the money comes out. We have never had them before. I was hoping for something Leacockian in the experience of getting a card from the bank. But no dice, as they say in the banking world. The banks are professional and user-friendly and Leacock himself, had he entered the Bank of Commerce on Sparks Street in Ottawa today to deposit his fifty-six dollars, might have come out with no story material at all.

We entered our secret codes into a secret code machine, then into the money machine, the money machine gave us money, and we were on our way, headed for Quebec City. To heighten the spirit of adventure we skip the usual route, the 417 on the Ontario side, because we have done it so many times before. It is flat and boring. Also, the 417 becomes the 40 at Montreal, a horror expressway through the city. It is a toss-up whether the 40 across Montreal is worse than the 401 across Toronto. Each is full of drivers who treat it with the contempt born of familiarity. Both give you that claustrophobic what-if-I-have-a-flat-tire feeling. The 40 probably wins in the horror sweepstakes because the people drive on it as if it were a lake, swooping from side to side.

The fact that some of its major exits are to the left doesn't help.

If I don't know what the trip is about yet, I do know that it is not about finding the quickest way to get to B from A, Quebec City from Ottawa. And while we are not going to be dogmatic about avoiding expressways, why would anyone take them if they had the time not to? What if we didn't have to get somewhere in a hurry, we are always asking ourselves when we drive, what roads would we take, what detours would we choose? Well. Here we are. We have the time. So we take 148, a much-travelled two-lane job that goes through Gatineau, Thurso, Papineauville, and Montebello. The drive is not memorable, but nice because it is the first day. And distinct. Even close to Ottawa, the towns, the houses, and the stores have a different architecture. Much of the first part of the drive is along the Ottawa River, which is in flood and looks the way Huck Finn's Mississippi might have.

If you live in Ottawa you are going to know Quebec a bit – particularly West Quebec, which is right across the river, and Montreal, which is only two hours away. You are also going to hear quite a bit of French, in and around the capital. But unless you drive a bus, work in a downtown store or a federal government department, you won't use the French you have and it will get rusty. That's what's making us a bit apprehensive about this part of the trip. Some years ago, the newspaper I work for, the *Ottawa Citizen*, offered its employees French courses through a local community college and I took a couple of years' worth. If I'd taken what I learned somewhere and used it, my French could have been okay. I know lots of words. But I didn't. I can follow hockey and baseball on the radio and for a time I, like an impressively large number of English-speakers in the late seventies, regularly tuned in to Friday night late movies on a Hull station, in which naked Scandinavians did one thing or another. As a result of this experience I was able to create for another book a wholly fictional character whose entire French vocabulary was derived from such activity; in the attempt to maintain his bilingualism bonus he would participate in meetings with such French-language utterances as "The sight of your proud breasts makes me feel like a mighty reindeer." Nancy, although she is less adept at such nuances, has taken courses more recently than I, and once spent three weeks in Jonquière on an immersion program.

We should know lots of French, but what we know diminished in disuse. We are like piano students who know all the scales but have never performed in public. Now we will be going to places where our inadequate French will have to be adequate. As well-intentioned Canadians, we can't just bellow loudly in English and expect satisfaction. As curious travellers we can't just go to the parts of Quebec – downtown Montreal, the Eastern Townships – where English is spoken. That leaves the course we have adopted: boldly go where no English is spoken – the Saguenay, the Gaspé – speak the best French we can, and hope for the best. "Maybe," I said to a bilingual friend, "they'll hear my French and answer in English."

"Probably they won't," he replied.

We stop for a picnic lunch at a roadside park near Lachute. It has bathrooms and picnic tables and a lame excuse for a river. Also flies and mosquitoes and a couple of fat people sunbathing. It is not the best roadside place we have ever seen, but it gives us a chance to try out the colourful picnic equipment we bought for the trip. The stuff works fine and the lunch is nice. We see our first wildlife, a chipmunk. I enter it in my notebook.

The determination to avoid Montreal leads us into construction at St-Jérôme, where we sit for half an hour with a view of the Taverne C Sexe C, open 13 to 3, with danseuses nues and Jours 2 pour 1 special draft. The enjoyment of Quebec signs (SuperGaz is another one I like) is not enough to promote contentment in all of our linemates. Some stand beside their cars and yell at the flagperson. I am resolved, on this momentous and sunny day, to remain Type B and think pleasant thoughts. Isn't it nice, I think, that so many people are working?

At Berthierville, now safely past Montreal, we get on the hated 40 to bypass Trois-Rivières. Driving through towns is great, in general; there is more of a feeling of driving *in* an area rather than *past* it. Still, every once in a while you need to get into cruise control and boot it a little.

But only so far. The map tells us that 138 goes closer to the St. Lawrence River. So we get off the 40 at La Perade and sure enough we get close and it is a great sight. A mile wide and surrounded by gentle farmland, it is as A. Y. Jackson drew it when he illustrated a book on the St. Lawrence for the Rivers of America series, for which my mother was art editor in 1942. We see chicken farms (but miss the tobacco farms around Lanoraie; it is instructive to read the guidebooks after we have stopped for the day and find out how much we didn't see).

The big psychological hurdle is to get over being performance-oriented. I had thought that without deadlines, without specific goals, we would be able to jump off the road and see all the interesting things that we would normally skip. But deadlines are self-imposed. We have decided we want to be in Quebec City for dinner.

We get massively lost on the way in because we don't really know what street we are looking for. Since I am driving and I am male, I don't stop to ask anyone. How could you ask anyone in Quebec City where the Château Frontenac is? The last time I was in Quebec was twenty-five years ago, roughly. I think at that time the Château Frontenac *was* the skyline and you could aim for it. Not now.

But we get there, change, walk out to the boardwalk to admire the view, then down the long stairs, with the other tourists, to Lower Town. We walk all the streets of Lower Town, and look at every restaurant before settling on the Restaurant Sous-le-Fort, which is small and reasonably priced and the proprietor speaks enough French to us and lets us speak enough to him to give us the feeling that we are trying. The more intricate ordering decisions are made in English.

It is a nice night – cloudy but warm and not windy and with no bugs. We sit outside and watch the people going by, deciding that teenage Quebeckers are indistinct from Americans, except that Americans are louder. When people dress up in tourist garb, unexplained things happen. Why do older men put on royal-blue pants and baseball caps just because they are in somebody else's town?

For two dollars, we take the Funicular back up the hill, knocked out by the setting and the way the city sits in it. Not far from here, no doubt, is an ugly city full of glass buildings and parking garages. But right here it couldn't be lovelier. Somebody had the good sense, back when good sense was hard to find and the word "environmentalist" had not been invented, to refrain from knocking down those old buildings to put up better ones.

The Château Frontenac is very expensive, but charming and grand. We will hit a few of the big railway hotels (as they used to be called when there were railways), to help balance out the roadside motels and bed-and-breakfasts. Besides, this is the first day and the hotel has to be momentous.

The hotel proves itself when we leave a plastic bag containing, among other things, Gordon's gin, sitting in the lobby. It is very difficult, even on the first day, for us to travel elegantly. In our travels there are always plastic bags resting in the lobby, sometimes even joined by green garbage bags full of dirty clothes. When we discover our grievous error, Nancy goes downstairs and finds that the hotel staff has it under wraps for us.

The lobby is great for strolling, much like the Château Laurier's in Ottawa, although without so many corners to turn. Nancy finds herself mistaken for an American when she uses English to buy stamps in a hotel shop. She is irritated, but at herself. In Quebec City, where the tourist trade is big and the merchants are obliging, it is too easy to get away with speaking English. Another of the things encountered in the lobby is a gift store in which mementoes of the hotel's railway past are for sale. I am mildly irritated by this: since the CPR couldn't wait to get out of the railway business, it has a lot of nerve now waxing commercially nostalgic about it. Still, it is the first day.

## Friends of the Plains of Abraham

It is raining fairly hard when we rise, Tuesday morning at 7:30, but there are things to see before we hit the road again. In two hours, you can walk along the Terrasse Dufferin, to the Promenade des Gouverneurs, up 310 stairs to the Plains of Abraham, around the Plains of Abraham, back down the stairs and to the hotel. Even in the rain it is an interesting, pretty, and even funny walk.

The terrasse is a boardwalk and you can feel elegant, even in your Ottawa Lynx baseball cap, walking it. It hangs high above the Lower Town and overlooks the river, two hundred feet below, and the ships. The Promenade des Gouverneurs was officially opened on September 9, 1960, by that great friend of Quebec, John Diefenbaker, two years away from losing most of his Quebec seats. At the Plains of Abraham there is a gazebo/lookout kind of thing where a guide is explaining the battle in French to the tourists. We English avert our ears. A marker nearby says: "The English victory was to make a decisive change in the history of the colony."

The guides and the markers tell the story of Wolfe and his men somehow scaling the cliffs and surprising Montcalm's forces. The cliffs look unscalable, particularly for guys in red coats and white spats carrying heavy muskets. Looking over them we watch the traffic driving alongside the river, on the way to work.

The Plains are so politically symbolic that we wince when we see a poster in a kiosk, inviting people, in French, to become "friends of the Plains of Abraham." In fact the Plains are a geographic fact of life in Quebec City, no more, no less, with soccer fields and football goalposts and signs showing some of the major events in its history, such as the landing of Lindbergh in 1928. The same kiosk is announcing a 10k Plains of Abraham jog.

As scenery, rather than symbol, the Plains is a great walk. To the north and east are highrise buildings, the combination of park and skyline reminiscent of Green Park in London and Park Lane. Beside the paths are lilac bushes and apple trees and humble dandelions.

Also humble is the spot where Wolfe was wounded, a small granite marker partly covered by a rose bush. But it is eloquent: "Here, on the very eve of victory, Wolfe received his mortal wound." That was September 13, 1759, of course. The main Wolfe statue, elsewhere in the park, is sillier and grander, a helmet and sword way up in the air. Nearby is the well where he was carried from the first marker, to die.

I like the fact that the Plains are named not after any momentous person but after Abraham Martin, a river pilot, who farmed some acres here around 1620, before they became famous acres. That is a nice, modest Canadian touch. Another nice touch, tinged with goofiness, is that the first prominent statue we encountered is that of Joan of Arc, burned at the stake by the English, as the plaque puts it, which was given to Quebec City by an American in the 1930s. Quebec City kept it, and put a sunken garden around it.

The best sign of the day is at the top of Wolfe's unscalable cliff:

DANGER, CLIFF
KEEP BACK

After only one wrong turn we are out of the city by 1:00 p.m. Away from the wall of the Old City, away from the river, Quebec City is like other cities, a tangle of traffic and expressways, its suburbs looking like suburbs. The rain continues as we head for Chicoutimi.

Why Chicoutimi? Because we want to get to the Saguenay and it looks like a good idea, on the map, to drive through Parc Jacques Cartier and Réserve des Laurentides, right to Chicoutimi. No towns, no people, and the promise of driving through a landscape we know nothing about.

Heading straight north, there is the Rivière Jaune, then the beginning of hills, not high but steep and close together, with clouds hanging in them. We climb constantly, into the Shield, dark pines against the light green of new growth. We climb from 323 metres up to 801, now seeing the odd patch of snow in the hills. Just this much farther north, winter can last another month and a half longer. Yesterday we had a very Canadian discussion, kicking ourselves for not bringing gloves and long underwear in June.

There is a fork in the road. If we stay on 175, straight ahead, we go to Chicoutimi. Left on 169 leads to Lac St-Jean. Lac St-Jean is where everybody votes separatist and nobody speaks English and we are making good time and what is this trip about but being spontaneous, right? – so left we go. Chicoutimi will come later, after we have driven around Lac St-Jean. Why drive all the way around it? It seems to be the old performance orientation creeping in again, the same thing that caused us to walk all the way around the Plains of Abraham. If it's there, we have to go all the way around it. If it's not round, then we'll go to the end of it.

Downward grades begin, marked by signs – 10 per cent, then 12 per cent, then the first highway signs warning of moose. This is almost as exciting as if there were moose, which there aren't. We cross the fast Chicoutimi River, see no signs of habitation, larger hills and deeper valleys. To see how remote this is, I run the SCAN function on the FM radio. It produces Vicki Gabereau, in English, on the CBC from Vancouver.

The decision to take this route is suddenly justified when we come over the top of a hill and, all of a sudden, fields stretch out before us, then church steeples, villages, and beyond that the lake. Nothing could be more dramatic and surprising than to find this big patch of farmland in the middle of the Canadian wilderness.

We take an expensive little detour to Val-Jalbert, a reconstructed turn-of-the-century village originally set up for pulp-mill workers. Admission is $17.00 which includes a bus ride around the surprisingly large town. The ride ends at an impressively high and powerful waterfall on the Ouiatchouan River. There is a téléphérique to the top, for another $7.50, but worth it for the ride and the view, over the falls and down the river and over the fields to Lac St-Jean. When you ride one of these things, like the Funicular in Quebec City, somebody closes you in, presses the button, and there you are, alone with the altitude and your thoughts, one of them being that if anything goes wrong at least the operator won't get hurt. At the top, there is a trail, constructed of treated wood, into the woods. So much of our day, beginning at Terrasse Dufferin, has been spent walking on wood.

We drive through Desbiens, home of the Musée du Motoneige. I decide I will visit a museum of snowmobiles when they are obsolete. I look forward to the Musée du Jetski. The north side of the lake is disappointing, less agricultural and a bit scrubby, saved by a great river at Mistassini, the Mistassibi River. We see the Saguenay, for the first time, coming out of Lac St-Jean. At a gas station in Alma, our meagre French proves temporarily inadequate. We had already figured out that stopping at a self-serve meant never having to say fill-'er-up in French. But neither of us has the slightest idea what to say when the credit card machine refuses to recognize Nancy's VISA. I am on the verge of the last refuge of unilingual scoundrels, namely talking loudly in English with an exaggerated American accent, when my credit card, which has the same number, somehow works. Meanwhile, I think I detect smirking as I recite my licence-plate number, forgetting momentarily how you say the letter J in French.

It is a setback and it doesn't help that the next town encountered is Jonquière, where Nancy spent some largely unpleasant weeks in 1991. She stayed with a woman who served dinner promptly at five, watched game shows on television, and whose conversational style varied greatly from that of the teacher. As the days wore on, Nancy spent more and more time in the swimming pool at the college where no language of any sort was required. This made her late for dinner. As we approach the town I want her to show me some of the places where she didn't learn French, but the road, Highway 170, doesn't go into Jonquière. "We must be bypassing the town, which is just as well," she says.

Although it is still light, it is late and we bypass Chicoutimi, ending up at La Baie, where we find a motel overlooking the Saguenay. I am now glad that I am not the business manager, as Nancy, the experienced Quebec hand, negotiates a room. It has an impressive view of the town reflected in the waters of Baie des Ha! Ha! and a restaurant that produces a good steak. The waitress is friendly and we feel better about our French, so much better that Nancy even manages to say: "Would you mind if we put our freezer pack in your freezer until the morning?" which is hard enough in English. Friendliness makes all the difference. Tomorrow, the Saguenay. I like the idea of waking up to a new landscape.

### Saguenay: The Top Ten Belvedere List Begins

The Saguenay is misted over as we hit the road at 9:05 a.m. After twenty minutes we pass a tiny lake on the right, whose name I forget to write down. It is notable for three features: (1) an immaculately manicured lawn, with retaining stone wall at the shore; (2) a shack; (3) a miniature chapel with the Virgin Mary, in the colour known as Virgin Mary blue.

The road becomes more hilly as we move away from the river, then steep, with signs recommending 45 km/h on some of the curves. But it is a good road, with passing lanes, the best of all driving worlds: The four-lane divided highway removes you too much from the scenery and is usually designed to avoid the best of it anyway; the two-lane highway puts you behind trucks and trailers; but a passing lane gets you around them easily if you are not too impatient.

Which we are not. It doesn't look like we have too far to go today. Today's goal is simply to get across the St. Lawrence and be ready for the Gaspé tomorrow. There are ferries in two places and we don't know when they go. This turns out to be a good thing for us, since it puts us in no hurry, enabling us to discover the first nominee for the Top Ten Belvedere List.

The name of the list honours a friend from Saskatchewan whose grasp of Canada's other official language is even more tenuous than ours. One day in the Gatineau Park we were having a discussion about the scenic lookouts the park features. He said: "I kind of like the Belvedere Lookout." Someone then pointed out to him that a belvedere *was* a lookout, the French word for it, in fact. Now a great view has become a belvedere to us. Since most roadside scenic lookouts are also equipped with toilet facilities, the notion of looking for a belvedere can take on an added and somewhat more urgent meaning.

To reach Belvedere Ainse-de-Tabatière, to which we were alerted by one of our many guidebooks, you leave the highway and drive through the pretty agricultural village of L'Anse Saint-Jean, follow some dirt roads over a covered bridge and up a washboard hill, park the car, endure a swarm of flies and walk along a narrow path. Once there, you find some big Quebec Hydro towers and some signboards with propaganda about the fine environmental work Hydro is doing. You also find, looking north and then east, two dramatic vistas of the Saguenay as it turns. The river runs through steep hills, covered with spruce. We are 160 metres up at this point. The river, we are informed, is 1.6 kilometres across. Our location, as best we can figure it, is east of Cap Éternité and north of L'Anse Saint-Jean. Way down below, someone is pushing a floating dock up the river, with an outboard, very slowly. There are no signs of cottages. The only sounds are the hum of hydro wires, the song of a white-throated sparrow, and the flapping of a Quebec flag.

We drive through the nice town of Petit Saguenay, then away from the Saguenay to meet the St. Lawrence at St-Siméon. Here we get the first example of how chance – let's not call it fate – can change the course of a trip. There is a ferry here, which goes to Rivière-du-Loup, and there is one farther north along the St. Lawrence, which crosses from Les Escoumins to Trois-Pistoles. Even farther along there is the town of Baie Comeau, which I would like to see, to satisfy some perverse political curiosity. It too has a ferry to the Gaspé. It is near lunchtime and the St-Siméon ferry doesn't go for two hours, so we decide to drive on to Les Escoumins and see what's happening there, checking out Tadoussac, where the Saguenay and the St. Lawrence join, on the way there, or the way back.

The road – it is 138 again – breaks at Tadoussac and there is a free ferry across the Saguenay, a pretty ride of just a few minutes. At Les Escoumins it turns out the ferry is leaving in only an hour. After an uncomfortable few moments, caused by our total lack of ferry vocabulary and inexperience with ferry lineup protocol, we luck into the lineup, assisted by a bystander who speaks a tiny bit of English. Then we wait there, in the car, hungry, hoping we are actually on the ferry and not the victims of a cruel hoax. In English Canada we are accustomed to signs telling us what to do, where to buy the ticket, where the lineup begins, whether or not you can chew gum in it, and other procedural matters. Facing a situation in which you are not quite sure, you develop instant empathy with those – such as many Québécois – whose travels take them away from their language, away from their areas of shared experience.

Aboard at last, we breathe a sigh of relief, as well as one of regret: we won't see Baie Comeau; we won't see more of Tadoussac. But we did see Belvedere Ainse-de-Tabatière. And we will get to the other side. Such are the mixed joys of unplanned travel.

The ferry is smallish. It can handle forty-two cars. Our fare, combined with the car's, is $42. It is very cold on deck and I'm amazed at how many people are dressed for it: despite its being tee-shirt weather on land, they have sweaters and warm jackets. We do too, but that's because we have most of our earthly possessions in the car. In addition to sweaters and warm jackets, we have baseball gloves, flashlights, and a mostly frozen freezer pack.

There is an enclosed lounge area on the ferry and a lunch counter, for which we are grateful, having spent the lunch hour sitting in the ferry lineup. In the one and a half hours of the cross-ing, we hear no English spoken. This is not surprising, given where we are, but we are surprised by something else – namely, that it is impossible to tell by looking at people what language they speak. English or French, we all dress the same and have the same appear-ances. This probably means that advertising and fashion know no boundaries. Does it also mean that we all look like Americans?

We are at Trois-Pistoles at 4:05 and rain begins. We see lush dairy land in the narrow spaces between the road and the ridges to either side. Now the radio scan test turns up no English voices at all. We have a quiet dispute (after thirty-one years, our disputes take place mostly by telepathy) over where we will stay. A mere two days into the trip I'm thinking that we had better find a little bed-and-breakfast where there is somebody interesting to talk to for the purposes of the book – some local colour, some travellers with wild tales, whom we will never find in fancy hotels. But we have already settled on another place picked out of the CAA book, a hotel in Matane, 150 kilometres down the road. I figure it will be too fancy and blame Nancy for the fact that I agreed to it earlier. After some telepathic grumbling, that's where we go and it turns out to be fine, not too fancy at all. There are no colourful characters but our room backs onto the St. Lawrence. We have seafood at dinner, and take a walk on the rocky beach as the sun goes down. There is a little wind and small waves hitting the shore. I like it when the loudest thing you can hear is the water.

## A Hunger for the Gaspé

One of the guidebooks has pointed us at Mt. Albert in Parc de la Gaspésie, just south of the highway that goes around the peninsula. The Chic-Choc mountains are in there, also moose, bear, deer, and maybe even woodland caribou. Since we have seen just the one chipmunk so far, away we go, first thing on a cloudy-but-not-rainy morning. Sure enough, although we see no woodland caribou, we do see two rabbits, or perhaps the same one twice.

Having filled up our Thermos with coffee at the hotel, part of the regular travelling routine, we stop at a picnic table in a quiet cedar wood beside a waterfall on the Sainte Anne River. There is nobody around. Our stroll takes us over a wooden bridge where our notion of the wilderness ends in a huge parking lot. Still, there are only three cars in it. There is also an interpretive centre, which is open. There we learn of a big hike to the top of Mt. Albert. We take a smaller one instead to another belvedere beside the river and it is a Top Ten, according to a hastily assembled meeting of the nominating committee. A strong and narrow waterfall runs into the river, foaming at the bottom, with high mountains above it, snow at the peaks. The woods around are full of cedar, large cedar, and smell the way woods should.

This highway, 299, would take us right across the peninsula in less than two hours to New Richmond and thence into New Brunswick. But we would miss the Gaspé. Still further behind us is 185, the Trans-Canada, which poor Edward McCourt – a slave to his publisher's contract perhaps – was forced to take in 1963. We drive back to Ste-Anne-des-Monts, which is said to be the start of the Gaspé. Saint Anne is, or was, the patron saint of sailors. It may seem odd to have a saint of the mountains who is the patron of sailors, but then the mountains are pretty close to the sea around here.

We have the St. Lawrence on our left now as we head north and east. Farms are wedged between the hills, to our right, and the river. The wind is making the river rougher. A new road sign appears, showing a wave knocking a car up onto its side wheels. What fun. There are also rockslide warnings and little waterfalls coming down the cliffs beside us. The sun is out, the sky is blue, and we soldier on.

Hunting for a place to eat shows us one of the drawbacks of travelling before the season. There are many communities along the road (their setting at the side of the river making them look more attractive than their actual buildings would warrant). There is, for example, Mont-St-Pierre where they celebrate La Fête du Vol Libre (that means hang-gliding). But the restaurants in the communities are not open yet. So the good news is that we have the road to ourselves. The bad news is that there's no place to eat. Worse, when we finally find a great-looking place, right on the river, it has only four tables and the only window faces the road. Why is that? Rudely, it would certainly appear, we step in and then step out, lacking the French to say: "We'd love to eat here if your windows faced the other way."

After several more attempts, we stop at one that still turns a blind eye to the St. Lawrence but looks a bit nicer inside. I order a western sandwich, which is what I always do when I'm not sure about a place. How can you mess up a western sandwich? There is wood on the walls, a model ship, some French country music playing, a TV tuned to the shopping channel with the sound turned down – the usual mix. The people are nice and don't mind our French.

Nancy, who has no appetite, orders soup. To make our life more interesting, she is taking mefloquin, an anti-malarial drug. Just before we began our trip, she was in East Africa. The drug, which can make people edgy and not so comfortable in the stomach, has to be taken once a week for another couple of weeks. Yesterday was the day. Today is the soup. The soup turns out to be wonderful. We will have mixed memories of this place. To Nancy it will be the place with the wonderful soup. To me it will be the place with no windows and the French country-music channel.

As we continue, the cliffs are right beside the road. And we begin to climb at Rivière-la-Madeleine, descending one hill at 14 per cent, a personal best. The combination of cliff and river is spectacular. We round the tip of the peninsula and drive through Forillon National Park, where the Appalachian Mountains begin, we are told, and the Chic-Chocs plunge into the sea. There is not much sign of any of that going on, nor do we get close enough to see any whales. We do, however, encounter Fort Peninsula, quite by accident, at our afternoon coffee-and-belvedere stop. It was built in 1939, a gun emplacement in the hillside overlooking Gaspé Bay to deal with German submarine activity. The fort has big guns and tunnels, now open to the sky and lined with wood. At the very end of the tunnel tour we find out that the guns were never used. But that's okay. A nice park surrounds the display and the would-be gunners had a lovely view.

As we head into the sun now, having turned the corner, the bay is sheltered and calm. The air is warm enough to require air conditioning in the car. We find the Jacques Cartier monument at Gaspé but the museum beside it is closed. There are two monuments: the nine-metre cross he put up when he arrived there in 1534 and an aggregation of six slabs upon which are carved details of the landing and some words, including these, from the natives he encountered: "As miserable as we seem in your eyes, we consider ourselves nevertheless much happier than you." Is there a metaphor we can work with here, or should we just drive on and find some dinner?

In the car we find CBC English, which is reporting on some kind of scandal involving Lucien Bouchard. It will not stay with us as long as Cartier's cross or the guns at Fort Peninsula or the cliffs of the Gaspé. The daily news is infinitely more fragile than the landscape in which it is heard. More relevant news is of an outbreak of legionnaires' disease in Quebec City where we ate two days ago.

Nancy drives while I scan the CAA book for motels. Traffic picks up around Douglastown. We have been spoiled: a total of one car in front of us all day. We begin a descent of a record 17 degrees and find Percé Rock, looking just as Percé Rock should look. The town of Percé, at the eastern end of the peninsula, shows signs of tourist activity. We find a hotel with a rock view for $55. In the restaurant we catch the sun setting over the rock and pay too much, but the setting is pleasant. There is a bus tour at the hotel and we overhear an American behind us asking the bartender if he is French. The American thought he might be Spanish. The bartender says he is Canadian. This leads to a minor epiphany – there must be epiphanies if this trip is to be worth anything, and here's one on only the fourth day. The epiphany is that we have more in common with these Gaspésians, whose language we don't speak, than with these Americans, whose language we do. It suddenly becomes important to speak as much French as we can. I fall into a conversation with our waitress, asking her questions about the names of fish. *Morue* is cod, I find out. You never can tell when something like this will come in handy.

### Out of the Gaspé, Through Two Pairs of Glasses

We are up at seven for a long walk along the beach to the pier. Whale-watching tours are available and we are tempted, but we decide to move on. We want to get the ferry to Prince Edward Island tomorrow. That means a long 700-kilometre drive through Quebec and New Brunswick today to catch the ferry tomorrow. So we are goal-oriented again.

We are on the gulf side now and the landscape is gentler. The rivers running into the sea are slower and wider. No more the steep climbs and steep drops. When we finally hit a steep-hill warning, it is only 7 per cent. I laugh at 7 per cent. In Chandler, we encounter the third traffic light we have seen in two days. There is a mall and the smell of a paper mill and we are getting back into industrialized civilization, which is always a pity. At Paspébiac it gets worse: a bank and a shopping centre, in addition to a stoplight. And paint stores. There seem to be a lot of paint stores in this part of the world and a lot of fresh paint on the houses, some of it a distinctive shade of light purple that you don't see elsewhere.

Now signs of anglo culture approach. The town of New Carlisle has a United Church and a main street called Main Street. There is less purple paint. New Brunswick is just starting to be visible to the south across the Baie des Chaleurs.

The highlight of the day is a side trip at Carleton, 582 metres up Mont St. Joseph to see the Notre Dame Oratory. The view is a killer: We see the Chic-Chocs coming down and gradually becoming fields. Baie des Chaleurs is in the background, with the town in front of it. Looking back east along the bay, we can see New Richmond and its paper mill. The church itself is nothing to write home, or Rome, about. Built in 1935, it has a blue tin roof, piped-in chants, strange paintings inside, many opportunities to donate money, a nativity scene showing the snow-capped Chic-Chocs behind the manger, and on the wall the legend "Si j'etait né a Carleton." It's the location that makes a believer out of you.

We have travelled 2,075 kilometres in all when we cross into New Brunswick, the last half dozen having been spent finding where we missed the turnoff into that province. It is hard to think that we could miss an entire province. When we finally find our way, we cross a bridge, upon which nothing is said about leaving Quebec or entering New Brunswick. There is a bewildering light-industrial route through Campbellton, until Route 11 is discovered, which is, like many main highways, a route through nothing. But that's okay. Today is a driving day. Our goal is Cape Tormentine, at the Northumberland Strait. The route through nothing will get us there quickly. Unfortunately, the route through nothing is also a route through no places to have lunch, so we get off it to grab some chicken at a fast-food place in Petit-Rocher. This is Acadian territory, with a lot of French spoken, though also English, which we are using, enjoying it like a new toy.

A word about methodology. When Nancy and I travel together, our mode of car travel, practised and refined in several Ottawa–Kenora trips, is to split the driving in two-hour shifts, stopping at gas stations, restaurants, or belvederes to make the switch. Where we can, we make picnic lunches. Sometimes we buy ready-made sandwiches in supermarkets and stick them in the small cooler stored behind the front seat.

Since this trip requires more maps than previous ones, there is a cloth bag of them on the floor by the passenger seat. We quickly realize that we have more maps than floor, so an extra bag is activated, to sit in the trunk and contain the maps we have already used or are not using yet. We have one of those book maps, in which each page has a different region; it is good for detail but not so great for the big picture. We have CAA maps – Quebec on one side, the Atlantic provinces on the other; Saskatchewan on one side, Manitoba on the other; and so on – which are good for perspective and don't have too much detail, which makes them easier to read. And we have detailed provincial maps, given out at provincial information centres, which vary in quality.

Then we have the books, the relevant ones in the active map bag, the others stowed in the trunk until their province comes. We borrowed a CAA hardcover called *Canadian Book of the Road*, which has two-page spreads on different regions, mapping them, giving some of the history and suggesting things to see. We will thumb through them at certain points, the passenger reading aloud appropriate parts to the driver. "Offshore from Percé village is another of Canada's most spectacular natural sights, the gannet colony of Île de Bonaventure," the passenger will read out, adding: "Shit. We missed the gannet colony."

The CAA also puts out tour books for the Canadian regions. These have some information on attractions. More important, they list CAA-approved restaurants and hotels, with addresses, prices, and other important details, such as whether there is a view of Percé Rock. So that's another important function of the passenger: later in the day, when a bed for the night becomes more important than historic sites at roadside, the passenger reads out motel descriptions and attempts to form a consensus with the driver on whether a given place sounds nice, or too nice, or not nice enough. Given the sketchiness of the descriptions offered, there is a lot of guesswork involved.

In the same bag are bed-and-breakfast guides and accommodation listings handed out at provincial information centres. Because many of the B&B listings are written by the owners themselves, they are not entirely objective. But reading them does give you an idea of the image the proprietors are trying to put out, and that can give you an idea of whether you want to have anything to do with them.

We are also carrying, because someone gave it to us, probably as a joke, a Fodor's, which turns out to be quite reliable in its assessment of hotels, although it mostly lists those at the high end.

This juggling of the maps and guidebooks also involves a juggling of eyeglasses, of which there seem to be at least three pairs in use at any given time. Those are the sunglasses, the prescription reading glasses, and some drugstore half-glasses. If you want to see out the window and read a map at the same time, what you really need is a bifocal with a reading glass on the bottom and a sunglass on the top. But no one makes that. I can approximate this by putting the sunglasses on over the half-glasses.

Glassy-eyed, as it were, I sit in the passenger seat, writing notes into one of those half-notebooks you can stick into your pocket. At one point, early on, it strikes me as strange that I am taking notes on scenery, sitting there writing stuff in a notebook as the

countryside goes by. "Tall trees on the right, a lake on the left," I
write. If I haven't seen the name of the lake, I madly consult maps
and various publications of the Canadian Automobile Association
to find out. It will be one of 7,000 names of lakes I check on this
trip. Then I write some more. "Bigger trees. Smaller hills." And
so on.

Back on Highway 11, we boot it, helped by a 100 km/h speed
limit and passing lanes. Highway 8 is the same, but with moose
signs. Since it is becoming evening and moose are alleged to be a
night danger, I am more attentive, eschewing the sunglasses and
ready with my notebook to write "moose" in it. But no such luck.
We do see fine bridges over the Miramichi and some tidal water-
ways, also the statue of a giant lobster at Shediac, which helps us to
get in a Maritime mood. "Giant lobster," I write in my book. At
Port Elgin is a striking roundabout: one sign points left to P.E.I.,
straight ahead and back is New Brunswick, and to the right is Nova
Scotia. What could be more exciting for a couple of near-strangers
to the Maritimes? The road we take, 16, turns out to be the Trans-
Canada Highway, the first time we have been on it.

At the Irving gas station in Cape Tormentine we check out the
times of the ferry. We could go tonight, but want to do it in the
daytime. So we check in, with some misgivings, to the Hilltop Bed
and Breakfast, our first B&B on the trip. The place is suburban, the
room large and comfortable, with what might be termed a pastiche
of decor influences, and a shared bath. This early in the season,
shared bath usually means it's yours, and this one is.

We return to the restaurant in the Irving station to eat. The fish
dinner is recommended to us, haddock, not fresh but frozen in
Newfoundland. It is pan-fried, unadorned and just right. The cost
is $7.50 each.

Taped to the wall of our booth is a certificate identifying
Norman Powell as recipient of the Bobby Big Wiggler Award.
Through the window and the rain we watch the cars coming off
the ferry.

# 2

## *The Missing Link*

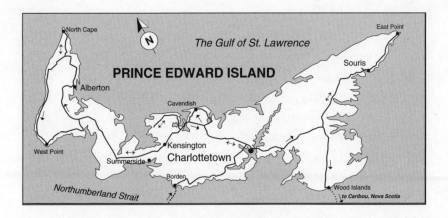

Up early for the breakfast part of bed-and-breakfast, we get a briefing on the Fixed Link from Joan Trenholm. Her Hilltop Bed and Breakfast is a two-minute drive from the ferry to Borden, Prince Edward Island. The Fixed Link will (a) cancel the ferry and (b) cut off the highway several miles before Cape Tormentine. She figures the Hilltop, which she and her husband Garth have run for twenty years, is doomed, but she has no intention of leaving. "We're here to stay," she says.

The B&B is not their sole means of support. Garth fishes for scallop and lobster. There is a painting of him in fishing gear and a captain's hat. He said last night that the Fixed Link has even hurt the fishing by ripping up some good bottom. But the Trenholms have found a way to make peace with the Link. One of their five children, Tony, runs boat tours out to view the construction of it, charging adults $25 and children under thirteen $10. He will have nineteen people today. Despite themselves, people are fascinated with the thing.

We drive onto the ferry with a minimal wait. If it were always so easy, there would be no need for the Link. But as we are often told, waits in the peak season can be three hours.

The ferry is called the *Vacationland*, one of four that do the trip, its crew among the six hundred ferry people who will lose their jobs when the Link kills the ferry. An FM-radio voice welcomes us aboard for the forty-five-minute trip and talks about the lifeboats, etc. The system of payment is interesting: You ride free over to the island, and pay (a total of $48.25 for the car and two adults) when you return. The ferry is well-equipped, with a gift shop and cafeteria. It is a hazy, sunny day, much warmer than when crossing the St. Lawrence three days ago. From the starboard side of the observation deck we watch the land recede, the banks reddish. On the port side we see the Link taking shape.

Our first Link booster is encountered in the cafeteria, where Don Barkhouse, an auto-repair teacher at a community college in Moncton, strikes up a conversation. He knows a lot about the Link, takes pride in the sheer size of it. He says it is not just truckers who are in favour of it. As someone who has waited as long as eight hours for the ferry, he says ordinary people want it too. The Link has created its own tourism, on the water and at the construction site on the Island side, where tourists marvel at the scale of the bridge components being assembled and moved, somehow, out into the water.

Barkhouse is not worried about the Island's identity being threatened by the existence of a bridge. "An Islander's an Islander," he says. With the thought of our long drive to get here firmly in mind, I'm impressed by the fact that a bridge alone is not automatically going to put millions of people onto P.E.I. They have to get to the bridge first, which is no easy trick.

That being said, it sure is one ugly piece of work, all the more so for overpowering such a lovely scene. This becomes clearer as we near the P.E.I. side where work is more advanced. Huge T-shaped sections rise out of the water, with massive prefabbed pieces lowered in to fill the gaps between the Ts. Seeing those gaps now would make you feel a bit woozy driving across it, but construction vehicles are already on, and will be able to drive all the way across by the fall. The thing will be opened to the public next spring.

Driving off is swift and easy and we are in Prince Edward Island, where we have never been, driving past the giant McCain factory on the road to Charlottetown at 9:20. It is a pretty drive, calming, in contrast to the rougher landscapes of the Gaspé. The earth is dark, the dirt roads red. A slogan on a billboard as you leave the ferry says: "Stay a few days. You've earned it." That works, and maybe the ferry ride itself contributes to the feeling: You've slowed down, got out of your car, had a cup of coffee, admired the landscape. Now you're in a slower, more gently paced world and you're ready for it. Will you feel the same way when you've just come off a thirteen-kilometre drive way up in the sky, hemmed in by concrete?

The feeling of relaxation extends to the Charlottetown traffic, on this Saturday morning, even for someone who has not the first idea where anything is. We find an information centre, pick up some stuff on B&Bs and begin to check them out. We stop at one in the centre of town called the Duchess of Kent (*all* B&Bs in the Atlantic provinces are called something like the Duchess of Kent, it turns out) but it is full. There is a convention of Presbyterians in town. Lock up your daughters. As we sit in the car at the curb pondering our next move, the proprietor comes out of the Duchess of Kent, asks if we need any help, takes one of our guidebooks and shows us how to get to all the good B&Bs in the neighbourhood.

This is our first encounter with the fabled Maritime friendliness and it is impressive. There was nothing in it for him.

In our search we encounter the full range – one highly rated place has a sign on it saying the manager will return at 1:00 p.m. Another has rooms that have a bad smell and need painting. And we find some real B&B professionals, people with many rooms to rent and an expert eye for antiques, art, and tasteful decor. Unfortunately their place hasn't opened yet. But Jordan and Judy Hill give us a tour of the Shipwright Inn just for the fun of it. While we stroll, we talk about the Link. You might not expect a man who values nautical tradition and honours it in his place of business to support such a newfangled contraption, but Jordan does. Prince Edward Island's economy rests on a narrow foundation of potatoes, lobster, and tourism, he says. Anything that helps one of those elements is good for the province. The Link brings the tourists to the Island and takes the lobsters and potatoes off, I guess.

We decide to do some laundry and wait for the proprietors of the highly rated place to return. At a laundry/café on University Avenue, I guard the laundry and write notes while Nancy goes off in search of tonic and other essentials. The laundry/café has a couple of couches, a lunch counter, some magazines, and a TV, which is tuned to a soccer game. The Swiss team, with what appears to be snow on the shoulders of their uniforms, is playing Britain. If I cared about soccer I would be annoyed when a guy picks up the remote control and begins zapping through the Saturday morning cartoon shows. But I'm too relaxed to be annoyed. I've earned it.

Returning to the highly rated B&B after 1:00 p.m., we find the proprietors not back yet. There are two ways of looking at this. First, isn't it nice that people aren't subject to the tyranny of the clock? Second, wouldn't it be nice if we could find a room? Eventually we check in, with our clean laundry, at Fitzroy Hall, which is downtown, old and beautiful. We have a rather dark room on the third floor, large, with old chests and cabinets and a floor made of wide planks. We are learning about B&Bs. Being in a beautifully restored old home costs. So does a private bathroom. And so does being in downtown Charlottetown. On the other hand, what good is a cheap hotel on the outskirts of town? Here we can walk everywhere. And there is, of course, breakfast. These are some of the ways people justify staying where they want to stay.

This one has six bedrooms rented out, each with a name. Ours is Miss Olivia. It seems to be a government regulation (surprise!) that bedrooms have names or numbers, presumably to keep people from wandering around, hopelessly lost, in heritage houses.

Charlottetown reminds us of Kingston, where we went to university and met. It has the same size and feeling, old houses, large old trees, and a sense of history. There are differences, though. University Avenue, one of the main drags downtown, is wide, like a Prairie main street, and has diagonal parking. A big shopping centre, the Confederation Court Mall, is hidden behind the storefronts. I enter and apply the shopping centre test. It is a perfect shopping centre if you (a) don't know what city you're in; (b) can't find out what time it is; (c) get lost; and (d) can't find the bathroom. My theory is that shopping centres are designed this way to disorient shoppers, make them so nervous and insecure that they have to *buy something* as a means of self-affirmation. Confederation Court Mall flunks the test because it has so much *Anne of Green Gables* stuff, not to mention signs in Japanese, that it couldn't be in any other town – at least not in Canada.

Even without a bridge link to the mainland, there is no way that progress, as it is defined in Central Canada, is going to be kept out of Prince Edward Island. "We now have cappuccino," a sign brags on an Irving station on the way into town. Eating places encountered in the city include a Beanz Expresso Bar and a Shawarma Palace. But there is still something delightfully Canadian about the way this cosmopolitanism is presented. Where else could you find a restaurant called the Stagecoach, which boasts "Steak and

Seafood, European Cuisine," and has a sign in Japanese in the window.

With all this diversity, the city is still very white, compared with Toronto, or even Ottawa. We walk downtown to the handsome Confederation Centre of the Arts and find out that shows – including, of course, *Anne of Green Gables* – don't begin until the end of the month. In the centre's art gallery, there is a display of a good local artist, Brian Burke, another example of the secrets Canada's regions keep from one another. There is also an exhibition of the works of the mid-nineteenth-century painter Robert Whale, a precursor of Robert Harris who did the famous painting of the Fathers of Confederation. (Whale's landscapes look as if he wished Canada's scenery was Britain's. As if to accentuate the point, he sticks wood nymphs and the like into Canadian scenes.) Harris's original painting of the Fathers of Confederation used Charlottetown as a setting but the government asked him to change it to Quebec City. So he had to add ten people and put in a window with a view of the St. Lawrence. Even in those days the relationship between artist and government was difficult.

One of the things that makes Charlottetown so attractive is that it is both a small city and a capital city. Without big-city traffic and noise, we get the big-time cultural amenities of the capital. The Confederation Centre, in addition to its fine theatre and gallery, has the paved spaces so inviting to skateboarders. Province House, right next door, is a joy of a different sort, the current legislative chamber elaborately done in the British style, with an olive curtain with gold braid backing up the throne, and gold trim. For some reason, the architecture and decor of legislative buildings appeal to me. Perhaps it is because I like politics, a shameful admission in this day and age, but there it is. I decide that we should visit all the legislatures. Too bad I didn't think of that in Quebec City.

We latch on to a young Parks Canada guide and get a bit of a tour. The chamber of the upper house, abolished in 1893, is preserved as it was when the Fathers of Confederation met there in

1864. In another of Province House's rooms is an extraordinary photo of the Fathers, taken at the front of the building, with Sir John A. Macdonald sitting on the curb. On the curb today, skateboarders are in operation.

We test this fine new, and very old, city some more. I go into what looks like the best bookstore and ask about P.E.I. novelists. The store has some Island poets, I am told, but no novelists, outside of Lucy Maud. Later, celebrating the fact that we are going to be in one place for two nights, we walk to a bad movie, like we used to do in Kingston, then walk to the waterfront, looking for a restaurant that has been recommended by Helen Doucette, our B&B host. Charlottetown is one of a number of cities that have made vigorous and expensive efforts to reclaim the waterfront for the people. Here there are well-lit lawns, boardwalks (indicated by a blue line), restaurants, bars, and ice cream shops. Also skateboarders. There is a big new CP hotel, maybe twelve storeys, that is too tall for the area. We find the Lobster Wharf, which is informal and friendly. Nancy has chowder and I have a lobster roll, which is sort of like a tuna fish sandwich in a hot dog roll, only with lobster, if you get the idea. It is fine. We walk home, a quiet walk for a Saturday night. Cars stop for us to cross the street. You could learn to like it here.

## Man of Green Garbles

The next day we are told that it was noisy last night outside Fitzroy Hall. You could have fooled us, but Don and Louise Thompson, Presbyterians from Stratford, tell us that over breakfast. They in fact are moving to someplace quieter. B&B etiquette says you chat with people over breakfast, which actually makes more sense than pretending they are not in the room with you, as happens in larger places. With the Thompsons, we demonstrate the Canadian principle that might be termed One Degree of Separation. "I see you're from the *Ottawa Citizen*," says Don, looking at my sweatshirt. "Do you know Audrey and Jim Ashley?" Of course, and that's how long it takes. We ask him if he knows Don Milne, a United Church minister in Stratford. Of course.

We chat about Presbyterian politics, then the Island, and the modernizing influences that may or may not be at work. Helen Doucette pops out of the kitchen to give an example of the pull of tradition: she says that every change made in the *Anne of Green Gables* play is controversial and that new costumes produced in a recent season had to be abandoned because people felt they were too unlike the old ones. The Green Gables craze is a fairly recent phenomenon, but it is powerful enough to have caused the province to put Anne on the licence plates. And the reaction to that is powerful enough to cause some Islanders to scratch her face off with a knife. Meanwhile, the road to Cavendish, where Anne hung out, has been widened. "They've taken away the flavour," Helen says.

We will see for ourselves. We drive out Highway 2 on a hazy day with the promise of sun. Because the towns and attractions are so close together, it doesn't seem necessary to drive very fast. You begin to see how a place can affect your inner rhythms.

The road is not full of signs hyping Green Gables, and the combination of seashore and farmland is wonderfully calming. Where else would you smell salt water and manure at the same time? After North Rustico, the nearest town to Cavendish, the tacky stuff begins beside Highway 6. Ripley's Believe it or Not Museum, Rainbow Valley, something about Santa Claus, an Enchanted something else. King Tut's Tomb, River of Adventure. We will have to examine, at some point, man's primal urge to build really ugly stuff beside national landmarks.

This particular national landmark is not well known to me, I have to admit. I haven't read the book, seen the play, or even the TV series. But I like the modest little National Parks sign at the entrance, and the nice surroundings of the parking lot, the grass and trees. In the lot, I notice, are licence plates from New Brunswick, Quebec, Nova Scotia, Ontario, Alberta, Connecticut, and Maryland. Once we have paid our $2.50 each to get in I stop and gaze at a building. "Is that the house?" I ask. But it is the gift shop.

The real house is right next to it, along with a plaque stating that Lucy Maud Montgomery lived from 1875 to 1942, which would make her a contemporary of my grandfather, Ralph Connor, and wrote *Anne of Green Gables* in 1908. Inside the house, which is quite nice in a sort of normal country-farmhouse way, a Parks Canada guide tells us that the house belonged to Lucy Maud's cousin but was the model for the house in *AGG* (as I have begun to call it). When the restoration of the house was done, it was to fit the house described in *AGG* rather than the house as it actually was.

Small knots of people go through as we are learning this, not many of them Japanese. The guide says that most Japanese tourists are in groups with guides to answer their questions. The ones most frequently heard are: Did Lucy Maud Montgomery really live here? and Which is Anne's room? Despite all the hype, the exhibit is put on with taste and restraint and the visitors (perhaps because there are not huge numbers of them this early in the season, perhaps because it feels like their uncle's farm) are showing good manners.

We see Lucy Maud's Empire typewriter (with three rows, the upper case being used for numbers) and we are entering the old farmhouse kitchen when a telephone rings and a guide pulls open an old farmhouse kitchen drawer to grab a cell phone out of it. Oh well.

In the gift "shoppe" the following Anne merchandise is available: fridge magnets; napkin rings; one of those glass balls that snows when you turn it upside down; salt-and-pepper shakers; toothpick holders; strawberry-rhubarb jam; sunflower, lupin, and wild-flower seeds; notebooks; hats; playing cards; place mats; books; spoons; tapes of Hagood Hardy's theme music from the TV series; and a CD of the musical comedy. These two play all the time. Asked about that, a guide says she doesn't get sick of the music because she is too busy to notice. Also some people don't have jobs at all, I suggest. "That's just the truth," she says.

Right now the house and the gift shop are operating with half the normal staff. In July and August it will be a madhouse. "I wouldn't be able to talk to you like this," she says.

Outside is a forest, which apparently is the Haunted Woods, and there is a Parks Canada trail through it, with signs giving literary references that are lost on me. The path intersects the path to the twelfth tee of the Green Gables Golf Course. The people teeing off there have to put up with the excited chatter from Green Gablists. I imagine one of them slicing a tee shot into the trees and exclaiming: "Frigging Haunted Woods!"

In the woods are bridges constructed of recent wood and a sign referring to Kate Maurice, an imaginary friend of Lucy Maud, "who was really just Montgomery's own reflection in the window of her grandmother's china cabinet." I imagine working for Parks Canada and having to write this copy.

Ahead of us in the Grove of Silver Birches is a woman, probably in her seventies, who is doing something to a birch tree. When we get to it we find that she has written her name, the date, and her home town in ink. This place clearly exerts a power that I don't understand. All around us, now that we look, are carvings and writings on the birch trees of the Haunted Woods.

Leaving Anne and the Grove of Autographed Birches, we find Cavendish Beach and buy a five-dollar pass for all the P.E.I. national parks. There are few people here and most of them stay close to where the boardwalk ends. We walk a mile or so down the sand. The surf is light and the water is too cold for swimming. The sand is beautiful, at times bright red under the water, the sun is out, and the walking is excellent. Afterwards we sit for ten minutes or so watching the water and little kids having what may be their first day ever at the beach. It is difficult to be more relaxed than this.

Another Island feature, quaint or not, depending upon your situation, is that many of the towns are so small that they don't have gas stations. They have marvellous wooden churches but no gas stations. I am not one of those for whom driving on Empty is a thrill. I like driving on Full. Since, as noted, the towns are close together, there is always the hope, the assurance, even, that the next town is just over the next hill, and that the next town will have gas. Finally, the next town is Kensington and it does. That leaves only our stomachs running on Empty. These are taken care of at the nicely named Little Mermaid Seafood and Dairy Bar in Summerside where we have an ice cream cone and note that poutine is on the menu.

Fortified, we now embark on more goal-oriented tourism, to reach the North Cape, the most northerly tip of the island. Such challenges are easily met on Prince Edward Island. Our drive takes us out of sight of the sea for a time but eventually brings us back near Alberton. There are four frame churches here. The United is called Gordon Memorial and we stop, to see whether it's anyone we know. But the church is closed. It is an odd feeling for people like us, who feel that we have deep roots in Canada, to spend time in a place where the sense of history is so strong and in which we have no roots at all. In most parts of the country, we know people, have ancestors, have some sense of connection. Here we feel like new Canadians and have a sense of how this country must seem to people who have not been here long.

The North Cape, when we reach it, is another Top Ten Belvedere nominee. Not only is it where the Northumberland Strait and the Gulf of St. Lawrence meet, there is also a lighthouse, the Atlantic Wind Testing Centre, and a terrific-looking restaurant at which it is too early to have dinner. We walk out on a long spit to the very spot where the gulf and the strait meet, the meeting taking place on my shoes for one weak moment. Not an hour from North Cape is West Point (another advantage of a small island) and it too has Top Ten possibilities, with the following elements: cliffs, fragrant fields, straits, cows, and a pond.

Driving east now, headed back to Charlottetown, having driven around half the province, we are on a tiny side road doing one of my fancy detours, when we see a small sign that says Elephant Rock, with an arrow. Elephant Rock is a famous rock that looks like an elephant. So we decide to see it. Soon there is a little sign that says PRIVATE ROAD, PROCEED AT YOUR OWN RISK, which we do for awhile. And sure enough, there it is: Elephant Rock, looking quite a bit like Percé Rock would look if it were smaller and shaped like an elephant. There are no knick-knack booths around it, no hot dog stands. No nothing. It is a nice thing, this Island understatement. In Central Canada, it would have been Elephant Rock Ramada Inn and Gaz-O-Bar du Elephant Rock and Last Gas Before Elephant Rock. Here it's just here. And a nice little Elephant Rock it is too.

We have dinner, by mistake, in a place along the highway that is too fancy. The chef's medals are on the wall, the muzak plays the theme from *Chariots of Fire* and it's the kind of place where the fish is built into tall columns on the plate and covered with spices that make the fish taste like spices. Island friendliness works against us when we try to retreat after sizing it up. We're not dressed for it, we say. Don't worry, they say. Since there's nobody else in the restaurant, we can hardly refuse. Or so we think. Two hours and $72.09 later we think again. If we had an itinerary, we would have arranged to be hungry at the North Cape, and there we would have sat by the window, looked out at the Gulf and the Straits meeting, and had a simple slice of pan-fried fish. But that would mean having an itinerary.

## One More Point

Nicely rested after spending two nights in the same place, we head east the next day and a bit north. This may not be the right decision. Nancy, in her business manager capacity, has been working the phones to get us on the ferry from North Sydney to Port aux Basques, Newfoundland, on Wednesday and she's in a let's-get-to-Nova-Scotia mood. But there is more P.E.I. highway to be covered. My growing obsession with getting to the ends of things is taking us now to East Point. The danger is one of anti-climax. We have seen a lot in two days and enjoyed every minute of them. Maybe this is pressing our luck.

McCourt, in 1963, fought against being impressed by the Island. "The farms," he wrote, "looked self-consciously well-groomed, as if waiting to have their photographs taken – not a crooked furrow or a ragged tree in sight, not a blade of grass out of place, nor a single pig wallowing in a mud hole." I can't agree. In the first place, who knows a farmer who has the time to prepare his acreage to pose for photographs? The farms look that way because that's the way they are.

Our drive to East Point is uneventful and the view from there is memorable, a Top Ten candidate – sandstone cliffs with the Îles-de-la-Madeleine visible in the distance. There are no signs warning us not to fall off the cliff, which is refreshing. Six or seven lobster boats are out on the water and we are told that there were thirty an hour ago.

On the drive down to Wood Islands and the ferry to Nova Scotia, I count up the things I like about Prince Edward Island. The ferries, the frame churches, the way waitresses say "shore!", the way cars stop for pedestrians, the ice cream chain called Cows. I like the age of the buildings. And I like the way the Island forces you to adjust your sense of distance. Now forty kilometres seems a long way.

I like the restfulness of the landscape, which calms the eye, rather than challenges it. We have had challenges in the Saguenay and the Gaspé and will have more. This is a nice contrast. I have been working on a plan to rearrange Canadian geography, putting the provinces in a different order. In this new Canada, you would arrive in Prince Edward Island just after leaving Toronto on the

401, when you most need it. On the other hand, now that I think about it, does P.E.I. want a bunch of frenzied Ontarians roaring in with the veins bulging on their foreheads, particularly now that they can get here, via the Fixed Link, without even slowing down? Maybe it would be a good idea to put a Prairie province, perhaps Manitoba, in the middle.

The Northumberland Ferry Ltd. ship leaves Wood Islands at 1:55. I've decided I really like ferries – strolling about, taking an hour out of a car trip to stand on the deck, watch one shore recede and another advance and to listen to the hiss of the foam above the noise of the engines. The mood of it suits P.E.I., which makes it sad that this may be the last P.E.I. ferry I'm ever on. Far off to the west, out of sight, is the Fixed Link. One of the ferry employees I talk to wonders how the Link will winter. There are many gleeful predictions of doom, I learn. Ice will build up around it and cause it to buckle. It won't be able to withstand the winds. And of course the ice problem brings to mind the highway signs so frequently encountered in Canada: "Bridge freezes before road." And if the whole road is bridge?

I wonder if there are ferry freaks, like train freaks. This is the third one in a week and they're all different, but all well-run by friendly, helpful people. Fortunately, the country is so large, the rivers and straits so wide, that they can't *all* be abolished.

# 3

## *Walks in the Treated Wood*

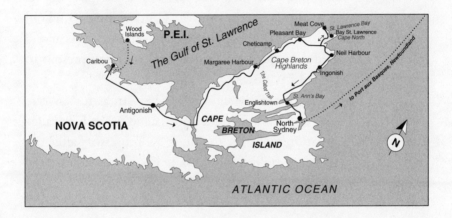

The plan, which may not make sense but is the only one we have, is to drive to North Sydney in Cape Breton, catch the ferry to Newfoundland, tour Newfoundland, then come back and "do" the rest of Nova Scotia. The way the Atlantic provinces are arranged forces you to choose routes like that if you don't want to be retracing your steps.

We will take the long way to North Sydney, around Cape Breton Island by way of the Cabot Trail. The idea today is to get near the start of the trail and find a place to stay. Getting off the P.E.I. ferry at Caribou at 3:00 p.m., we drive through Antigonish and suddenly think of Bobby Orr. That is our connection with

Antigonish. Fifteen years ago, my father got an honorary degree from St. Francis Xavier University. We all came out for it and stayed in a motel in Antigonish, the Wandlyn Inn. Also there was Bobby Orr, perhaps the best hockey player in history, then not too recently retired as an active hockey player, who was getting an honorary doctorate at the same convocation.

I remember that it was warm for January, by our Ottawa standards, wet and foggy. And I remember that Orr, despite the many awards that had been heaped upon him, was genuinely thrilled to be getting an honorary degree and that Antigonish, including the university community, was thrilled that Bobby Orr was there. Among the people thrilled were the two Gordon kids, to whom Orr paid particularly kind attention, seeking out twelve-year-old John in a crowded restaurant to talk hockey, making a present to ten-year-old Mary of the flowers from his room.

Orr was amazing, patiently signing hockey sticks for anyone who brought one to the hotel coffee shop, standing in his academic robes to sign autographs for the St. F. X. professors after the convocation ceremony, smiling and looking like there was nothing he enjoyed better. I particularly savour my memory of the banquet that night, where we watched from a distance as my mother and Bobby Orr laughed and wisecracked with each other at the head table. Not long after, I read a magazine article about how unhappy Orr was in retirement, a viewpoint impossible to reconcile with my recollection of a magnetic and gracious man charming an entire community.

That strange association with Antigonish causes us to take a detour so we can drive past the Wandlyn Inn, which we don't recognize at all.

From there, it's across the Canso Causeway to Cape Breton. There is a good government information centre, with helpful people and many brochures, which are particularly useful in indicating places to stay. We are out on the coast road, Highway 19. When it turns inland briefly, we turn onto 219, which hugs the shoreline. Prince Edward Island seems to have rested and reinvigorated our eyes, and we are knocked out by the hills and the sea. We stop at Margaree Harbour, about a hundred kilometres up the island, at a rather ordinary-looking fifties-style roadside motel, the Duck Cove Inn. It turns out to have a perfect dining room, informal, friendly, woody, and with a great view. We sit by the window and look at the Margaree River, watching an eagle fly over it. There is a two-for-one special: if we both order the same thing, we get two dinners for the price of one. Here is a test of the relationship. We have no trouble agreeing on the trout, which is from a nearby trout farm, but dessert is more difficult. A compromise is reached on lemon meringue pie, and we've done it. It's all delicious, leading to the establishment of a new category: Top Ten Motel Meals.

In the room, I look for a ball game on TV and am perplexed by the selection of channels offered. How come NBC is from Detroit? Why is Edmonton's ITV on it? There is much to think about on such a trip.

## On the Trail

The next morning's meditation is about motel showers that have the curtain on the left, as you stand with the water hitting your back. This is one. Why aren't there more? Is there a Bureau of Shower Standards that decides such things?

We pack up the car in the way that we've been perfecting – big suitcases in the back, the computer on top of the black suitcase; the small suitcases in front, then, piled around them, the laundry, the books, the gin, the bag with all the disks and notebooks, jackets, the maps we're not using. The cooler goes behind the front seat, beside the IKEA picnic gear. The bag with the Atlantic Canada maps, the CAA books and accommodations books and all the spare pens, goes on the floor in front of the passenger seat, the notebook wedged between the seat and the centre tapes compartment, a pen clipped onto the spirals.

The first part of the trail is scrubby, not at all slick and touristy. Fog is beginning. After Cheticamp, which features Acadian flags and a big church, we climb for thirty kilometres up into the clouds, past many scenic lookouts with nothing to look out at. It is creepy, but it eventually begins to brighten and there is a moose warning sign, which always cheers me up.

We drive into Cape Breton National Park, past a closed toll booth. The park is full of walking trails, long and short, and we have a good brochure listing them. We stop at one called French Mountain Bog, which is supposed to take twenty to thirty minutes. To keep people off the bog, which is fragile, and to make the trail wheelchair-accessible, it is completely covered in treated wood. I am thinking that you could travel across the entire country on treated wood. We walk through, looking at wild orchids and other flowers and reading signs telling us about the surroundings. "Sphagmas – Small But Mighty," one says. Is that good or bad? There are strange stunted trees, blue spruce and eastern larch. The fog hangs in their branches and we can watch the wind blowing it around. There is a different kind of beauty in this.

Driving on we leave the fog and the little trees as we begin a steep downhill climb into Pleasant Bay, a more touristy place with many gift shops. An hour later we hit another trail, called Lone Shieling. This one is in a hardwood forest, one hundred acres of it, built around a shieling, which is a crofter's cabin. It was all donated by a Professor Donald S. MacIntosh in 1934. The maples are tall and there is an impressive hush to the forest as we walk through it. We stop beside a stream that flows along a gravelly bottom, absolutely clear in its deeper pools. Above it are the hills, and the nominating committee is struck by its belvedere potential. It definitely helps for there to be more than one element in a belvedere – hills plus water plus the light green over the new maple leaves. This one establishes the fact that a Top Ten Belvedere (or TTB, as I am now calling it in my notes) does not have to be high.

This is turning into a terrific day. Sunny but not hot, sweatshirt weather. There are so many scenic lookouts beside the road that we get picky about where we want to stop. When the highway exits the park, near the island's northern tip, I decide I want to go to Meat Cove, which is at the very tip and looks – as well as sounds – like a good place to eat. We stop at Food Town in Cape North Village and look around for picnic fodder. A man making lobster sandwiches says they are better on white bread and we accept his advice. At last, white bread gets some respect. While he makes the sandwiches, we look around the store, which has nuts, screws, battery cables, and videos, as well as food.

Somewhere between Cape St. Lawrence and Meat Cove we get lost, the dirt road becoming increasingly narrow and eventually non-existent. Retracing our steps, we find Meat Cove, but there is no good place to stop. So we pause for a second to admire the view off the northernmost part of the island, then drive back into the park and find a picnic spot at Neil Harbour. We have the ocean to the left, the river in front of us and a hill across, and the lobster sandwiches are delicious. There is one other car there. We have the sandwiches, some iced tea and apples, topped off by some leftover Prince Edward Island fudge. Life is good.

It is not even spoiled by the ranger who drives up and asks us if we have our Parks pass. Oops. We didn't know we should have gone into the information centre at the spot where we passed the empty toll booth. He is nice about this. We tell him we want a pass that will work in all the national parks. He says there is no point in paying him for today (six dollars) if we are going to be buying one of those. We can pay on the way out. Whether we are trusted because Parks Canada is trusting or Maritimers are trusting or this particular ranger is a nice guy, it is nice to be trusted, a feeling we constantly have in this part of the world.

(When we get to the park gate at Ingonish, we find that there is no such thing as a cross-Canada pass. So we pay our six dollars.)

The driving is challenging, as well as staggeringly beautiful, with steep climbs and descents around hairpin curves. We quickly learn that when the sign says 40 km/h, it means it.

Meanwhile, we keep doing Cabot Trail walks. The next one, encountered soon after lunch, is the Jack Pine Trail, and it has everything (including, of course, lots of treated wood). There may be a few too many signs, with headlines like "Flourishing Ferns" and "Life Blossoms" – imagine being a headline writer for Parks Canada – but the signs and the information they carry may do more than convey information: they may convince visitors to take the place seriously, as evidenced by the complete lack of litter and graffiti along the trail.

The trail moves through a jack pine forest, which grew out of seedlings released in a 1921 fire. The Parks Canada writer goes over the line with this one, telling of a little jack pine seedling taking life in a crevice and growing into the sunlight. "At the edge of the rock, other jack pines towered over him. They seemed to jeer at him in the breeze." I am pondering this new form of literature, when the air abruptly cools on the ascending path, and the ocean – and it really is the Atlantic Ocean here; next stop Ireland – suddenly becomes visible. Rocky outcroppings jut into the sea, the water surging into the gaps. Under the water are light-coloured rocks, turning the ocean a lighter shade of green. Lobster traps are out there and three black coastal birds fly by in formation. There is the smell of the sea. Looking inland we see tall jack pines and when the trail goes back into the forest, the ocean noise suddenly disappears.

The trail is marked by piles of small boulders, cairns, rather than by arrows or signs nailed to trees. As the trail ends we come to a fork in it and I check our map. We have started to speak a new trip language.

"That belvedere will get us a waterfall," I say, pointing left.

"Want to do it?"

"I hate to pass up a waterfall."

The afternoon's meditation is on the taming of the wilderness by Parks Canada and whether it is a good thing. It is a blow to Canadian vanity to find out not only that people have been here before us but that they have laid down a boardwalk through the forest for us. On the other hand, it protects the forest and makes it accessible for people who can't walk or who walk with difficulty. We stop at one more trail, which features a steep climb, and on our way out we encounter an older woman who says: "It's hard on the knees." That's probably as good an argument as any for the treated wood. Those who want to blaze trail can find lots of other places to go, places no one has been.

As we head south now, through the east side of the park, we see the French River. How many French Rivers are there in Canada? We saw one in Prince Edward Island and know there is another in Northern Ontario, near Sudbury. Should we start a list of Top Ten French Rivers?

My ferry obsession lands us on one that would have been completely unnecessary had we not taken a little shortcut. This one goes across St. Ann's Bay and it takes eight minutes from the time we arrive at the line on the east side to the time we arrive at Englishtown on the west. The fare is fifty cents and there is a staff of two. The ferry carries an average of 800 cars on a weekend and can take as many as 1,000.

If there is a problem with a ferry obsession, it emerges when the person possessing it also has an obsession with not missing the ferry. I came by this one honestly, travelling the world as a UN brat with a father who thought, sometimes wrongly, that trains and planes would wait for him. Most of my adult travelling life has been an act of rebellion against this aspect of my upbringing. Much of Nancy's adult travelling life has been an act of accompanying me, patiently but (arguably) hours too early, to train stations, airports, bus depots, and now ferry wharves.

Arriving at North Sydney in the early evening, we check into the first motel we find, a bit too fancy and expensive for us but we're not about to argue. We have driven only three hundred kilometres but they were memorable ones. Searching for that elusive right place, the seaside motel, the picturesque B&B, takes time and energy, and we left ours on the trails. Besides, the hotel is really close to the early morning ferry to Newfoundland and we have a good chance of not missing it.

# 4

The Bottom Half of Newfoundland

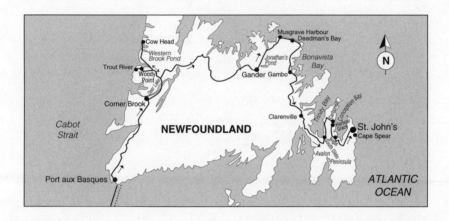

The MV *Caribou* is big – 179 metres long, 25 wide – and can hold 1,200 people and their cars. It is holding nothing like that today, but it still takes a while to load it. It has two parking decks and two decks for passengers. It is big and comfy. There are lounges with railway-type seats, a gift shop, a bar, a nursery area, a cafeteria, a restaurant that operates in busier times. The aisles are wide. One of the lounges is a movie theatre, with two large television screens. The movie is called *Outbreak* and quite a few people are watching it. There are also sleeping cabins and we have one, on somebody's advice, perhaps because the trip takes six hours. The room has four bunk beds, a bathroom, a desk, a Bible, and a sickness bag. We don't need it (the room), but it is nice not to have to carry our stuff every time we move. And there is stuff: map bag, purse, camera, computer.

This ferry wasn't our first choice. What we wanted to do was take the fourteen-hour ferry to Argentia, closer to St. John's, and work our way west. But that one doesn't run until June 21. So we are adjusting. We will arrive at Port aux Basques and drive east.

Outside you can walk around on several decks, but it is cold and foggy and there is nothing to see. We go inside to the cafeteria and have the breakfast special, which consists of two eggs, sausages, toast, and coffee. What the hell – we didn't miss the ferry. This is a triumph to celebrate.

As we are finishing, we see some familiar faces. We smile at them and they at us. It is the couple from Green Gables, the woman who wrote on the birch tree. They have been following the same route: the ferry to Nova Scotia, the Cabot Trail to North Sydney. What fun that I know her shameful secret and she doesn't know I know. Where are you from? I ask, knowing full well. She tells me. This is my moment to say: And I hope you treat the birch trees there better than you treat the ones at Green Gables. But she is so nice and friendly and maybe she just had a weak moment. Maybe that's the only tree she will ever write upon. I decide to pardon her. I've been there, I say. Pretty little town.

There is a tourist information booth on board and we load up on maps and travel guides, which are very good. Nancy settles in to write postcards and I prowl the wide aisles of the ship, accumulating information about it, such as the fact that its predecessor was torpedoed by a German U-boat on October 14, 1942, with 137 lives lost. I find a quiet place to read, just outside the empty bar, and am into a very dark Newfoundland novel, *Nine-Tenths Unseen*, by Kenneth J. Harvey, whom we will visit in a few days, when somebody nearby begins playing a video game that goes YAHOO and BOOIIOOOIIING! Then the bar opens and somebody feeds the jukebox, which plays "Little Surfer Girl" quite loudly. I move, checking out the gift shop, which has quite a few Newfoundland books, including some novels, but none by Kenneth Harvey, who might, presumably, frighten the tourists. I buy a witty and rather grouchy guidebook by Patrick O'Flaherty called *Come Near at Your Peril* and I notice that the Newfoundland flags in the gift shop are made in Taiwan. The Inner Journalist emerges and decides that this must mean something. Then the traveller pushes the Journalist aside and says: So?

I overhear some men talking about fishing. The man doing the answering says there is some lobster and crab but the cod are gone and there seems to be no sign of a return. I think the Journalist is back today because I keep overhearing conversations. In another lounge people are talking about other trips they have made. One woman talks about a boat trip up the British Columbia coast, fifteen hours without a berth: "Well, we just about went nuts," she says. "There's only so much scenery you can look at."

I go outside on deck, where there is no scenery at all, just fog, and meet a woman from Rockland, New York. She is sitting on the stairs with her camera, hoping to see whales. She tells me about taking her aunt to the Grand Canyon. People talk on ferries. They also smile and nod when they pass you, the etiquette seeming to be that the smiling and nodding begin on the second meeting.

On a long ride like this there is time to notice things. I begin noticing the baseball caps old men wear. CABOT TRAIL, one says. Another says WINSTON CUP: 1991 DAYTONA 500. There is FARMERS' DAIRY, CFB SHEARWATER, and THE WORST DAY FISHING IS BETTER THAN THE BEST DAY WORKING. I remember reading somebody saying that if you're old enough to have seen Mickey Mantle play, you're too old to wear a baseball cap. But I think I understand the dynamic. A son or daughter or wife didn't want the old guy's head to get sunburned. The old guy dutifully wears the hat, more or less oblivious to what is written on it. So a Journalist (down, boy!) can't draw any meaningful conclusions from what people wear on their hats. This is a comforting thought when I consider all the in-your-face slogans that have begun to crop up on hats and tee-shirts. It helps me to believe that the tee-shirt that says OUT OF MY WAY, ASSHOLE was a present from some-body. The guy puts it on in the morning not even aware of what it says, only that it's black.

But I digress, which ferries let you do. We reach Port aux Basques at 3:00 p.m. and drive off, having seen nothing in the way of scenery but nicely rested by the ride and excited to see Western Newfoundland. I am driving, more or less north. Quickly and almost painfully, I absorb two lessons of Newfoundland highways: (1) When you are in a passing lane and YIELD is written on the pavement, it means you've run out of passing lane; (2) when it says 50 for a bump, that is the correct speed. Bumps here are not like Prince Edward Island bumps, which you don't notice. They are breaks in the pavement.

We stop for gas and wait a bit while the Winnebago in front of us pumps more than a hundred dollars' worth in. I ask the server if it's always like this when the ferry comes in. She says: "This is nothing compared to July month. They're lined up back to the road."

Aside from the odd bump, the highway, which is the Trans-Canada, is great to drive on. It is smooth and has lots of passing lanes. The only thing is, you can't buy a belvedere. The scenery is amazing – broad valleys and large bald hills. There is a wide sweep to it, the view not cut off by sea or cliff. So the big-sky phenom-enon is at work in a most remarkable way. We stop at an Irving near Deer Lake, to replenish our junk-food supply. Some of the staples – tonic, soda, and jujubes – are missing. We settle for red licorice. There is a fine statue of a giant moose, billed as the largest in the world. It is called Howley and, expecting lore, I ask the kid behind the counter what the story is on it. "They just put it up for looks last summer," he says.

We leave the Trans-Canada and head west in the direction of Gros Morne National Park. The highway forks at the entrance to the park and we head towards Woody Point. This is because a Toronto friend told me: "Don't go to Rocky Harbour. Go to Woody Point." I wrote this down on a piece of paper, which I filed in a little envelope labelled "Nfld." By chance, I find the piece of paper, although I have no longer the faintest idea why we are supposed to do this. Sometimes decisions are made like this. Cabot probably did some stuff he couldn't explain too.

When we arrive at Woody Point we find a village in which the most likely-sounding motel, according to the guidebooks, is closed, apparently forever. The Victorian Manor, a B&B, is open and we get a nice homey room and a recommendation from Jenny Parsons to eat at the Seaside Restaurant in Trout River. It is a small world here. Jenny and her husband, Stan, own the restaurant and her mother cooks there. Trout River is fifteen or twenty kilometres away, reached by driving through the Tablelands, weird and beautiful flat-topped hills, unlike anything we have ever seen. The restaurant could not be more ordinary-looking. It is in a one-storey frame building beside a small strip of beach. Inside, the carpeting is inexpensive, the tablecloths are covered with plastic. The Irish-sounding music of the region plays too loudly. But the sun is setting over the water, a fishing boat is heading out, and the fish is delicious. I have cod, which fishermen are allowed to keep if they catch it accidentally while fishing for something else. This news briefly awakens the Inner Journalist, who then decides to put his notebook back in his pocket and eat. Nancy has salmon. Both are cooked in the simplest way, pan-fried. On the way out we give our compliments to the chef. She says that we should let them know at the B&B if we want lobster tomorrow night.

## Soap for the Moose

The Victorian Manor is about sixty years old and has as much of a Victorian look as you can get in a Newfoundland fishing village. But there is something about Newfoundland that resists the trend to the boutiquey, the B&B-ish. For example, this Victorian Manor was plagued until recently by a moose that hung around in the front garden. It was discouraged from further attendance by the device of hanging some scented soap in a tree.

We tell Stan we're going back to the Seaside Restaurant and he says he will lay in some lobster. There follows some chat about the B&B business. Right now, on June 13, it doesn't appear to be too hectic. The only other guests are two German guys who work for Lufthansa. But Stan says he is 60 per cent booked for the summer already. When I talked to the Germans last night they pointed out that Newfoundland is the same size as West Germany, with a far more varied landscape. (Also, roughly one-hundredth of the population.)

Our goal today is Western Brook Pond, from which a boat will take us into the fjords. On the way there we drive through Rocky Harbour and begin to notice how interchangeable are all the names of these communities. Rocky Harbour. Trout River. Woody Point. When we get to the parking lot for the trail to Western Brook Pond, we see a sign saying the boat doesn't go if there are fewer than five people. The trail begins with a boardwalk curving across a marsh, the curves a nice touch with some tricky saw cuts. The marsh is beautiful and so would be the mountains behind it, if we could see them, which we can't because of the fog. The marsh, which is full of wild flowers, gives way to spruce. There are moose tracks and poop. We see two Arctic hares, one of which wanders up quite close to us. At the end of the trail, at the pier, there is a group from Pennsylvania. One of the older men was stationed at Stephenville and has a thirty-one-year-old son who was born there. Hearing that we are from Ottawa, one of them asks if we got here by ferry. We say sort of. He seems to remember that there was a ferry from Ottawa to Newfoundland. Actually, what a great idea!

We wait for the boat driver to come. He doesn't. The boat won't go if it is too foggy, which it is. We walk back and in an open stretch see a moose, perhaps fifty metres off the trail. I am overjoyed. The moose is eating something but stops to look at us and its ears go up. This spooks Nancy, who has a healthy respect for moose, from her youth in Thunder Bay. Once she was in a car that was chased by a moose. We stand around long enough for her to take a picture that may have both me and the moose in it.

The trail is three kilometres long and beautiful, even though we can only see the bottom half of the landscape in the fog. When we get back to the car it is past lunchtime and we meet a guy from Mississauga who recommends the food at the Shallow Bay Tourist Motel just down the road at Cow Head. So we go there. It is funny how the tourist jungle-telegraph works. Here's a guy I've never met before and will never see again and I will value his advice over all the guidebooks and other available information. Of course, I want to go to Cow Head anyway, because I like the name and want to send a postcard from it. Also the Inner Journalist wants to use it as a dateline on a column for *Maclean's*. When we get there, we see the Germans from the B&B and also the whale-watching woman from the ferry. We are a funny little group, following each other around.

No matter how far off the beaten track you think you are, the cold fact is that you are simply doing something today that some-body did yesterday and somebody else will do tomorrow. Rather than bemoaning this, maybe we should celebrate it as evidence of a national shared experience – not that many of the people we're sharing the treated wood and belvederes with seem to be our countrymen.

On the way back to Woody Point we see another moose, in the bush beside the road. Moose are not a thrill for Newfoundlanders. There are too many of them. Many Newfoundlanders will not drive on the highways at night for fear of a collision that can be fatal both to moose and car, not to mention passengers. Jenny Parson told us yesterday that she recently counted twenty moose between Woody Point and Deer Lake, a drive of less than an hour.

At Trout River, sure enough, the lobster are waiting for us. The waitress, Lisa Brake, tells us that lobster are in season but her husband put out twenty-five lobster pots yesterday and only caught three lobsters. This is not totally bad. "Usually when we only get one, two, three we take them home and eat them ourselves," she says.

There is a lobster pot in the restaurant as decoration. We walk over to it and Lisa shows us how it works. There is time for this, since only one other table is occupied. The lobster walks in one end, attracted by the bait, which is usually herring, stuck on a spindle. Once in, it can't get out, perhaps because it is stupid.

Nancy asks Lisa how the lobster would get to the restaurant. Could a fisherman sell directly to it or would he have to go through a middleman, a fish processing plant or marketing board? Lisa says the fisherman can sell directly. We, in fact, have just eaten two of the three lobsters her husband caught yesterday. Small world. Smaller than that, actually: Lisa cooked them; she is the only staff in the restaurant today.

## Worse than a Moose

Just east of Deer Lake, back on the Trans-Canada and heading northeast, Nancy slams on the brakes. Oh good, I think, a moose. Rather, it is the Royal Canadian Mounted Police. She had carefully set the cruise control for 118, which turned out to be too fast. I begin searching for the registration and insurance, which I can't find, as the Mountie pulls up behind us. The Mountie delivers no lectures, asks no rhetorical questions about did we know how fast we were going. Nancy hands over her licence. I keep hunting for the registration as the second Mountie checks the front licence plate. Most of me is panicking, except for a small part, perhaps the Inner Journalist, which is saying: Oh good, an adventure.

Finally I find the registration, in a place where it is not supposed to be, namely my wallet. The Mountie gives us a warning. Nancy resets the cruise control to 110. We don't talk about this, owing to a rare display of tact on my part, until a few miles later when we notice that there are flies in the car. "It's from the cops," says Nancy, never one to hold a grudge.

Day 12 is going to be a driving day, probably seven hundred kilometres or so. In two days we have to be on the other side of the Rock. The drive has taken us out of the mountains and through lake country. Now the curse of the Trans-Canada Highway has hit the scenery again, causing it to disappear, except for a couple of lakes. We stop at Gander to pick up some supplies. The Fraser Mall at three on a Friday afternoon is a bit like dropping into civilization. We buy fixings for a picnic and I try out my bank card, which works here too. I find, on the first attempt, Highway 330, which loops up to the coast then follows Bonavista Bay back to the Trans-Canada. We picnic in a provincial park at Jonathan's Pond, which is a lake, of course. In Newfoundland, a pond is a lake and a brook is a river. This morning over breakfast someone talked about kitchen hearing and I finally figured out it meant catching herring. What we have been hearing (not herring) is partly a different way of using words and partly a different way of pronouncing them. Thank heaven. Why would we travel all this distance to hear people talk the way they do at home?

I travelled this road – it is called the Road to the Shore in the guidebooks and The Loop by the locals – once before, when I was working on a feature story about Newfoundland's strange experiment in Double Daylight Saving Time in 1988. Now I am anxious to show it to Nancy. Aside from Quebec City and Antigonish, it is the only place on the trip I have visited before. The beginnings, however, are inauspicious. We are away from the sea and the vegetation is scruffy. Have I remembered it wrong, or have the bushes and spruces grown up, blocking the great view I remember? Or have all the great belvederes of past days dwarfed what's here? We emerge briefly for a fine vista at Musgrave Harbour, which is home to the Banting Motel, in honour of the plane crash that ended his life here. This is a weird way to name a motel.

The scrub disappears and we turn a corner just west of
Deadman's Bay and see two icebergs. Ah yes. There is no formal
stopping place here, no plaque, no picnic tables, none of the trap-
pings of the belvedere. But this is Newfoundland in June. No one
is around and no one owns the coast. We pull onto a gravelly bit,
get out and walk over grass and moss strewn with large red boulders, to the water. There may be no other place on earth that looks
like this. The sky is blue. The ocean is crashing in. Icebergs. A sea
of red boulders on the shore. The nominating committee doesn't
even have to take a vote.

The rest of the Loop drive takes us through Deadman's Bay,
Lumsden, where we see that donairs are available, Newtown,
where there are more saltboxes and fewer bungalows than in most
towns. Most of the stores in these smaller communities are convenience stores, selling a bit of this, a bit of that. They are called
Mini-Mart, Kwikmart, Food Stop, Bishop's Hilltop Superette. A
great one in Gambo – birthplace of Joey Smallwood, of course –
advertises beer, snacks, movies, wedding supplies, and tuxedo
rentals. We see no supermarkets, or, for that matter, banks or furniture stores. We also see none of the boutiquey stuff aimed at
tourists. Typically, the towns expand sideways. The sea keeps them
from growing forward and the hill keeps them from growing back.
So the towns go on for a long time, even though there may be only
one or two streets.

As we turn south and inland, the landscape changes, with hills
and a wide horizon. This has been a long drive and the day's addition to the trip lingo is the phrase "I feel motelish." This means,
let's stop somewhere where we don't have to interact with people,
just flop and maybe even eat room service. I have to do the
*Maclean's* column, which means I need a telephone in the room
and a three-prong plug for the computer. It is getting late, at least
for us. Eventually we find the motel we want in Clarenville. It
is a big place, right on the Trans-Canada, and seems to have a

bureaucratic system that causes the check-in to take a long time. Big places are like that. I haven't missed them.

## Too Bad It's Not Nicer

Heading south next day, toward the Avalon Peninsula, which hangs off the east side of Newfoundland, we see another moose statue at another Irving station, which looks just like Howley, and we see the Putt 'n Paddle, whatever that is. We see cars and trucks pulled over to the side of the road, so that people can get out and fish. In Northern Ontario, when people are pulled over to the side of the road, it means someone has seen a moose. Here it means fishing. There is cloud and fog, quite dense at Chance Cove on Trinity Bay. Then it brightens a bit.

We decide to take another long way, and turn onto the Baccalieu Trail, Highway 80, which will take us north beside Trinity Bay then south beside Conception Bay. We drive past Dildo Pond, South Dildo, seeing lots of kids with baseball gloves, riding their bicycles on the road without bicycle helmets. Much of small-town Newfoundland has a Fifties' feel to it, which I don't find unpleasant. We pass Heart's Delight, Heart's Desire, and Heart's Content. With Ken Harvey's novel in mind, it occurs to me that the same town that looks picturesque when you drive through it, could be oppressive if you lived in it. On the other hand, more and more of us will be seeking out just such towns as we age and weary of the city pace. We have a discussion in the car about whether it would be better to live in Heart's Desire, Heart's Delight, or Heart's Content. I say it depends on how old you are. Heart's Content's slogan doesn't shine much light on the subject: Site of the First Successful Transatlantic Cable.

At Carbonear, where pirates hung out in the seventeenth century, we begin encountering signs of what might be termed civilization. There is a long lineup of cars waiting to get into a shopping mall. Instead of the skull and crossbones, there is a more fearsome sight – a billboard advertising a country music station, always a sign that you are nearing a city. There is a traffic jam near a Canadian Tire at Harbour Grace, a decor centre at Bay Roberts, plus a fancy-looking B&B, a McDonald's, and a Tim Horton's. But you would not mistake this for Ontario. For one thing, no one in the town is speeding.

My novelist friend Ken Harvey says his house is in Burnt Head but Cupid's is the mailing address and it is reached by the Brigus turnoff. These are very old villages, perhaps close enough to St. John's to be affected by the urban conservationist ethic. Fewer old buildings have been torn down. After we drop our bags at the house, Nancy, Ken, and I drive to Brigus and walk around. It is old and charming, with narrow streets and sidewalks and houses built right up to them, in the Old Country manner. City people are moving in, but Brigus has resisted boutiquing, so far. There is a graveyard overlooking the harbour from a height, the tombstones leaning and many of them barely legible. I check dates: 1856, 1873, 1892. I see

MARY JANE BUSH

Who fell asleep in Jesus
31st June 1889
Aged 23 years 7 months.

Ken and Jan have three kids and a big black dog, Cheever. Ken's output includes three novels, two short story collections, a volume of poetry, and many unpublished works. For a person with a reputation for dark and violent writing, he has a cheery nature and a fondness for kidding. He is no fan of the way Newfoundland has been treated in the arts – the whole happy fisherman thing – terming it "cultural bigotry." After dinner we sit around and talk about that, as well as other, happier things. It is cold enough to light the wood stove.

We are up early the next day for a walk on Burnt Head, which is the headland. After our walk yesterday, it is clear that one of the great virtues of having friends in places you don't know is that they can make presents to you of places you would never see otherwise. No highway goes by, no plaque marks them, no guidebook points to there. Burnt Head is like that. We park at a church and begin walking on the grass, seeing a brook and a pond down to our right, the sea and the headland ahead. It is a mauzy old day, in the Newfoundland phrase that Jan taught us: warm but cloudy. We can't see the sea because of the fog. "We are poisoned with the weather," is the way some people put it.

Except that here the fog creates a kind of magic. There is no one but Nancy, Ken, and me. And Cheever, who sees sheep ahead on the grass and takes after them. We are not on anyone's land, as far as we know. People and their sheep just use it. Ken calls and Cheever comes back. I congratulate Ken on having a well-behaved dog and Cheever takes off again. The sheep learn that they can walk out on the cliff and down it a bit, finding some rock they can stand on where Cheever can't get them. It is quiet enough that we can hear the clack of their hooves on the rock. There are no other people in sight, not another dwelling. Just us and the fog and the sheep and this ancient-looking landscape, truly a scene out of another century.

We pass piles of rocks that are the foundations of the original dwellings. The first English colony in Newfoundland was around here. At the water's edge the drop is deep, the water clear. Ken says he saw whales from here just the other day. "Too bad it's not nicer," he says, and I think I've heard other people use that exact expression in the past few days. How much of Newfoundland have we missed because it is covered in fog?

Yet, much seems to be *added* by the fog. Or am I just being too cheerful?

With Jan and young Emma added, we drive to Upper Island Cove, another pretty little town with horrible curves. We stop at

the Tim Horton's in Bay Roberts, then at the fish store, which
doubles as the video store. A sign says: "Movies, Loto 649, Worms."

That night, I finish *Nine-Tenths Unseen*, which is not about
the Newfoundland we have seen, except that it is haunted by the
rough landscape of the towns. Just before we got to Cupid's yesterday I took a detour to the village of Bareneed, which is depicted
in Ken's novel. I wanted to see the church looming over the village
and the narrow opening in the harbour where the iceberg – nine-
tenths unseen – could block it. But Bareneed looks nothing like
that. Later Ken said he loved the name of the village and fixed his
own landscape onto it.

### Perfect Inn, Flawed Guests

Getting lost is not a good idea in St. John's. In other cities a rough
knowledge of the landmarks and main streets will do. Not here. It
is said that the streets were laid out in order to spare the horses
difficult climbs. Consequently, the streets wind up and down the
steep hills of the city and there is no such thing as a right angle.
That also means there is no such thing as just going around the
block if you miss your turn. A cute little system of one-way streets
has been added just to complicate matters. We don't have a good
city map and only a vague idea of where we are going. Where we
are going is, in fact, any one of several B&Bs listed in one of the
many publications in the car.

It is, of course, a beautiful city, the harbour being its most striking feature, as we notice every time we find ourselves driving
downhill towards it, which is more often than we would like.
Probably none of this would have happened had I not spent a few
days here in 1988. That made me think I knew my way around.
That and the fact that it is a port city, so you always know where
the water is. You'd think that would help, but it doesn't.

Eventually, because the city is small, we luck onto one of the
streets we are looking for, and find the Winterholme Heritage Inn.

It is a beautiful old mansion, green, with turrets and gables and pillars holding up the front porch. Inside it is big and comfortable, almost a caricature of the country inn, with paisley bedspreads, a bottle of wine in the room, with a corkscrew, lots of wood, hundreds of paper flowers, high ceilings, those dressed-up dolls here and there, hardwood floors, French-provincial-style desks and chairs. The whole thing.

It is the kind of perfect place that deserves perfect travellers. Unfortunately, we are not like that. Here is how you desecrate the perfect B&B room. First you throw the suitcases onto the paisley bedspread. Then you grab one of the richly coloured towels out of the bathroom and spread it onto the glass-topped desk so the laptop won't slide on the glass. Then you raise the computer screen in front of the paper tulips, run the power cord to the outlet, which unfortunately causes it to nestle in the basket of ivy, open the potato chips and place them on the French-provincial bedside table, dump some of the digestive potion you've been taking into the wine glass, fill it up with water and use the reverse end of the corkscrew to stir it up. Dick and Ruby Cook who run this place deserve better than us.

We compound our insensitivity by ignoring Dick's recommendations for places to eat. Having been here once eight years ago, I know better, and decisively lead us halfway up Signal Hill to a restaurant with a great view. The food is not as great. In my defence, I say this trip is not about gourmet food. And the view of the harbour is terrific. Behind us is a table at which a well-dressed father who seems to be visiting his children persuades each of them that, despite the many interesting things on the menu, such as a mooseburger, they should make the salad bar their entire meal. I think this may be the first dislikeable person we have encountered in two weeks of travelling. Charitably, I decide that he is from away. I don't know where all this charitability is coming from. Can it last?

## Finally, the Beginning

Two weeks into the trip we are about to enact the symbolic beginning to it. Cape Spear, twenty-five kilometres away, is the easternmost point in North America, and we drive there, after heeding
Dick Cook's warning to take jackets despite the sun. "It's cool in
the air," he says.

Cape Spear is a National Historic Park, dedicated by the Prince
and Princess of Wales in June of 1983. More important, it is a collection of impressive vistas – steep cliffs, rocks, a rugged coastline
to either side, the full, unbroken Atlantic before you and perhaps
Ireland over the horizon. Ignoring the caution signs, you can strike
out on your own and walk on grassy little paths made by people
who largely ignored the caution signs. The interminable warnings
are annoying. Not that you couldn't fall down and hurt yourself
quite badly, but every time you check out a vista there's a danger
sign in the foreground of it. "The cliffs and seas in this area are
dangerous," says a sign that greets you on your arrival. "Utmost
care must be taken, particularly with small children." More
effective is a small cross erected to memories of three people who
drowned here.

Turning and looking west, you see all of Canada, beginning
without trees until the first hill is reached and the trees begin. I
take a picture of Nancy with all of Canada behind her.

This was also Fort Cape Spear, from 1941 until 1945, with
heavy artillery emplacements, never used. A guide is taking some
kids through it. "They were, like, fighting against who?" he asks,
hopefully.

"Germans," say a few kids. I wonder about the reaction of
German tourists, of whom we are seeing more and more.

"How loud was it?" asks a kid.

"Really, really loud," says the guide.

There are corridors dug into the face of the hill as part of Fort
Cape Spear, apparently a very good place to write your name, over
the years.

There are a couple of lighthouses and a gift shop, which features a display on lighthouses, including the information that the four thousand remaining in Canada are not called lighthouses any more. This may have something to do with the fact that they are no longer inhabited. Now they are officially called "lightstations." Imagine being at the committee meeting which produced that one.

On the way back we take a detour to look at Petty Harbour, the closest thing Newfoundland has to a picture-postcard village. Ever alert to the encroachments of big-city ways, I spot Petty Harbour Unisex Hairstyling. The Inner Journalist stirs and I tell him to calm down.

Back in St. John's I begin to experience big-city irritability. I have to do a phone interview with an Ottawa radio station in a couple of hours and I also need to pick up a phone gizmo for my computer. In the Radio Shack on Water Street it is lunchtime and there is only one clerk on duty. He is showing a woman how to change a battery in her phone, first testing the one that is in there. I get grumpier and grumpier at the fact that this guy is alone in this big store and finally walk out (without, however, announcing that I am doing so; this is another telepathic rage). We walk to the Murray Premises, a beautifully reconditioned eighteenth-century building on the waterfront and the first restaurant we encounter informs us it is no longer serving at 2:15 in the afternoon. My grumpiness increases, as does the realization that it is having deadlines that does this to me.

Eventually I cheer up. We find a restaurant and later we find the *Scademia*, a sailing tour vessel I rode on eight years ago, and Charlie Anonsen, the skipper, who remembers me and something I wrote about him. We make a reservation to take a harbour cruise and I feel better about life. Maybe we will see a whale, or a sunset, or both. All of this only goes to show that your trip is what you bring to it.

It is upon returning to the hotel that we receive word of my mother's illness. Nancy makes arrangements for us to fly back to

Ottawa and Dick Cook tells us to leave the car here, for however long. It will save us the twenty dollars a day it would cost at the airport. I can't get over how nice people are. I also like leaving the car here, a tangible commitment to the idea of completing the trip.

# 5

## Another Beginning in Newfoundland

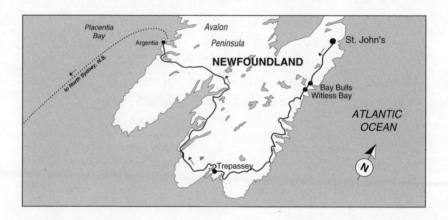

The weather when we return is cloudy and cool. We have just time to unpack and get to the waterfront before the *Scademia* departs for its evening cruise. The departure, as it turns out, is delayed for the arrival of the ship's two musicians. Finally, it leaves without them. I'm just as glad, although I like the notion of a ship waiting for musicians. Life seems to be a bit less organized here. Charlie Anonsen is not coming but introduces us to the skipper, Brian O'Neill.

A dozen other people board (capacity is seventy-five) and we motor, rather than sail, out of the harbour, past docks loaded with containers. Bosun, the six-year-old Newfoundland dog, is along.

I met his mother, also Bosun, on my last voyage. Dave, one of the crew members, takes the microphone and introduces the safety features, which seem to include a bar, as well as extra parkas and a furnace, which will come in handy. In the harbour are some freighters and four British minesweepers. Dave directs our attention to the starboard side, where a dock is being constructed for the Hibernia oil field out in the ocean. "There's not much action here now but this used to be the site of many fishing wharves," he says.

He says that this is one of the best-protected harbours in the world and you can see what he means when we leave it through the narrow opening and begin pitching and yawing and whatnot. Brian O'Neill says this would be a small sea for the wintertime but is a pretty large one for the summer. Whales may be hard to spot in a rough sea but we are told to yell "thar she blows" if we see a waterspout. I see one but can't bring myself to utter the phrase. "There's one over there," I say. We head for it and get alongside, just northeast of Cape Spear. It is a humpback and it comes up once, so we can see how large it is. Once it dives, showing its tail. I ask Dave if, taking as many as five trips a day, he gets blasé about whales. He says no. There is something mystical about them, the notion that there is something so big in the ocean around you that can appear at any time.

We see a couple of puffins (which I add to our running wildlife catalogue), then go in to get warm, after an hour and a half outside. I ask the whale question to Brian, who is at the wheel, and his answer is the same. He never goes Ho-hum, another stupid whale. That's encouraging. Somehow it is important that the thing that excites us does not bore the natives.

Brian is aware of my mother's death and asks about her. He talks about his mother, Ellen, whose kidneys failed some months ago and for whom dialysis didn't work. He has seven brothers and sisters and they were all tested to see who could donate a kidney. "I was fortunate enough to be chosen," he says. Seven or eight weeks ago they went to Halifax for the operation. She is fine. He is fine too, and very proud.

I like this story better than the "colourful character" stories some people have been urging me to seek out. Here is a prototypical colourful character, the skipper of a ship sailing out of St. John's harbour, but behind the colour is a real person with a real life, a mother, and the kind of quiet heroism that I suspect exists all across the country and never makes it into feature stories. In the *Scademia's* off-season, November to April, Brian teaches at the Marine Institute at Memorial University. Maybe this is *his* off-season.

We talk about the cod. He has read somewhere that they have been sighted in abundance close to shore. He doesn't think the seals are to blame for the shortage. Very little of what they eat is cod. He blames the federal government for letting foreigners overfish. Although he is a young man, he remembers the glory days of the cod fishery which were not too far back. The fishermen would fish twenty-four hours a day, refuelled and replenished by supply boats from home. At night, the water would look like a city, with all the lights.

Now seven thousand people a year are leaving. If he was a kid, he'd be thinking of it. Brian has a ten-year-old daughter and wonders what she will do. But he's encouraged by Hibernia and the copper and zinc findings at Voisey's Bay.

Other passengers wander into the wheelhouse and he demonstrates his radar, showing the coastline and other boats and even the waves. I say: "But you can see everything now, why do you need it?" He answers: "The tourists like it."

The screech-in ceremony, in which we decline to take part, is rather low-key and almost ironic. Three guys from Manitoba drink some screech, eat some bologna, kiss a wooden fish, and say something that is supposed to be in Newfoundlandese, something like: "Indeed I is. Me old son. And long may your big jib draw." Is that it? Anyway, they get a certificate for it, as we sail into the harbour, which looks pretty in the fading light under a three-quarter moon.

## Another Beginning at Signal Hill

Signal Hill is where McCourt began his coast-to-coast journey in
1963, the beginning, or the end, of the Trans-Canada Highway.
Everybody goes there, but that doesn't mean you shouldn't. From
the top of the hill you can look west and see the harbour, the city,
also Quidi Vidi Lake and Gibbet Hill, where they used to hang
people. To the south, the other shore of the harbour. To the east,
Ireland. It is warm and foggy, mauzy. There are paths all over the
hillside, boardwalks and steep staircases. Signboards at the top of
the hill display historic photographs, including one taken from this
very spot in 1884 showing icebergs, lots of them.

The people are of all types. A couple of young fellows from the
British minesweeper are there and they chat with a couple of
Canadians who did the same thing during the war, fifty years ago.
One of the older fellows has a great hat – NANAIMO TRANSIT. He
and his wife are driving across the country with another couple in
RVs. They've been on the road sixty days, with ninety to do. I sud-
denly feel like a trifler. They stay at truck stops. He has a book, *The
Truck Stop Guide*, that tells him which truck stops are RV-friendly. I
ask him what's the best thing he's seen. "I guess the best thing I've
seen is the friendliness of the people," he says.

There is a trail down Signal Hill with many stairs. The grass and
dandelions are bright in the sun and I see a whale. As I grab the
binoculars for a closer look, two Newfoundlanders ask if we've
seen any whales. We say yes and they say that last week they were
a stone's throw away. Now they've moved, following the little fish
they eat by the thousands. "The caplin is at Outer Cove," one of
the men says. When they hear we are from Ottawa they want us to
take Brian Tobin, the premier, back there. And they accept our
compliments on St. John's by saying: "When the weather's nice,
there's no place nicer. It's clean, the people are friendly, like us."

From Signal Hill you see the Confederation Building off in the
distance, far from the ocean, and you wonder why it is where it is.

When we get there we find it has a commanding view of the harbour, although a couple of large new buildings have cut off its view of the narrows. The statue of John Cabot is looking out over the scene. He landed in 1497. Inside, a guide tells us, as many others have, that next year, the 500th anniversary, will be a really big one for tourists.

We see the marble lobby with the many flags representing Canadian Legion branches. We see a peculiar mural depicting Cabot, the Indians, a Mountie, a soldier and sailor, some sailing ships, loggers, fishermen, an airplane flying overhead, Mackenzie King, some children, a Newfoundland dog, and Sir Humphrey Gilbert, first colonizer of Newfoundland, wearing Joey Smallwood's face. We see a plaque with the names of all the Newfoundland members of the Order of Canada, including Christopher Pratt, the designer of the Newfoundland flag. You can learn a lot about a province by what it displays in its legislature.

There is a display marking what the guide calls "our saddest day" – July 1. Oh no, we think. But it is sad for another reason. It is the anniversary of the Battle at Beaumont Hamel in 1916, in which 798 members of the Royal Newfoundland Regiment went out of their trenches into no-man's-land and only 68 came back.

Outside the legislative chamber on the third floor, Newfoundland art, including that of Pratt, is on display. In the chamber we find that the government in Newfoundland sits to the *left* of the Speaker. In an earlier, pre-Confederation legislative chamber, that's where the wood stove was, making it a better place to be on a cold day. When the new building was put up, no one saw any reason to change.

The legislative chamber's colour scheme features a kind of flat green, with a darker green carpet accented by pink squares. The chairs are lined with leather from seals, this being an attempt to counter-propagandize the anti-sealing lobby. The desks are covered with papers. The members get until Tuesday to clean them off. This is Friday. The premier's, it is encouraging to note, is clean. When Joey Smallwood died, in December, 1991, he lay in state here or, as the guide puts it, "He waked here for three days."

### Disarmed in Witless Bay

We leave St. John's again, this time to Argentia, on the western edge of the Avalon Peninsula, where we will get a different ferry to North Sydney. This one takes fifteen hours and we can't get a berth on it, one of the first signs we have had that we are no longer the only people on the road. In this case, the road is Highway 10. We have time and are taking the long way, around the bottom of the peninsula and up. We go through Bay Bulls and stop at Witless Bay for something light to eat. Nancy orders fish and chips, even though she is told that the cod is from Norway. I order cod tongues, which I have never had. It turns out I don't like them all that much and when I am finished, I ask the waitress where they are from.

"Norway," she says.

"No," I say. "I mean which part of the cod."

"The tongue," she replies.

Oh. I thought cod tongue was just a figure of speech, a colourful regional expression, like figgy duff or toad-in-the-hole. When in Rome, they say, do as the Romans do. This is what I do in Witless Bay.

The drive down the east coast is pretty, hilly, a lot of low trees, good vistas, sun, blue water, and one deep harbour after another, each with a village. There are moose signs, then an animal beside the road – what is it? – then another sign: CAUTION: CARIBOU CROSSING. Aha! That's what it was.

I get another good sign for my collection: CRAFT SHOP, T-BONE STEAKS, BUILDING SUPPLIES, LOBSTER.

As we approach the southern tip of the peninsula the scenery opens up to big boggy prairie, spongy to walk upon, with lovely wild flowers, ponds and hills and a great sweep to the horizon. Chance Cove, Portugal Cove, Biscay Bay, Trepassey. A causeway

carries a sign saying: HIGH SEAS, ROAD MAY BE COVERED BY WATER
OR DEBRIS. I like any and all indications that life is not as I'm used
to it. So far most of the great drives we've done have been recommended by a friend or a book. This is a great drive, one that no
one has prepared us for.

At Argentia we are early, of course. We buy our ferry ticket then
drive the car into a kind of carwash, where the Camry is searched,
vacuumed, and run under a high-velocity spray to get rid of the
golden nematode and potato wart, two serious potato pests that
don't occur on the mainland, and which I might have ordered for
supper, given my current level of culinary alertness. Failing that,
we split a club sandwich in the terminal's cafeteria, have coffee and
candy bars and wait. And wait. Travelling with me is a real joy for
people who like waiting. There is an announcement that your gas
tank should not be more than three-quarters full, which is a new
one on me. Now I begin thinking about that, and the fact that we
gassed up not too many miles back. Then I wonder how you get
gas out of your tank, quietly. Perhaps I could drive around the
parking lot about five hundred times.

When we are in the lineup to drive on and I see an official with
a flashlight looking into the cars ahead of us I figure the jig is up.
He'll look at the gas gauge, pull us out of the lineup, and people
will drive by pointing at us. Then if we get on the ferry at all, all
the seats will be taken and we'll have to spend fifteen hours sitting
on the floor. Then the ferry sinks and survivors tell the major television networks that the disaster was the fault of a dark green
Camry with Ontario plates.

What the official is really interested in, we find out, is matching
up the number of people in the car with the number of people on
the boarding pass. In fact, he pulls someone else out of the line and
motions us ahead, with our three-quarter-tank of gas. We board at
10:45 and look for a quiet place to spend the night. This is a huge
ferry, the *Joseph and Clara Smallwood*, and we find some comfy
chairs with a table on the 7 deck, then move when a travelling

teenage boxing team sets up in a nearby space. The other side has lots of room and we find reclining airline-type seats upon which to sleep, awakened occasionally by public address announcements telling us where it is permissible to smoke (mainly outside).

It is a bit like sleeping on an airplane, or a train, the sensation coming not from the motion of the vehicle but the vibrations of the motor. There is even an occasional shake, like a plane hitting an air pocket. The boxing team is up all night, wandering about, chattering, playing little games, looking for a lost bag, which they finally find at 6:40 a.m. I'm awake at dawn, get a cup of coffee and read the Nova Scotia guidebook, learning that 1996 is the year of the wooden boat. Peace is shattered at 9:00 a.m. by the movie beginning, quite loudly. If I ran a ferry I would promote peace and quiet on board and then advertise it. I bet it would draw.

As North Sydney comes in view, so does a whale, perhaps a minke, says the guy who spotted it. This is right after he told his teenage son one would be showing up just about where it did. It's nice to watch the two of them, the guy really pleased with himself, the kid knowing that his father had no idea what he was talking about, but happy for him.

At 12:30 we are told we are about to dock and should go to our cars. Some people wander about the car decks in confusion. You can see how it could happen, with all the cars, all the decks, and the inevitable confusion between port and starboard, bow and stern. I can't think of a worse panic than hearing about 150 cars blow their horns while you look for your car. Fortunately, we find ours easily. And it has lots of gas.

# 6

## Thrice Across Nova Scotia

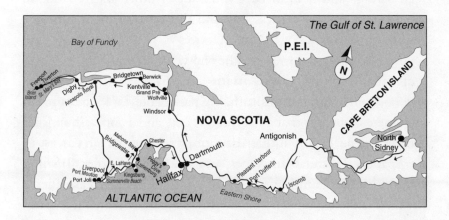

It is the Saturday of the Canada Day long weekend. To make matters worse we are into what may be the most screwed-up section of the trip so far, in terms of planning. We land on Cape Breton Island. Tomorrow we have to be out on the Digby Neck, precisely as far away as it's possible to be and still be in Nova Scotia. Then we will come back across the province, toward Halifax, then drive back across the province again and out into New Brunswick. I planned this myself, in accordance with my notions of the people we want to see and when they are going to be where they are. At least it is a workable-sized province, not Manitoba or Alberta, that we have to drive across and back.

Facing this and running on about four hours of sitting-up sleep, we are not in an ambitious frame of mind, which is why we drive away from, rather than toward, Louisbourg. How could we skip Louisbourg? It's how decisions are made on an unstructured odyssey like this one and a lot of it has to do with luck and timing. If we had reserved earlier on the *Joseph and Clara Smallwood*, we would have had a bed, and hit the day rested, anxious to do a fort. On the other hand, at the time when we originally intended to leave Newfoundland, the Argentia ferry wasn't running. We would have driven back across Newfoundland and perhaps have seen Salvage and Port au Port and a lot of other places. And we would have missed Witless Bay and the caribou: next time for Louisbourg, we say.

It is becoming tee-shirt weather now. We are on country roads, tamer than Newfoundland's, with some habitation, nothing too steep or rough, but lots of brush. We pass a cute-looking tea room and discuss why it is that a tea room is cute and a coffee shop isn't. Stop at a general store in East Bay for provisions, which consist of newspapers, lobster sandwiches, and ice for the cooler. Turning south from Antigonish, we stop for coffee at Lochiel Lake Picnic Park. I like the expression "picnic park," perhaps because it is accurate. We sit down beside the lake, which is quiet and reminiscent of one of Ontario's smaller ones. This is calming scenery, still water, sunshine, trees, as opposed to challenging or awe-inspiring.

We stop at a resort at Liscomb, on what is known as the Eastern Shore, and find tennis courts, a putting green, and no vacancy, which induces a mixture of relief (how much does it *cost* to stay in a resort that has its own putting green?) and mild anxiety (it *is* the long weekend). Nancy uses the phone and finds one room available at the Marquis of Dufferin a couple of towns down the coast and we take it sight unseen. We are lucky again. The room, one of the older ones, across the road from the ocean, is small and dumpy, proving once more the adage that the fancier the name, the plainer the establishment. But it is clean and quiet, we are too pooped to care, we have a little balcony and a nice view of Beaver Harbour. And the halibut, in the dining room of the main house, built in 1859, is great. We take a little stroll beside the water and into an ancient graveyard at dusk. The graveyards in this part of the world always have the best view.

The next day feels better, although it is mauzy and the fog comes and goes as we drive along what the guidebook calls the Marine Drive, past some of the great place names of the trip – Mushaboom, Pope's Harbour, Pleasant Harbour, where the fog breaks, Murphy Cove, Musquodoboit Harbour, East Chezzetcook – southwest toward Halifax. We have to get all the way across the province today, which seems like a daunting task, but it is in fact only about four hundred kilometres. Around here the ocean looks like a lake, closed in, the shore featuring boulders and lawns. There is sun in the air and fog on the water and we seem to have Highway 7 to ourselves.

We bypass Dartmouth and Halifax successfully and turn northwest. This road, 101, is one of several that cuts straight across the province, efficiently and at the expense of scenery. To compensate, I collect town slogans, which Nova Scotia seems to have in abundance:

WINDSOR: HOME OF SAM SLICK
WOLFVILLE: LAND OF EVANGELINE
KENTVILLE: SHIRETOWN OF KINGS
BERWICK: NOVA SCOTIA'S APPLE CAPITAL

I think my favourite, for sheer lameness, is BRIDGETOWN: GATEWAY TO FUNDY AND VALLEYVIEW. If I was the mayor, I would immediately construct something memorable, even if only a big sign, which could then say something like BRIDGETOWN: HOME OF THE WORLD'S BIGGEST SIGN.

We stumble, really, into Grand Pré National Historic Park, just looking for a picnic table where we can stop for coffee out of the Thermos. What we find is a moving memorial to the expulsion of the Acadians, in an attractive setting, with gardens, ponds, and weeping willows. We wander into the Grand Pré Memorial Church, which was built in 1922. It has paintings depicting the expulsion in 1755, plus letters and documents of the time, including a rather touching one by the British governor in which it is clear that he doesn't much like what he is doing. There is a guest book, the inscriptions contrasting strangely with the sombre message of the church. "Nice!" writes someone from Sweden. "Beautiful – stained glass lovely," adds a visitor from Buffalo. "Interessant" (New Brunswick). And someone has drawn eleven happy faces.

To this unfortunate juxtaposition is added the typically Canadian irony that it was an American, Henry Wadsworth Longfellow, who got to tell the tale of the expulsion in his epic poem *Evangeline*, and that he did so without ever having visited Grand Pré.

The way Nova Scotia is oriented, it is difficult to say with accuracy whether you are north or south. Let's just say we are at the top of the western part of the province, heading further west, out to the end of Digby Neck where my friend Andy Moir has a place. We pass through the beautiful old towns of Wolfville and Annapolis Royal. There are stunning old houses, painted interesting colours, and few signs that the onrush of boutiquedom has arrived. We thought Ontario was pretty old when we moved to Ottawa from Brandon, but this is older. The oldest dwelling in Annapolis Royal goes back to 1709 and everywhere we turn we see references to the 1600s and 1700s.

It is low tide when we hit the Digby Neck, a narrow strip of land poking out into the Bay of Fundy. Sandy Cove has no water in it. It could be Sandy Mudflats. A number of signs advertise whale-watching tours. Judging from what I have seen on the Gaspé, the north shore of the St. Lawrence, Western Newfoundland, the Avalon Peninsula and here, whale watching may be the growth industry of the decade. It may be the Nineties' version of the baseball card stores of the Eighties, with everybody getting into it, oversupply undercutting the value and the public gradually losing interest. It's hard to imagine losing interest in whales, although it is not hard to image whales being driven off by the constant buzzing harassment of tour boats.

When we get to East Ferry, for the trip to Long Island, we just miss the ferry and have to wait a whole ten minutes. The ferry, the *Joshua Slocum* (named after the first man to sail around the world by himself, from 1895 to 1898), takes three minutes and forty-five seconds, before depositing us at Tiverton. On the drive to Freeport we see an ancient Nash Rambler in someone's yard.

Andy worked with me at the *Brandon Sun* twenty-five years ago. Before that he was a campus radical and after that he was a CBC television producer, one of the founders of "The Journal." Every once in a while he gets the urge to scale back, take the pressure off. He can do carpentry for a living when that happens. Then the CBC calls, or at one time the CTV "National News," and he goes back. He has had the Freeport property since the late Seventies and always the thought of moving to it permanently. One day, while working in Toronto, he got stuck in traffic on the Don Valley Expressway and decided it wasn't worth it. He phoned CBC Maritimes to see if there was any part-time work. There was only full-time, running the evening news for CBC Halifax. So he took it. Now he is ready to leave for good. The house he and Chris Callahan share is a big old thing and they are making it into a bed-and-breakfast. Make-Your-Own-Damn-Bed and Breakfast, Andy wants to call it, but Chris will show a less grumpy face to the customers.

Looking southeast from their hill, Andy and Chris can see St. Mary's Bay. Looking northwest they can see the Bay of Fundy and Grand Manan Island. When the fog comes in, as it will, they can hear the otherwordly sound of an electronic foghorn (from a light-station, no doubt).

We go for a walk in the late afternoon haze, to Beautiful Cove. The two dogs, Slick and Shetland (both named, with the journalist's gallows humour, for environmental disasters), lag behind. We climb on rocks, look at the remnants of a dead whale, and hear tales of the islands. There are two of them: Long Island, where we are, and Brier Island, the next one. Population of the two islands is about 1,500. When the kids on Brier Island take the school bus on the ferry over to the consolidated school in Freeport, they must wear their life jackets, but not their seatbelts, since school buses don't have them.

Although it is hard to think of a more beautiful, more stirring spot, the locals, like locals everywhere, see the grass greener elsewhere. Many of them go to cottages at lakes. Andy fights isolation by listening to marine radio for the weather and the local gossip. He picks up more gossip on the ferry and keeps track of visitors. Last year they were from all the provinces and all the states of the continental U.S.

Dinner that night is Digby scallops, broiled on a skewer with bacon. We stay up too late, talking not so much about old times as about this part of the world. How do people live? What do they do? Meanwhile, nothing seems inappropriate, not the turtles warming themselves in front of the fire, not the cat, Chlöe, eating her food on a little pedestal hung high up on the wall where the dogs can't get at her.

Sometimes the island has an old-home week around the July 1 festivities. There is a parade, usually with about a dozen people in it. And there is a beauty pageant. Once Andy got roped into being a judge for it. He and one of the two other judges took it quite seriously. They compiled a checklist of positive attributes for the contest winner to have. They attended a lunch in order to get to know the candidates. The lunch was ham with olives in it. Finally, the most experienced judge took the other two aside. "Look," he said, "Miss Brier Island won last year, Miss Tiverton Fire Hall won it the year before. This year the winner has to be someone from Freeport." So they looked at the Freeport candidates, decided which one deserved a break most, and gave it to her.

## Too Bad It's Not Nicer: Part Two

After absorbing more such lore the next morning, we set out for Port Joli. We will drive across Nova Scotia once more, foiled once again by the weather. We want to drive around the southwest corner of the province, the Lighthouse (sic) Route and the so-called French Coast, but there is fog and the marine radio says it will last. So we pick an overland route that will take us more quickly to Liverpool. Next time.

There's also a balancing rock we miss, rushing to catch the ferry off the island, but we figure there will be more balancing rocks. Canada must be full of them. The cars on the ferry have licence plates from Quebec, Ontario, Maine, and New York. There is fog at Tiverton, water in Sandy Cove. Everything has changed since we saw it last. At Liverpool, the end of Highway 8, we turn west in the direction of Port Mouton, which Nova Scotians pronounce Port Muttoon. Apparently Champlain, who named all the bays around here, gave this one its name, probably in 1604, because it was here that a sheep fell overboard.

Now we begin following a terrific set of instructions to get to a place at Port Joli. The directions include nothing like an address or a street number, just little landmarks someone has accumulated along the way. We are not to take either of two signs to Port Joli, but a turnoff to the left after a dirt road, community hall, and convenience store, not follow down to the right but take the left fork at the mailboxes, passing a barely discernible road, then a small graveyard, which we may not be able to see either, then find a clearly discernible driveway, a garbage box, and a metal gate that may not have the name on it. We find it. We only get lost in easy places.

The place we call Port Joli, which may actually not be at Port Joli as such, belongs to Anne Carver, widow of my uncle, Humphrey Carver, who died last October. He was a huge man, towering over us all, in both physical and intellectual presence. The place here, which we are visiting for the first time, reflects him. He was an architect, a city planner, and also a landscape architect. The property is full of paths he cut through the grass and the white and purple lupins, and the paths contain places to stop and sit on a bench and have a look, out and down, at the ocean. There is a long walk down through the woods to the beach, which I instantly recognize from his watercolours, with the walls of boulders that appear from time to time. Many members of the Carver clan are there. I am related to them because Humphrey's first wife, Mary, who died almost fifty years ago, was my father's sister. Humphrey's son, my cousin Peter, is not here, but his sister Debby is, along with her husband, Tim Matthews. Peter's ex-wife, Penny, is also here, along with their two daughters, Stephanie and Kate, and Stephanie's husband, Bill Greenlaw. I find it amazing that I have never seen them here, at their gathering place, but it is the old business of spending all our summers at Lake of the Woods, where the Gordon summer place has been since 1905.

Most of the younger Carvers were born in Ottawa, where Humphrey and Anne lived, but several have migrated to Nova Scotia. Some of the Carvers maintain a Gordon orientation, which takes them west in the summer to Lake of the Woods. Others have opted completely for Nova Scotia. They are not alone. The list of Ontario expatriates seems to grow daily.

The beach is deserted except for us and we all walk and stop to sit in the sun, then walk some more. When we arrive at the place where the path enters the woods to go back up the hill, there is a horse standing there. A horse does not belong beside the ocean, the way I look at life, but this one seems to feel right at home. Up the hill, we meet the horse's owner, Dirk van Loon, a writer and editor and publisher and pioneer expatriate. He arrived in Nova Scotia from the United States in 1969. His first summer here was also the first for his new next-door neighbours, Humphrey and Anne. Both of their places had been farms.

Dirk now publishes four magazines, one of which, *Rural Delivery*, has subscribers all across the country, to judge by its letters section. His latest venture is a kind of museum, the Hank Snow Country Music Centre in Liverpool, which is drawing visitors, despite not even having a sign on the highway. Atlantic Canada likes to celebrate its country singers. Already we have passed markers commemorating Stompin' Tom Connors in P.E.I., the Rankin Family on Cape Breton, and now this. And there is still Springhill, home of Anne Murray, to go.

What kept Dirk here, got him inventing magazines and museums to have an excuse to stick around, was the beauty of the place, followed gradually by what he calls "life's investment," the accumulation of experience and memory. "Maybe when you live out in the country like where we are and most times you look out the window and see nothing walking along, when you do see something walking along it sears your brain. There is not a window in the house I can not tell you a story about what I once saw 'out there.' A moose, bobcat, mink, fox, porcupine, deer." Humphrey was part of that landscape too, and Dirk still sees him, the first summer he has been gone, walking over the crest of his hill.

Dirk's philosophy on the expatriates, the influx of full-time residents, is less alarmist than some, perhaps because he has seen what expatriates, like himself and Humphrey, can bring. "Full-time residents invest full-time in a place, enjoying the pleasures, enduring the pain," he says. "Maybe some other areas have so many newcomers they lose their identity. Once again, moderation in all things is what to strive or hope for."

Our sense of time, like our sense of place, grows rather approximate after weeks on the road, so it is a bit jarring to be reminded that this is Canada Day, as well as the Monday of the long weekend. All the Nova Scotia Carvers, of whom we count eight, have to return to their homes, most of them in Halifax. We leave Port Joli in the early evening in separate cars and reassemble for a restaurant meal at Somerville Beach. The restaurant has a marvellous location on the water, but is overdecorated and has three kinds

of butter, always a bad sign. Then we split up, with most of the
gang heading for Halifax and our car following Penny Carver's to
her home at Rhodes Corner, which is equidistant, she tells us, from
Bridgewater, Mahone Bay, and Lunenberg, as if that would help.
We drive perhaps fifty kilometres through the dark and the gathering fog, with the gas-tank warning light on again, wondering if
we will make the last ferry from LaHave across the LaHave River.
We do. This is another fifty-cent ferry. It was threatened with
extinction until a protest meeting at the LaHave Fire Hall saved it.
Now it, like the one we took earlier to Englishtown, will have its
fare go up to $1.75. On the other side, at East LaHave, I find gas
and we get to Rhodes Corner and Smith Mountain, where Penny
Carver's house is. The next morning we learn that the fireworks in
Halifax were cancelled because of the fog.

### Too Bad It's Not Nicer: Part Three

We seem to be missing quite a bit of scenery, but I like the idea of
the weather not cooperating. There is something quintessentially
Canadian about it. The next day is an even better example. We set
out the next morning for Kingsburg, where some friends are building a house. As we near it, Penny has me slow the car at the crest
of the hill. This is the place where we always pause to admire the
view, she says. There is no view. There is fog. Despite that, Penny
describes where, in the fog, the interesting sights would be, if we
could see them.

We drive around Kingsburg and see big houses owned by
people from Ontario and the foundations for houses put in just in
time to beat development restrictions. Then we walk along the
beach where the breakers roar through the fog, and up onto a
headland. This development is controversial with the locals who
think there should be nothing at all on the hill. Our friends are
sensitive to that, but say that if they didn't build on this lot,
someone else would have, which is true enough. Their house,
almost completed, is beautiful, in the shingled Cape Cod style,

and looks like it belongs. If you have seen enough big cottages and big summer places you know the people of that world can be divided into those who want their houses to dominate the landscape and those who want their houses to blend into it. This one will be in the latter category. Abstractly, I regret that it is here. Realistically, I wish I lived in it.

Penny guides us into Lunenberg, which is picture perfect, but also a functioning community. The distinction matters to me for some reason: Would the community disappear if the tourists disappeared? Not Lunenberg. It is old, of course. It has boutiques, some of which smell of potpourri and play new-age music, and some of which don't. It has a wonderful harbour with real fishing boats and fine old churches playing chimes.

We drop Penny off and begin towards Halifax, thinking that we might see what Chester looks like, and Peggy's Cove. We drive through Mahone Bay, where I suddenly remember that Rose Potvin, a writer who once edited a volume of Graham Spry's letters, now has a B&B here. On the grounds that old CCF connections should be sought out wherever they exist, I find the B&B, the Manse Inn, and stop.

We barely know Rose and she had no notion that we were coming and yet when she greets us at the door she says: "I was just thinking of you." During renovations she has discovered a 1916 newspaper with an article about my grandfather, and was looking for my address to send it on. Indeed the clipping is on the table when we enter the living room.

The house, built in the 1860s, was a Presbyterian manse. It has four rooms, all attractively done up, two in the house and two in a carriage house. "The front room, where the christenings got done, has good floors," Rose says. She and her husband, Allan O'Brien, arrived in Nova Scotia about a year ago and this is the inn's first year of operation. She likes being busy – "We weren't coming to Nova Scotia to look at trees" – and she likes the local custom of people dropping in to visit.

As we near Halifax, the fog thickens. We are running late, and decide to skip Peggy's Cove – SKIP PEGGY'S COVE!?! – and blame the fog. People have been saying that there are prettier places anyway, although how will we know? We find Debby Carver's house in the university district of Halifax and the three of us head for Dartmouth to see the new house of Penny's daughter Stephanie and her husband Bill Greenlaw. On the way we run into a traffic jam, caused by people trying to get to the Halifax Metro Centre to see the Nova Scotia Military Tattoo, a reminder of the impact of the armed forces in this area.

The fog continues, blocking the view from the Citadel. We can't even see across the harbour to Dartmouth. We have decided to regard fog as our friend, since there is no feasible alternative. We cross the Angus Macdonald Bridge, which costs seventy-five cents each way. At dinner that night at Debby's she does something that reminds me so much of her father, Humphrey, and the way he would reign over the table and try to steer the conversation in stimulating directions. She has been giving some thought to what I should know about Halifax, she says, and she wants everyone at the table to contribute an idea about what distinguishes the city from other places. She begins by talking about Halifax as a North American centre for Buddhism and the impact Buddhists have on the arts in the city. Stephanie, who is twenty-nine, talks about the separation of black and white in Halifax/Dartmouth, which might not seem odd if blacks were recent immigrants, but they are not.

Tim Matthews, Debby's husband, thinks it's remarkable that a city of 300,000 has seven universities and colleges. And he reminds us that the Nova Scotia College of Art and Design was founded, more than one hundred years ago, by Anna Leon Owen, who was Anna of *Anna and the King of Siam*, later to be Yul Brynner.

Bill Greenlaw notes that, as one who lives in Dartmouth, he is aware that some Haligonians never get to Dartmouth and vice versa. Not everyone will know, therefore, that one of Dartmouth's stoplights is located inside the fence around a cemetery, giving new

meaning to the expression "dead stop." I am struck by how ener-
getically all the people I have seen in the last few days, the natives
and the come-from-aways, have soaked up the culture of their
province.

## Memo: Need Another Week in Halifax

We have designated the next day as a driving day, meaning that we
will get into New Brunswick and to St. Andrews, where we have
reservations. But we have to see more of Halifax before we go. We
begin at Province House, a modest sandstone building on modest
grounds, three blocks up from the waterfront. It is also the oldest
legislative building in Canada, opened in 1819. The layout is familiar from Charlottetown. There are portraits in the red chamber of
various queens and kings. A Province House librarian once noticed
that what was supposed to be a portrait of King George II was
really a portrait of King George I. Another portrait is of Judge
T. C. Haliburton, better known as an author, creator of the Samuel
Slick stories, such as *The Clockmaker*, and inventor of many phrases
we could not do without, such as "It's raining cats and dogs" and
"Six of one, half dozen of the other."

The legislative library, with its fine hanging staircase, was at one
point the Supreme Court of Nova Scotia, scene of Joseph Howe's
famous libel case in 1835. In the legislative chamber, which has a
curved wall at the back, we learn that the location of the wood
stove also determined where the government sat, although in this
case it was to the traditional right of the Speaker. On the wall is a
portrait of Joseph Howe. Behind the Conservative and Liberal
benches sit portraits of Sir Charles Tupper and W. S. Fielding,
respectively. When the government changes and the parties switch
seats, the portraits switch walls. I am a sucker for this stuff.

We walk to the waterfront in the rain, cars stopping for us at
intersections, a nice gesture that it would be fatal to get used to.
The Historic Properties is yet another impressive example of a city
reclaiming the waterfront for its people. Both Charlottetown and

St. John's have done the same thing, and it is arguable that the restoration of Lower Town in Quebec City belongs in the same category. At the Historic Properties, three blocks of restored warehouses, we also see our first beggar in weeks. The Dartmouth ferry terminal is here, along with many businesses, the law courts, restaurants, and stores, not all of them touristy. There is dinner theatre and a bookstore with a fine selection of regional titles. I think we need another week in Halifax, and could stand a year.

# 7

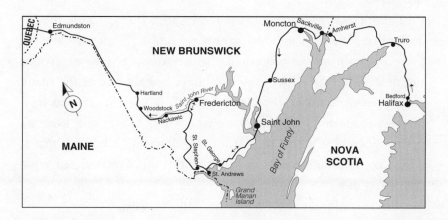

## Skipping Magnetic Hill and
## Other Crimes Against New Brunswick

Once more we go across the middle of Nova Scotia, back up to the Trans-Canada Highway, a route enlivened mainly by the most half-hearted town slogan yet – BEDFORD: A TRADITIONAL STOPPING PLACE. Once again, New Brunswick is entered with little fanfare on New Brunswick's part. For the first time, we have a real deadline, namely to be in Montreal Saturday night, and it looks like New Brunswick is going to suffer for our haste. Or, rather, we are going to have to suffer for hurrying through New Brunswick. We bypass Moncton, skipping Magnetic Hill. This will leave us a lot of explaining to do. Bore View Park tempts us, partly because of the name, but the time is wrong for the Tidal Bore and the weather is lousy. It is a driving day. We turn on the radio. The CBC afternoon show is called "Main Street." It features a summer song contest, during which you might want to hear your name, and an RCMP tourist alert, during which you wouldn't.

Late in the afternoon, 560 kilometres later, we are in St. Andrews, registering at the Algonquin, one of the grand old railway hotels we've decided no book about Canada should be without. The hotel's grandeur is intact, at least from the outside, the red roofs of its many wings broken by turrets and gables, the walls and windows framed in the Tudor style. The lawns and flowers are elegant.

The spell is broken quickly when I return from parking the car and realize that I've forgotten our room number. Nancy has already gone up with the luggage and the key doesn't have the room number on it. I go to the long front desk and ask one of the many young people behind it if they will tell me what room I'm in. I give my name and that doesn't seem to work. Then I give Nancy's name, since it was she (the Business Manager) who registered. There is more hesitation. "Is it difficult," I ask, "to find out what room I'm in?"

"I'm sorry," the young clerk says. "It's security."

I mutter something appropriate to being denied one's room number after driving for six hours. "Oh, for Christ's sake," is about it, the words not enunciated as clearly as they might be, but the tone giving the clerk the general idea. I am given the key and hear three people offering apologies to my back as I walk away, remembering all those trusting bed-and-breakfast operators and thinking bad thoughts about large institutions.

This frame of mind is then applied to an analysis of the accommodations which, for the amount of money we are paying, are quite ordinary. In these old places you get a high ceiling, which is nice, but the shape of the room has not been made appropriate to the furnishings in it, most notably that wooden monstrosity all CP hotels have decided the room needs, the oversized cabinet that encloses the television set, the mini-bar, and the ice bucket, along with several other things. It sits at the foot of the bed, a big clunky thing, impeding the flow and shrinking the room.

We go for a stroll in the town, my grumpiness coming along. About 1,500 people live here in St. Andrews and from the look of the business district, all they do is eat, drink, and buy gifts. Cars cruise slowly up and down the main street, in a style reminiscent of the movie *American Graffiti*. It is gradually dawning on us that summer has arrived, probably sneaking in some day while we were in the car. The kids are out of school and they are in a little resort town and there is nothing to do. We walk out onto the long pier, look out on the low tide and the remains of the old pier, which burned.

The buildings are old. My heart has not been hardened against old buildings. We see one dating back to 1808. Walking past a hotel, we see a sign saying LODGING VICTUALS AND BEVERAGES. Cute. A smaller sign identifies it as a Best Western. Clearly there is money in this stuff, which may or may not be a good sign. Well, it's a good *sign*, but it may not be a good omen. On the plus side, all the trav-elling yuppies are demanding quality in their victuals and lodging, which will help everybody. On the minus side, there is this ten-dency for everybody to want to be adorable.

We find a good restaurant, the Lighthouse (sic) at the end of town, and eat seafood while we watch the sun go down over misty islands. And I find an ice cream place open on the way back. Clearly, there are some advantages to being in a tourist town.

Despite my grumpiness, or perhaps because my grumpiness has been diminished by infusions of seafood and ice cream, we decide to stay an extra day at the Algonquin. We learned in Quebec City that one night is not long enough to pick up the flavour of a grand hotel. In and out in a night, we got a sense that the Château Frontenac was a neat place, but had no time to explore it. So we will give the Algonquin another chance. Also, we will jump at any excuse to spend more than one night in the same place.

## The Four-Hour City: Saint John

The next morning I do a small prowl around the hotel before breakfast. The main lobby is big and wide, with cane chairs and round tables. There is a gift shop off the lobby, as well as a bar, in which breakfast is being served. At night, a guy plays standards on the piano. The elegance of the place is undercut by the guests, who underdress in the contemporary manner, and by a young boy playing hacky-sack in the grand lobby.

From the outside, the building reminds me a bit of Château Montebello, an equally grand and rather overrated place down the river from Ottawa. Its best feature is the finest hotel lobby in Canada, with a huge, many-sided fireplace.

The Algonquin's lobby has fireplaces at either end, a high ceiling, and some nice touches, like the display of New Brunswick art on the walls. The muzak plays string-quartet muzak. The effect is one of nostalgia for the days when these places mattered more than they do now. It is a funny kind of nostalgia, because most of us who feel it would not have belonged in that kind of society anyway. Perhaps it is a regret not only for the passing of those days, but for not having belonged to them.

And also for the passing of the train, which was a big part of the success of such places. Shamelessly, given the fact that the railways themselves were instrumental in the demise of transcontinental passenger travel, they seek to cash in on people's fond memories. We find in our room a glossy catalogue, with a picture of The Canadian on the cover, the dome car passing beside a river, with a mountain in the background. Inside a poster of it is offered for sale, for $24.95, or a tee-shirt at the same price. There are other posters offered, as well as a replica of a conductor's hat (for $95), a switch lamp ($495), a pair of conductor's button brass cufflinks ($95), a CPR soup tureen ($695), a set of napkin rings and salt-and-pepper shakers (all of these illustrated by a photograph of the kind of dining car service that the CPR never offered in the days it was trying to get out of the business). There are historic photographs –

Ginger Rogers sketching an Indian Chief at Banff; Roosevelt, Churchill, and Mackenzie King at the Château Frontenac in wartime.

Enough. I hated it when the railways bailed out of transcontinental passenger service and I hate it even more when they try to sell back to us the thing they abandoned. On top of that the breakfast buffet is cold and I am shown to a table away from the window, even though there are window tables available. We finally make a point of asking for a window table and get it but I am convinced that in a smaller place a guest would not have to ask.

There we sit, over our cold and expensive breakfast, watching the rain and our fellow guests. There is a look younger men get in a place like this – bored and unimpressed, as if to show they're not intimidated by the rich surroundings and the prices. But you suspect they don't really think they belong. Maybe I'm just projecting. Maybe they do belong. Maybe we all do now. That's what democracy is all about. The wives are more natural about it; it is impressive and they are not afraid to show they are impressed and glad to be here.

We ponder our options. Grand Manan and Campobello islands are out, because it is pouring with rain. We decide to spend the day in Saint John, which is roughly one hundred kilometres away.

The fog and rain are with us all the way. In the absence of beautiful sunny vistas, I content myself with adding to my slogan collection. ST. GEORGE: THE BEST DRINKING WATER IN CANADA. That, and the discovery that Saint John is having a jazz festival, lifts my spirits. We find Market Square, park underground, and walk through a series of connecting corridors – pedways, they call them here – right into a noon-hour jazz concert, then stroll some more into the atrium of the Brunswick Square Court, another shopping centre, with all the stores you would see in any other shopping centre in Canada. Except here, four guys from Kennebecasis Valley High school – drums, piano, guitar, and bass – are playing, among other things, a jazz version of the theme from

"Spider Man." There is a small audience – this is the first day of
the first year of the festival, and shopping centres have never been
the hippest of venues – but high in quality, consisting of music
teachers, mothers, and girlfriends. Two video cameras are trained
on the group. The musicians – three of them will be studying
music at McGill, I'm told – are wearing white shirts, ties, and
matching slacks.

Applying the shopping centre test I walk into Coles and look
for New Brunswick literature. I'm shown to a shelf that has three
books by David Adams Richards, including the new one. There
are also books by Bill Gaston of Fredericton.

Now we have established that Saint John has jazz and bookstores
that have real books in them. But we haven't been outside. So we
walk out to King Street, seeing a fountain dedicated to the SPCA in
1882. Is it the Maritimes that causes me to take notice of the dates
of things? We see a new city hall, attached to the mall complex, but
also old warehouses, spruced up with restaurants. Eventually, I
realize that what I am seeing is the exterior of the shopping
complex we were in. That seems clever, hiding the ugliness of a
shopping centre behind the beauty of refurbished older buildings.

We were here for a few days about twenty-five years ago when
I worked in Brandon. It was a conference of newspaper editors
and, given that it was a conference of newspaper editors, I don't
remember much about it, except that at the time waterfront redevelopment was just beginning. Now we can see how well it was
done. Many old buildings were preserved – we see an old ad for
Shamrock Plug Tobacco painted on the side of one – and the
working nature of the waterfront has survived as well. Along with
the beach volleyball court at the waterfront, we see a pile of red
and green buoys, a reminder that people still work on the water.
We walk up the steep King Street to King's Square, the best kind
of city park because it sits in the middle of the traffic, bringing an
inner calm. In that way, it is reminiscent of a London park, like
Berkeley Square. In the middle of King's Square is a bandstand.

The statues are a varied lot. The Glorious Dead are there, as well as John Frederick Young, who died at nineteen in a rescue at sea in 1890. A cross marks the founding of New Brunswick in 1784. A statue honours Sir Samuel Leonard Tilley, a minister in Sir John A. Macdonald's first federal government and later the lieutenant-governor of New Brunswick. There are many begonias, an abnormally large number by Ontario standards, says Nancy, who knows begonias a bit better than I.

The Old City Market Building connects with all the other downtown markets by means of the same interior corridors. That probably gives it life at the same time as the market building gives the malls character. It is a high-ceilinged old building, looking a bit like an armoury from the outside and a bit like Covent Garden inside, three storeys up to the roof, with ceiling fans working hard against the muggy day. The interior is painted white. Three aisles are crowded with junky souvenirs, crafts, coffee shops, and real market stuff, particularly food. The overall effect, the people, the merchandise, the food, the smells, the setting, is very pleasing. In the middle of it is Linda M. Cooke, selling sketches by her husband, A. R. He draws and she tints the drawings. The sketches are not idealized; some of them show ugly new buildings in the background of heritage scenes. She has been in the Old City Market three and a half years. It is not – yet – open on Sundays. "I'm just as glad," she says.

We are working on what we call the Four-Hour City. On the assumption that suburbs and shopping centres are the same everywhere, you measure a city by its downtown, look at its museums and other public buildings. If it is a capital, you look at the legislature. All of this you do on foot, if you can, to avoid the tendency to judge a city by its traffic. Then you head back into the country. Saint John is a great four-hour city.

The New Brunswick Museum has just moved into the Market Square complex, which has boosted its attendance. Admission, which is $5.50, gets you not only into an historical museum, but into a natural history museum and an art gallery as well. We watch a film on whales, then walk through exhibits of sail and industry (at the end of which we find four guys – real guys, not part of an exhibition – trying to start a Bricklin). We continue through the exhibition of birds and whales. At one point there is a little girl standing under a whale's suspended skeleton, and she's saying: "I can't believe I'm under a whale's skeleton."

There is a Discovery Room where children can find out things on computers. I look out the window there and see fog. There is a little television studio, a replica of a local station, CHSJ. Children can sit at an anchor desk and say things for the camera. A four-year-old boy gets up there and discovers he has nothing to say. This upsets him greatly (a fact that upsets me greatly; why should it matter so much?). "I didn't know what to say, Daddy," he sobs to his father, who tries to console him.

The art gallery is fine, with works by Jack Humphrey, Molly and Bruno Bobak, and a 1940 Alex Colville. There is a New Brunswick section, a Canadian section, and an international section. The Canadian section has Mary Pratt, Stanley Cosgrove, Ronald Bloore, Goodridge Roberts, John Lyman, and Dennis Burton.

On the way out of our Four-Hour City we stop at the famed Reversing Falls, perhaps out of guilt that we have missed the Magnetic Hill. It is sad to have to characterize the Falls as the bride's third major disappointment. Mind you, we got there at neither high nor low tide, when the reversing is supposed to happen. A splendid observation station has been put up for it, in which you can eat at a restaurant, see films and everything. But all we saw was some water swirling oddly under a bridge. The information desk has charts of all the tides, including high slack and low slack. We could have seen high slack had we waited another fifteen minutes. Instead we drive back to St. Andrews through the fog, wondering what, exactly, high slack would have been like and whether it can be used as a metaphor for anything.

In keeping with my notion of getting the whole grand hotel experience, we dine in the luxury hotel dining room. Our disappointment continues. It is not that the food is bad; it is pretty good. But a meal should be great if you pay $84.05 for it, given that Nancy doesn't eat dessert and I don't drink wine. This one isn't great, particularly contrasted against some of the excellent forty- and fifty-dollar dinners we've been eating in Atlantic Canada.

## To B&B or Not to B&B

It is not the money, we decide the next day. It is the feeling of not getting value for it. It is, in short, the feeling of having been ripped off. This assessment comes about the time we discover that we have been charged $1 for each phone call. I think I won't buy the CPR soup tureen after all. Just before we leave, Nancy takes her first picture of the Algonquin. This is a sign. She really looked forward to staying here, but when she likes a place, she takes lots of pictures of it.

We head north for Fredericton in what may be the best fog yet. Perhaps it is the fog that is causing me to turn against this national institution. But I don't think so. I think I like the fog. We pass through Dewolfe, Baillie, Harvey Station, eventually reaching the Trans-Canada, which is Highway 2, and turning east to Fredericton. The Saint John River shows up on our left. Too bad it's not nicer. We hear on the news that Lester the Lobster, some kind of giant creature, has died. In the last couple of days we have followed this story, plus news of an albino lobster and an albino salmon. These feel like Toronto ideas of Maritime news stories. Are CBC Radio people from away?

Driving into Fredericton we unaccountably fail to get lost. On the recommendation of a friend, we check in at a large and gracious bed-and-breakfast.

Fredericton, like Charlottetown, is a city that combines the amenities of a capital with the advantages of small size. About 50,000 people live here. The older part of town is lovely, compact and easy to walk about. We walk to the Saint John River, then along Queen Street to the legislature, an 1882 sandstone building, where we are offered a guided tour but are also told that we can have the run of the place if we want to stroll around by ourselves, which we do. The legislative chamber is traditional and the most ornate of the ones we have seen so far. It has a high ceiling, brocade wallpaper, satin draperies around all the windows, portraits of George II and Queen Charlotte, high-backed seats, like pews, in the visitor's gallery, pictures of the Queen and Prince Philip staring at the Opposition. In the quiet, we can hear the ticking of a grandfather clock. The upper chamber, used for ceremonial occasions, is reached by a curved hanging staircase of wood. There are a few cracks in the curved walls.

We look for traces of Dick Hatfield, perhaps the province's most colourful leader, but the honoured places on the wall are reserved for lieutenant-governors and former Speakers. Tradition and the British connection still matter in this place but we know we are in bilingual New Brunswick because of the translation equipment on the legislators' desks, the first we have seen.

Right across the street is the Beaverbrook Art Gallery, built in 1958. There is a pre-Confederation exhibit in the basement which we are in the right frame of mind to absorb after spending so many hours in Atlantic antiquity. To my completely untrained eye, the paintings are most interesting for their depictions of the way people lived. The Beaverbrook is best known for its huge Salvador Dali painting *Santiago El Grande*, which dominates the gallery's main hall, along with two smaller Dalis. I buy the tee-shirt. But I connect best with several paintings by Pegi Nicol MacLeod, who knew my family and once did a portrait of my mother. It is funny how, in this country, you can find traces of yourself in places you have never been.

There is a new wing, the Marion McCain Atlantic Gallery. I overhear someone joke that the Irvings will be donating money soon, so as not to be outdone. Colville is here, along with Christopher Pratt and Jack Humphrey. There are some impressive recent acquisitions – *Oka Warrior*, by Shirley Bear, and *Cyclist*, by Peter Sabat, who was born in 1970. Elsewhere, there is a formidable-looking Churchill, by Graham Sutherland, and many Krieghoffs.

Continuing along Queen Street we see the York County Courthouse (1855) and Officers' Square, a grassy oasis beside the Saint John River, which here has a pastoral, English look to it. We walk by two blocks of the Fredericton Military Compound, the City Hall (1876), and find an excellent bookstore, the Kingfisher, with Coltrane ballads playing quietly on the sound system and an up-front display of Atlantic novelists, including Ken Harvey, in anticipation of his upcoming stint as writer-in-residence at the University of New Brunswick. The co-owner, Frances Giberson, is angry at the much-discussed harmonization of federal and provincial taxes, which will cause "twice as much tax in the poorest part of the country." Among other things, it will bring the provincial sales tax, which is higher than the Goods and Services Tax, to books. It is a shock to find people angry in such a peaceful setting, but we are easily persuaded to be angry too.

The back of Piper's Lane opens up into what was once a parking lot but is now the entrance to a number of shops and restaurants, another nice restoration idea, extending the reach of the older city. The walk home takes us past many fine old houses preserved by the institutions occupying them – the Ombudsman's Office, the Liberal Association of New Brunswick, the Nurses' Union, the Human Rights Commission. Christ Church Cathedral, which is getting a new copper roof, has the feel of a large European cathedral.

The walk is so nice that we do it again later in the day. This is partly because I treasure every moment spent out of the car and also because I sort of underestimated the distances involved. Nancy makes polite comments to this effect. We wind up at a good Swiss–German place on Queen Street, where the waitress, showing that nice marriage of Old and New World, says: "Der vetter could be nicer, eh?" We pay about half what we paid last night and don't feel cheated. Then, however, we have to walk back.

Later, I'm sitting in the television lounge by myself watching a ball game with the volume turned down, when I notice a book on a table cluttered with magazines of all sorts. The book is called *Establishing a Bed and Breakfast Business: A Beginner's Guide.* Aha! I say to myself. Now we'll find out the truth. The book begins promisingly. "A rule of thumb seems to be to price your room a little less than a good local hotel or motel," it says. Imagine leaving this dynamite stuff lying around. And then: "You have to be the type of person who regards as a challenge the unique problems that may be encountered by your guests." But there isn't much about those unique problems. In fact, what I find is a fair bit of common sense, plus twenty-two pages of menus and recipes. There are rules that we have seen honoured mostly in the breach, such as "provide at least two comfortable chairs in the bedroom" and "a double bed should have two [reading lamps], one on each side." We are getting to the stage now where we could write our own book about B&B World. Within it there is great variety, but there are certain constants that can be stated:

1. Many of the entries in the guidebooks you see are written by the B&B owners themselves. That means you don't get an independent assessment, but you do get an idea of the establishment's self-image – antiquish, New Age, outdoorsy – and act accordingly. You can also get an idea of the location – downtown or not – and, most important, whether the bathroom is your own and whether there's breakfast or just a muffin. Some B&Bs skimp on the second B.

2. You can't put too much faith in the provincial accommodation guidebooks, particularly the number of stars they give an establishment. One very fine place we stayed in was marked down

in the provincial guide because it didn't have a television in the living room, although it had TVs in all the bedrooms. Art and decor and the full breakfast it served didn't seem to count. Are the inspectors demanding too much? As one of our B&B hosts pointed out, some of the things that get a hotel stars are precisely the things people don't want in a bed-and-breakfast.

3. Are the customers demanding too much? We saw a fax machine in the same living room that didn't have a TV. The original idea of the B&B was to get away from all that stuff, but now some people are wanting all the facilities of a large hotel, only cheaper. As more and more people get into the business, there may be an escalation that will eventually cause the simple B&B to become the thing to which it was once the alternative.

4. Know that B&B owners are going to be gregarious. They would not have invited people into their homes if they did not like people. Be prepared to talk, or check in at a motel. I am not normally (ever, now that I think of it) a gregarious person at breakfast. But B&B etiquette demands that you chat with your fellow guests and your host/hostess. This is good for my purposes, providing contact with both locals and fellow travellers. "You are the touchstone to the community and all its services in emergencies," says *A Beginner's Guide*. And that's quite true. We routinely rely on the proprietor for advice on the best restaurants, the best attractions, the weather, the best way to get to the museum or out of town.

5. In fact, on the rare occasions when a host/hostess goes quietly about his/her business, I feel a bit cheated. This happens most often in the larger B&Bs, establishments with more than five rooms, which of necessity operate more like hotels. There is a staff, which comes between the owner and the guests. The differences between such a place and a hotel are reduced to size and decor.

6. Smart B&B owners make sure their guests are aware of the house etiquette, such things as how to avoid crashing into other guests in the shared bathroom (knocking on the door will do it). If

the prospect of such occurrences disturbs you, you should know that the difference between having your own bathroom and not having your own bathroom is somewhere between thirty and fifty dollars a night. The odds are that if you are travelling in months other than July or August (assuming you are in a place where the fall-colours frenzy does not strike), the bathroom will be all yours anyway.

7. A lovingly maintained heritage home full of treasured antiques is not necessarily a guarantee of a warm welcome and a comfortable stay. Some of the B&B business, particularly in the older parts of the country, seems to be based on the notion that what people want most is to sleep surrounded by really old furniture. If all you want is a warm welcome and a comfortable room, you are just as well advised to pick someone's new suburban split level, where the rooms are big, the beds are new, the shower has lots of pressure, and the host/hostess is not worried about antique chairs breaking under you.

8. This means, however, that you have to prepared for some irregularities in decor. Here is a partial list of the things that were in a large and comfortable room we rented for the night in a large newish house: plastic flowers in a net hanging in the corner by the bed, a Gibson Girl print over the bed, framed photographs of various old-timers and a girl in a graduation hat, imitation French-provincial furniture, except for a chair that may be Queen Anne (the patron saint of chairs?), a folk art wooden clock in blue, a modern ceiling fan, and, best of all, a fringed bedside lamp, the stand of which is a porcelain sculpture of a man and woman, in colour, kissing and grabbing each other's rear ends. It is as if someone phoned the B&B warehouse and said: "I need twelve yards of decor, please, by next Wednesday."

9. On the other hand, it's not your house.

10. You have to be careful that the place you think is a B&B really is one. It used to be easy: you looked for a wooden sign, painted a deep red or green with lettering that looked like flowers.

It is sad to report that such signs have been seen on boutiques, restaurants, a church, and, in one case, a chiropractor's office. Since such signs are unreadable except up close, you can be in the chiropractor's driveway before you really know what's going on.

## At the Potato Festival Parade

Next morning there is no room at the breakfast table and we have to wait a while. But then we get the full range of travellers' tales you only pick up at B&B breakfasts. There is an American teacher, a self-described "schoolmaster" from a prep school in New Jersey. There he teaches, of all things, Can-Lit. In 1988, when both Canada and the United States were holding elections, the school asked him to find someone who could talk about the politics of both countries. He invited Richard Hatfield. It was through Hatfield that the schoolmaster learned of Timothy Findley, whom he seems to regard as a Maritimes writer. We talk a little Can-Lit, as much as you can over breakfast at a long table in a B&B. He is using *Two Solitudes* in his course and *The Diviners* as an example of Prairie literature. I try to interest him in Guy Vanderhaeghe of Saskatchewan and in New Brunswick's Bill Gaston, whose *North of Jesus Beans* I have been reading as part of my attempt to be familiar with the literature of the area we're visiting.

It may be hard to keep the reading up, what with all the typing of notes and reading of guidebooks and old guys' hats, but it should provide a balance. We know we're seeing the pretty half of every province we visit, the places that have been cleaned and polished for display to the outside world. There is another, grittier side and the novelists are better at showing that. Walking the quiet, tree-lined streets of Fredericton gives one picture. Reading the tragic stories of David Adams Richards gives another. It is not that either picture is false. It is just necessary to remember that there are two pictures.

Also at the long table is a guy from New Mexico and four retired women from near Montreal. "We're retired, no men, we're

free," one says, happily. I ask – in English, of course – if they have
encountered any difficulty being served in French. They say no. In
fact, one tells of being in a Halifax store, asking a question in
English and being told: "Ici on parle français." This gives us a
warm feeling to take back to Quebec.

We set off before ten, do a swing around the attractive U.N.B.
campus, with its hills and red brick buildings, then head north and
west up Highway 2. The day's entire journey through New
Brunswick, about 270 kilometres of it, is beside the Saint John
River, making it one of the most consistently pretty drives in the
country, the valleys gentle, the hills rolling, the potato-farming land
lush and green. Along with the Cabot Trail and Gaspé drives, we
will remember this one.

We pass Nackawic, Home of the World's Largest Axe, which
we don't see. The next highlight is Hartland, Home of the World's
Longest Covered Bridge, which we do. Although we almost don't.
Driving up to it we are stopped by a sign that says BRIDGE CLOSED.
There is a picnic area beside the bridge and we stop there for
coffee, during which we see a few cars coming off the bridge, and
try to reconcile that with the bridge being closed. This may be
some local custom we don't know about. Reading various interpretive panels, we learn only that it is "by far the longest covered
bridge extant in the world" and that the real reason covered
bridges are covered is to keep their foundations from rotting.
Then we hear sirens and other odd noises indicating a parade on
the other side of the bridge. So we cross it on foot, travelling
390.75 metres or 1,282 feet. The bridge was opened in 1901. In
1906, you could cross it for three cents. The cover was put on in
1922. It is fun to be walking across it, looking down at the river,
on the way to a parade.

The parade, we soon learn, is in honour of the Hartland Potato
Festival which is in its last three days. People are lining the street –
not too many people because there are only 925 people in the

town. The Hartland Fire Department goes by, followed by a convertible carrying Miss Hartland High. The crowd applauds. Then Harold Cuthbert, member of Parliament. "Hi folks," he says from his car, which you can hear, easily, over the applause. There is also a Miss Hartland, and she goes by, followed by a float from N.B. Tel, a racing car shaped like a telephone or a telephone shaped like a racing car – these things are hard to tell. Then there are some people driving golf carts and John Deere tractor mowers. Manufacturers Life Insurance has a wagon pulled by Clydesdales. A GMC truck pulls the Perth Andover Bandwagon, the band playing the theme from "Hogan's Heroes." The Upper Valley Shriners are in trainman outfits, for some reason. One of them yells "Wave!" to the crowd and we all do. The Lakeville Volunteer Fire Department's siren is going, which is probably the one we heard earlier. The Florenceville Fire Department features Smokey the Bear.

People have warned us that we should never say we're from Ottawa, but we always do and the response is always friendly. Today a fellow tells us that the police chief is from Ottawa. We see an Old Guy's Hat. BATH, N.B., it says. We walk back across, a nice hike, and observe how traffic works on a one-lane bridge. There is no traffic light, no one to say which direction has the right of way. What seems to happen is a game of covered chicken: You peer through the bridge. If you see no one at the other end, you start. Then everyone behind you starts too. According to the guidebooks, there is also supposed to be honking and kissing involved on covered bridges, but as we drive off in the other direction I have no idea how that happens. The bridge is closed after all. Later we cross on another bridge, an uncovered one.

As we move north it becomes hillier, although the hills are of the rolling kind, with a lot of birch and poplar. The weather is uncertain, alternately bright and rainy, the kind of day in which you run your windshield wipers and wear your sunglasses on top of your head, the better to put them on and take them off.

The state of Maine is just to our left and there are many available border crossings promising short cuts to Montreal. We won't
be tempted. Just east of Edmundston the land flattens and it begins
to look like Northern Ontario away from the lake. The rain is
harder, the river smaller, and the churches bigger. We see a sign: 16
KILOMETRES TO GAZ–O–BAR.

# 8

## *Jazz, Baseball, and Canoes:*
## *Back to Quebec*

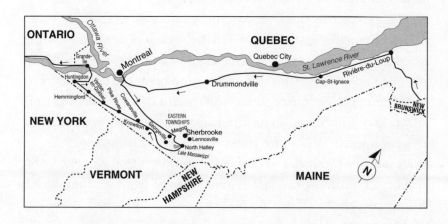

Just inside Quebec, we stop at an Irving. Except for a seafood crois-sant, there is no fish on the menu. We miss the Maritimes already. Suddenly, all of the conversation around us is in French. It's always amazing to me how rapidly the culture changes. Two kilometres to the north and everything is different. Walking around the gas station, I bump into two people I know from Ottawa, one from work, one from the neighbourhood. What are the odds on that? Each is heading to Nova Scotia, both to places we missed. Small world, big country.

Today's idea is to go as far as we can. We want to be in Montreal for a ball game and the last day of the jazz festival tomorrow. Maybe

we can get that far today. We drive northwest on the Trans-Canada
and pick up Highway 20, the expressway to Montreal, at Rivière-
du-Loup. The first glimpse of the St. Lawrence from the south
shore is spectacular and it stays that way, although the highway
often goes away from it. We stop for coffee at a rest stop near Cap-
St-Ignace and are somehow surprised to see that many other
people are there. But it is, after all, a Saturday afternoon in July. All
our days on the road have produced a sense of isolation, a difficulty
in keeping track of time. For the most part that is pleasing.
Occasionally, as now, we are brought up short, when we suddenly
find ourselves in a crowd we didn't expect.

We look across the river to Quebec City as we pass it. About
thirty kilometres east is a Top Ten Belvedere – farmland leading
down to the river, across the river the hills and, above the hills, five
distinct rain storms. After that, civilization begins to encroach. The
road leaves the river, straightens and flattens out. For the first time
in weeks, we notice, in an unflattering way, other drivers – hogging
the passing lane and other tricks. We stop at Drummondville, an
hour out of Montreal, and decide we could get to the city tonight,
maybe see more of the jazz festival. Nancy begins calling hotels
from a pay phone. There are no hotel rooms to be had in the city
of Montreal.

We take the last room at the Drummondville Quality Inn, on
the edge of a concrete sea of highway and the parking lots of the
fast food places that are on every corner. Our room is a meeting
room, dominated by a huge table, the bed placed, as an after-
thought, off to the side. At 7:45, lacking all ambition after driving
733 kilometres, we reject the allure of the Drummondville Folk
Festival and decide on the laziest of evenings. We'll grab a fast bite
to eat and watch the Expos on TV. We leave the car and walk across
the concrete sea to the St. Hubert chicken place. There is a long
lineup outside the front door. Nancy says: "I think I want to go
back to Newfoundland."

## The Jazz and Baseball Doubleheader

Montreal, approached from the east on Highway 20, is impressive. From this new vantage point, the city's role as a port stands out. We see Île-Ste-Hélène and the former Expo '67 site as we cross on Pont Cartier, then find a parking lot within walking distance of the jazz festival, which takes up several city blocks around the area of the Place des Arts Metro station. It is 11:45 and volunteers in FIJM (Festival International de Jazz de Montréal) tee-shirts are getting ready for the day, scurrying through this empty city of jazz, the streets lined with posters, last night's litter not yet picked up.

Eight Metro stops and we are at the Stade Olympique, a place I know well from many two-hour trips from Ottawa. Like many other baseball fans, I have never warmed to the place. You can love it when the Expos are in a pennant race and the place is packed and jumping. But most of the time it is two-thirds empty and has a hollow sound. The seats are too far from the field, the air has a dead feeling, the faded orange roof hangs over the plastic field, which is symmetrical in the style of sports facilities built in the seventies. But I love baseball and I have loved the Expos since I first began following them, around the time this stadium was built. Before that I confess to having been a New York Yankees fan.

We are nicely early for the game and use the excuse of the trip to buy the best seats we can. These cost $26 each and put us on the third-base side in the second row, probably ten feet from the mound in the visitors' bullpen where two young pitchers are warming up. At the same time, the Mets coach, Frank Howard, a former star with the Dodgers and even the Washington Senators, hits fly balls to the outfielders, a sixty-year-old man with an easy, powerful swing. A four-man relay is set up to return the ball to him, using pitchers who will not be in the game today. Meanwhile, batting practice is going on and infield practice too. It is intricately choreographed: everybody gets to practise; nobody gets hit with the ball.

One of the many great things about baseball is how different it looks from different perspectives. I am very much a first-base-line type of fan, I realize. Usually I can anticipate what will happen when the ball is hit and say something irritatingly knowledgeable to the person I am with. Not so today. Also, because of our location, I am thinking, as I chomp on a smoked meat sandwich, about how a line drive hit foul could take our heads off.

All the Mets seem solemn – the pitchers warming up, the catchers, the pitching coach, the left fielder, Chris Jones, who warms up by playing catch with a ball girl between innings. She's grinning and laughing, perhaps because she gets to play catch with a big-league ballplayer. He, who gets a chance to play catch with a pretty young woman, couldn't look gloomier.

All of this is new to me, from my unfamiliar vantage point. The Mets pitching coach comes out and solemnly lays five balls on the bullpen pitching rubber. One of the Mets fans yells to the starting pitcher, Pete Harnisch: "You're the man, Pete! Be the one out there today!" Where do we learn this stuff? How does one go about being the one out there today?

It is all an education for me. I note the existence of what seems to be a Behind Third Base community, consisting of the ball girl, the guy who fetches drinks for the people in the VIP seats, and the security guard. They meet at the rail and chat away. They probably do that all the time, considering they work in the same neighbourhood for eighty-one days a year. Towards the end of the game they are joined by another security guard, who stands with the waiter facing the crowd between innings. I ask the guard what they are there for. "To prevent runners," he says, and I think, Runners? The pitcher's supposed to do that. Then I get it – the people who jump the fence and run out on the field late in the game after the beer kicks in.

Being this close to the field has other effects. The air feels better, somehow, and I am less aware of being in a crowd, since most of it is behind us. Fletcher hits a two-run homer to put the

Expos ahead, and Rheal Cormier – a francophone, although a New Brunswicker (from Shediac, where the big lobster is – we drove through there!) – is pitching well and everybody feels good. One guy behind us feels so good that he tries to organize the Wave. I hated the Wave the first time I saw it, and continue to do so, but there is a fascination in seeing up close how the mentality works. The weirdest thing to me is that, in order to succeed in his mighty mission, the wave-maker has to turn his back on the field, at the height of a Montreal rally, and devote his attention to the fans. He counts down, five, four, three, two, one, then implores them to leap up with their hands in the air. To my delight, almost no one does. Finally, on about the tenth try, he gets it to work. The Wave begins in front of him, then ripples around the stadium. I watch the guy and think I understand. He can look way over to right field, where the fans are leaping to their feet, and watch the thing he created. "That's mine," he can say to himself.

At around the same time, activity begins in the Mets bullpen. Steve Swisher, the bullpen coach, is involved, as well as a pitcher, a catcher, and another player standing behind the pitcher with a glove, in case a foul ball is hit in that direction. After a while, Swisher looks over to the Mets dugout, unclenches his fist twice, and waves his hat. Then the pitcher sits down.

When Cormier bats in the eighth, the fans (all 16,076 of them) give him a standing ovation, not thinking that it might be a good idea to pinch-hit for him. The first pitch he throws in the ninth is hit for a home run and he is lifted for a relief pitcher, Mel Rojas. After Rojas gets the second out, the Mets bullpen people stop working. They stand and watch the last Mets batter ground out to third. We win, 4–3. Time of game: 2:38, which is very fast. It is 4:13 when the game ends. Taking our time getting out we are on the Metro at 4:42 and at Place des Arts at 4:53. For getting around a city, you couldn't ask for better. There is no shortage of digital clocks either.

### Swinging in the Rain

The subterranean nature of our existence – subway to domed stadium to subway to indoor mall – means that we have lost sight of the elements. We should have known. About the time we hit Jeanne-Mance and Ste-Catherine it begins to rain. But there is a big crowd at the festival anyway, big enough to be difficult to walk through. This is the free stuff the Montreal festival is known for, an eclectic area of interesting music on free stages within sight of each other, and it draws a crowd, even on a nasty day.

Montreal crowds are not like other North American crowds. The threat, the edge you find in large crowds elsewhere, does not exist in Montreal – except on rare occasions, usually having to do with hockey. The first time I experienced this was about ten years ago when I emerged from Théatre St. Denis about 1:30 in the morning from a Horace Silver concert to find a goodly number of young people, many of them with beer bottles in their hands. Uh-oh, I thought. But the people were good-natured and friendly, low-key and relaxed. This is not what happens in Ontario when large numbers of people get together and drink outdoors. Maybe it's the history of beers served in windowless rooms, the repressive notion that drinking has no place in the sunlight. Whatever the reason, when the restrictions are temporarily lifted in Ontario and the lads can have a beer outdoors, stand back. The fighting will start any minute.

I have heard that this tradition is not completely lacking in Quebec, that, for example, the Quebec Winter Carnival is avidly avoided by some of the city's peace-loving residents, but as far as Montreal and its jazz festival are concerned, the street is cool.

So it is on this day as the Vic Vogel Big Band, which is what we've come to see, sets up at the stage called the Scène du Maurier. Tobacco sponsorship gets us this. Now the government, which cuts back its support of the arts and doesn't have the guts to collect a prohibitive tax on cigarettes, is talking about punishing arts groups that take money from tobacco companies. I think I said I *like* politics.

Vogel's band, another of Canada's best-kept secrets, has been a fixture of the Montreal scene for years. Because it is not in Toronto, it doesn't get the recognition it deserves (just as bands that *are* in Toronto don't get the recognition they deserve in the United States). Vogel, who plays piano, arranges and leads with the infectious enthusiasm of Dizzy Gillespie, who is one of his heroes. The band has great soloists, great spirit, and the support of the crowd. Above and beyond the stage is an old building with a painted sign: GOOD CLOTHES AND NOTHING ELSE. The rain pours down but the people stay. Those who have umbrellas are considerate with them, which is not easy in a big crowd. The trick is to keep them high enough so that people behind can look underneath.

I read an article in the Montreal *Gazette* this weekend about the unwillingness of Montrealers to support good jazz clubs, despite their massive attendance at the summer festival. This festival syndrome is affecting the whole country, with people flocking to see folk music, fringe plays, Shakespeare, and jazz outdoors in the summer, then bunkering in for the winter in front of their VCRs, while artists, actors, and musicians desperately seek an audience.

Be that as it may, as we trudge to the car we are happy that we have seen some of the best of Montreal. We are also happy that the car has a roof, as we find our way out of the city, over the Pont Champlain and into the Eastern Townships.

North Hatley is about an hour and forty-five minutes from Montreal, much of it along a well-engineered four-lane highway, No. 10. Leaving 10, near Mount Orford and the town of Omerville, you are soon on a series of very hilly and extremely bumpy roads, on which you will find out what the bottom of your car sounds like. The hills continue into Vermont. It is pretty country, known for its lakes, its fine skiing, and its beautiful autumns. It is also known for having a large English-speaking population.

We began coming to Hovey Manor in the mid-eighties for part of a week in late February or early March. We cross-country ski at Mount Orford, which is nearby, doing just enough skiing to justify all the fine food we'll eat at Hovey Manor and all the time we'll spend lying around reading books.

I like the idea of seeing the seasons change at North Hatley. Around the first week in March the sun can be warm, melting the snow and closing some of the south-facing trails at Orford. For someone who doesn't mind seeing winter end, that's not so bad. When there is skiing, there are spring smells in the woods and streams running freely. Meanwhile, over breakfast there is the *Gazette* sports section, with news of the Expos at spring training. It all ties in.

The town of North Hatley, which has a New England look in its architecture, has been the summer home of a number of major Canadian cultural figures – Hugh MacLennan, Blair Fraser, Ralph Gustafson. As a kid, I knew North Hatley as the place to find my father's friend Frank Scott. His house there, high above Lake Massawippi, was where you got the latest on Quebec politics, from a constitutional lawyer and socialist, or on Canadian culture, from one of its best poets – the lawyer and the poet happening to be the same person.

Scott and my father, King Gordon, were active in the Montreal left scene in the thirties, working together in the League for Social Reconstruction, which became known as the intellectual wing of the CCF. When my father moved to New York and then overseas, Scott stayed in Montreal, fighting against Duplessis, fighting for the CCF and then the NDP. He remained an intellectual touchstone for my father, on our visits to Montreal or North Hatley. What was the best university in Canada now, I remember my father asking, in the year I had to choose where I would apply, whether I would go to an American or a Canadian university. "Queen's," said the McGill professor, and I'm sure that's why I wound up there.

Sitting beside a pitcher of pre-lunch martinis, Scott would speak as if for the compilers of *Bartlett's Familiar Quotations*, in elegant, witty, and perfectly constructed paragraphs. I was impressed as a teenager and am even more impressed now, as I think of the combination of intellect and sense of fun that is so rare today in this country.

For the longest time, I had difficulty locating the Scott place when we visited North Hatley, thirty-odd years later. I had a mental image of where it was and what it looked like, which was completely, as it turned out, at variance with reality. Somehow, it was important for me to find it, perhaps as the kind of link with the past we begin looking for as we get older. I could have asked somebody where it was, of course, but there is a reason I am not the Business Manager. Finally, I learned that Graham Fraser, the *Globe and Mail* writer and son of Blair Fraser, had taken over the place his parents had shared with the Scotts. I looked up the address in the phone book and found the house, not where I expected it at all and looking less like it than a lot of other North Hatley homes did.

One of the things I remember about Hovey Manor is that Scott took our family there for dinner one summer evening in the late Fifties. It has been expanded a bit since, but it is clearly the same place, approached the same way, over a long driveway winding through the woods down to Lake Massawippi. Built in 1900 by an American southerner, Henry Atkinson, in the manner of George Washington's home at Mount Vernon, the manor has a broad verandah and white pillars, rooms with canopy beds, a comfortable library with a large fireplace, a dining room with another stone fireplace and window tables overlooking the lake. Much of the style of North Hatley derives from that period, when wealthy southerners, reluctant to summer in Yankee New England, built large summer homes on the west side of the lake. In 1900, there were more than a dozen inns and hotels in North Hatley. Now, there are as many bed-and-breakfasts.

## Not the Same Townships

We are in an unconscionably fancy room, probably the fanciest we will ever see, but our conscience is clear. Arriving late last night from Montreal, we found the room hot and the air conditioning not working. Without even pausing to think about it, the night manager put us into one of the fancy rooms in the new wing, at the same price. While I ponder the two king-sized beds, the TV set, jacuzzi, fireplace, balcony, table, two couches, and walk-in closet, I inwardly explain to my socialist forebears and the spirit of F. R. Scott that I really had no choice in the matter.

I do like that about Hovey – that there is no hesitation in simply assigning us another room, no red tape, no phoning the manager. I feel, perhaps wrongly, that in a larger institution this would have been a lot more difficult.

We have the huge breakfast that comes with the price of the room, then borrow a green aluminum canoe and paddle into town, which is three or four kilometres away by road, but closer this way. Lake Massawippi is windy and wavy and we have a nice tailwind going in. Being Canadians, we know we will pay for it on the way back. There are many grand places on the lake, some of them hiding their grandness in the trees, others flaunting it. It is partly a clash between old and new money, partly the constant struggle on any lake between those who want to be seen and those who don't.

It is warm, sunny, and hazy as we walk around the town. There are some fancy restaurants and some unpretentious little ones, boutiques, galleries, a post office near the tennis courts, across from the war memorial, a laundromat, a little church or two, a tiny library, and a general store. Some years ago there was a controversy over the acquisition of a good chunk of the town by a man from the Middle East. Whatever great things he was planning to do didn't work for him and now the town is back where it was.

Actually, not exactly where it was, because North Hatley, like the townships generally, has been changing, becoming, if not more French, at least more open to French, more bilingual. Even in the ten years we have been coming here that has been obvious. The Eastern Townships are no longer the anglo bastion they once were. Later, after we have fought the wind to get back, this impression is confirmed in a discussion with Steve Stafford, who owns Manoir Hovey. When he was growing up in the fifties "hearing French was an oddity," Stafford says. His parents bought Ripplecove Inn, at the other end of the lake, when Steve was three years old. Twenty or thirty years ago many of the smaller towns, like Ayer's Cliff, were overwhelmingly English-speaking. Now even those with an English-speaking majority have only a bare majority and the English-speaking percentage in the region as a whole is only 10 per cent. It seems like more than that, partly because of image and partly because of the presence of Bishop's University in Lennoxville, one of the region's most prominent institutions.

Particularly in dealing with his suppliers, Stafford speaks French more and more of the time. "You don't do much in English," he says. All of this improves his French skills, so that he now speaks French to people with whom he used to speak English, because their English was better than his French.

Meanwhile, Stafford, from the vantage point of a parent, sees advances in the way the young French and English interact. "They mix more than they did in my day." It would be nice to think we are seeing a microcosm here of Quebec's development – an expanding French population meeting and working with an increasingly French-speaking English population. Mind you, it is happening at the upper end, and there are many parts of Quebec where English and French don't mingle. And the constant politics gets on people's nerves, particularly on the English side. "This is my homeland," Stafford says. "I love the Eastern Townships. But I love Canada too."

With another night to spend at Hovey, we have an afternoon to drive around aimlessly. We find some little highways that are not on the map and we find Georgeville, a truly lazy little town. Parking at the village square, we walk down to the wharf. On the dock are some kids and an old guy fishing in the following outfit: purple shorts, black shirt, blue baseball cap, brown shoes, and blue dress socks. He looks good. Out in the water, someone is tanning on a floating dock. The haze gives different colours to the near and far hills. It is another calming scene.

The French–English contradictions are all around us. We visit Les Artisans McGowans, a handicraft gallery where the language (inside, of course) is English, then have coffee at Bistro Les Amis de George Bar, where we are served in French. The bulletin board at the tennis court has some information about the village, including the fact that it was settled in 1797 by homesteaders from New England. Other notes ask for books for the library sale, offer tennis memberships, tickets for the strawberry social and the chicken pie supper. There is also someone wanting to set up a group to take French lessons.

Nicely lost on the way back, we find some places we've never been, including Fitch Bay, Graniteville, Beebe Plain, and Stanstead. When we figure out where we are, we are at Katevale – or Ste-Catherine-de-Hatley, as it is now known – and a view that is as stunning in summer as it is in winter: we are on the side of a steep hill overlooking a deep valley. To the northwest is Mount Orford. In the valley are farms. We nominate it for the Top Ten Belvedere List, then drive back to our modest little room and get ready for a modest little dinner. Because it is part of our modified American plan it is hard to know exactly what it cost. Probably more than at the Algonquin. But worth the money this time.

### An Extra Hour for the Shortcut
We tootle along the bottom of the townships, near the Vermont border, going from one small road to another, trying to get across

the St. Lawrence without driving through Montreal. This is something I've always wanted to do but never had the time to try. We see an excellent sign near Bolton: CAMPING LAC TROUSER. We go through all the Boltons – East, South, and Centre. We see Knowlton, Cowansville, Pike River, Hemmingford. Our big surprise is finding a huge summer community, with hundreds of trailers, stretching for miles across the top of Lac Champlain. This is Venise-en-Québec. There are many signs concerning a bridge being closed but we are not sure it is our bridge. We are not even sure there *is* an our bridge. Then we find one, a lift bridge to Grande-Île, then another one, and we are on the 20, heading for the 401, and into Ontario. Five provinces down, five to go. With a stop for coffee the trip to the Ontario border took three and a half hours, about an hour longer than doing it the normal way. But where's the thrill of discovery then, eh?

- · — · — · — · — · — · — · — · — · — · — · — · — ■

## *Men and Women from Glengarry*

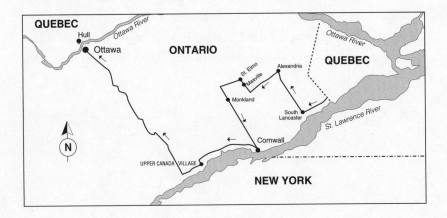

The section of the 401 we're on, from the Quebec border west, is tolerable. There is not much traffic and the scenery is pretty. Occasionally there is a glimpse of the St. Lawrence to the left. This is Day 28 of the trip. Although we are anxious to get home and rest for a couple of days, there are some places to see first. One is my great-grandfather's church, the Gordon Free Church at St. Elmo, in the heart of Glengarry County, near Maxville.

Outside the church, which stands at the top of a rise on the Highland Road, is a plaque that was unveiled in 1959, honouring my grandfather, who was born here in 1860 when it was called the 19th Concession, Indian Lands.

"The Rev. Charles W. Gordon, 1860–1937," the plaque says.

> Born at Indian Lands (St. Elmo), Gordon was ordained a Presbyterian minister in 1890. He served as a missionary in the North-West Territories until 1893 and the following year was called to St. Stephen's in Winnipeg. A chaplain during the war of 1914–18, he was moderator of the Presbyterian church in Canada in 1921–22. Under the pen name of Ralph Connor, Gordon became one of Canada's leading authors and wrote such books as *The Man from Glengarry*, *The Sky Pilot*, and *Glengarry School Days*. The theme of many of his novels was drawn from his missionary experience and boyhood memories of Glengarry. – Erected by the Ontario Archaeological and Historic Sites Board.

I was there for the unveiling, along with my father, my aunt Lois Gordon, and a few more distant relatives, a fair-sized crowd and an impressive turnout of local dignitaries. Because there wasn't room for us all to stand on the steep bank in front of the plaque on the church side of the road, we moved to the other side as the speeches were made from the church side. Police were stationed down the Highland Road to either side and, while a speech was going on, would stop the traffic. So the member of Parliament made a speech, then the police let some cars go through, then stopped them again as the member of the legislature made a speech. And so on. There were lots of speeches. History could stop traffic in those days.

Researching an article for the *Ottawa Citizen* last year, I found that the church, a small building constructed of red brick, is only open for two services a year now, but the residents keep a lively interest in it and there is a group of people who make sure the church is cared for. I found one of those people, Dr. Wallace MacKinnon, and he let me into the church, first peeling off the plastic protecting the door. The church looks much as it did then.

There is one wood stove now, instead of two, and there are not the chandeliers holding the kerosene lamps. Today the wooden floor is painted. But the layout is the same, the standard two aisles of the Presbyterian Church, with a dozen pews in each of the three sections. I stood up in the pulpit, the first of four generations of Gordons not to have a licence to stand there, and tried to imagine what it was like back then, when 300 to 400 people would come for services in the summer months.

My great-grandfather, Daniel Gordon, whose church it was, built it in 1864 after having been kicked out of the Church of Scotland building in Maxville in one of those disputes Presbyterian sects used to have. Dr. MacKinnon's *History of Gordon Church, St. Elmo* gives an understated account of what happened there: "In 1860 the Free Church was granted permission by the Presbytery of Glengarry to use the Church of Scotland Church building at Maxville on alternate Sundays. There were disputes with the Rev. Daniel Gordon over the use of the Church building and on one occasion Mr. Gordon found the church locked and a new lock on the church door. The arrangement had proved unsatisfactory for the Free Church and Mr. Gordon, and plans were made to build a new Free Church."

The version in my grandfather's autobiography, *Postscript to Adventure*, is more colourful. When Daniel Gordon found the new lock on the door, he asked the parish officer, Donald McEwen, for the old key, asking several times if it was the key to the church. Upon being told that it was, and upon finding that it didn't open the door, Gordon said: "Donald, and you Mr. McNaughton, and all of you will notice that there is something wrong with this lock. The key will not open it. Stand clear!"

Whereupon he kicked open the door and led his Free Church congregation in. For this, he was summoned to court. He escaped a jail sentence but lost access to the church and had to build a new one.

I have never been bothered by the image of the stoic, deadpan Scot, but I like this story too, the story of someone who will kick down the door for what he believes. And I like dropping by the church on important occasions. One such day, about ten years ago, was when our son, John, was leaving home. I drove him down to the Townships where he was beginning university at Bishop's. I would discover later that Mary Robertson, John's great-great-grandmother, came from the Eastern Townships to marry Daniel Gordon. Because this seemed like an important occasion, we stopped at the church, his first visit. I showed him the plaque and tried to think of something appropriately stirring to say. Being Scots, neither of us came up with any emotional words that we would remember years later, but both of us remember the moment.

In my *Citizen* article, I wrote about all this and immediately began hearing from Glengarry people, some of them liking the attention, some of them pointing out inaccuracies, and, more terrifying, some of them inviting me to speak to the historical society. There would be people there who actually knew something about Glengarry, had qualifications that go beyond having the same name as the church and the same nose – strong, I like to think of it; others would say large – as the church's founder.

I prudently turned down all such invitations, until one day in November when the invitation was accompanied by the assurance that I would not be asked to speak, just attend. John and I drove out to St. Elmo, to the church hall around the corner, which is the former Congregational church, even older than "our" church. Just before the auction of a couple of items, we were introduced to the gathering. One of the items was one of my grandfather's lesser known works, called *The Angel and the Star*. That meant I had to bid, which I did. But others were bidding too and my eventual win was costly. Then I was invited up onto the stage after the presentation to answer questions. People had some. Then John and I were interviewed by the *Glengarry News*. It was a peculiar experience, pleasant, but strange to be among people who know all about your history and care about it.

The oddest moment came at the end of the proceedings when the president of the Glengarry Historical Society, David Anderson, introduced me to a local trapper, the last descendant of "Alan the Dog," a trapper who figures prominently in *Glengarry School Days*, which was written almost a century ago. That he should be known in this room as the descendant of Alan the Dog and that I should be known as the descendant of Ralph Connor, speaks volumes of the power these Glengarry stories have after all these years. It is the power to turn men into historical artifacts, and to sprinkle bits of notoriety down through the generations. I guess it shouldn't be amazing, considering what we have seen at Green Gables.

This time Nancy and I approach St. Elmo from the southeast, driving through Alexandria, Dominionville, and Maxville. The land is neither the lushest nor the most scenic and I wonder what my ancestors found so compelling about it. But we no longer see it as lumber country, only as unimpressive farmland. "There is forest everywhere," my grandfather wrote, in *The Man from Glengarry*. "It lines up close and thick along the road, and, here and there quite overshadows it. It crowds in upon the little farms and shuts them off from one another and from the world outside, and peers in through the little windows of the log house looking so small and lonely, but so beautiful in their forest frames. At the nineteenth cross-road the forest gives ground a little, for here the road runs right past the new brick church, which is almost finished and which will be opened in a few weeks." We can recognize the spot, except for the forest, which is no longer there. It is not a big hill the church is on, but the church is at the very top of it. We stop, take some pictures, walk around, and don't kick the door in.

Instead we head south again, to Cornwall, then west to Upper Canada Village, another place I have never been, and would never go except for the built-in aimlessness made possible by this trip.

The village has been put together from historic buildings brought in from all over the province, although mostly from close by. There is a Ralph Connor thread here too: the schoolhouse is often described as the schoolhouse from *Glengarry School Days*. It is not: in fact it was brought from the village of Athol in Kenyon Township. But the resemblance is close. "The 'Twentieth' school was built of logs hewn on two sides," the story says. "The cracks were chinked and filled with plaster, which had a curious habit of falling out during the summer months, no one knew how; but somehow the holes always appeared on the boys' side, and being there, were found to be most useful, for as looking out of the window was forbidden, through these holes the boys could catch glimpses of the outer world . . ."

This schoolhouse looks like that, typical of the schools of the 1860s. There is a boys' side and a girls' side, the students sitting on benches, their desks facing the windows, the boys away from the girls. This made the best use of the light, since the school was too poor to afford oil for the lamps. The date on the blackboard is July 9, 1866. There was corporal punishment and a ban on writing with the left hand. The charts on the wall show the upper- and lower-case script letters of the alphabet and a guide to the currency of the period, a farthing (a word much tampered with in those days) being one-quarter of a penny. A potbellied stove sits in the middle of the room.

There are no indications in the schoolhouse that it has anything to do with *Glengarry School Days*. The "teacher," a Trent University student, is aware of Ralph Connor, but the role he plays as teacher to groups of tourists does not draw on the book. He watches me taking notes as we talk. "I see you're writing with your left hand," he says.

The village, in the warm late afternoon, has an air of calm. We walk on Church Street, Mill Street, and, of course, Queen Street, looking at the houses, stables, stores, the church and the hotel. In the bar is a poster: BRISTOL'S SARSAPARILLA IN LARGE BOTTLES. THE

GREAT PURIFIER OF THE BLOOD. Part of this peaceful feeling is something like nostalgia, the feeling of a simpler time. Much of it is the absence of automobiles, I think, as we trudge back to the car.

## Ottawa: A Triple-A Kind of City

We are back in Ottawa, 28 days and 9,600 kilometres after we started. We can do some laundry without going to a laundromat, spend a couple of days not driving the car, get an oil change, stock up on Scotch mints for the glove compartment, reconsider all the stuff we packed, and do some errands. I drop by the lawyer's and the funeral home. There I encounter the small world again, in the person of a minister, Mark Caldwell, who is a big Ralph Connor fan, even to the point of being knowledgeable about his mother's family, the Robertsons. Mark "pastored in Saskatchewan," as he puts it, and admired Tommy Douglas. The other day he was driving back from Montreal and he too stopped at St. Elmo to see the church. They must wonder there about all these cars.

Thinking about what to see in Ottawa and what to say about it, I remember dinner in Halifax and Debby Carver's suggestion that everybody come up with something people wouldn't know about the city.

What wouldn't you know about Ottawa? Well, a large part of its existence has nothing to do with government. To take one very important example, it has a minor league baseball team, the Lynx. On summer nights, anywhere from 4,000 to 10,000 people go out to a new ballpark near the train station to watch the games. The stadium has natural grass, as it is now called, and no roof. The best seat costs about $8, the parking $5.50. Because it is a new stadium (it was completed in 1994), it lacks the charm of some of the older ballparks. But it is still sport on a human scale, the antidote to the rip-off that professional sports has become.

You always meet someone you know at the stadium. It is called "the stadium" or "Ottawa Stadium" by default because no one has given it an official title. Like other modern professional sports facilities, the stadium has put its name up for the highest bidder. For a brief period in the second year there was a rumour that the stadium was going to be named after a kind of minivan. Miraculously, it didn't happen.

We all meet there and enjoy the brand of ball, which is very good. These are Triple-A players, on their way up to or down from the major leagues. In Ottawa's case, they are Triple-A players who belong to the Montreal Expos, so we know them well when they come down and watch them with affectionate interest when they go up.

We are Triple-A fans too, which means that our attitudes and emotions are different. We know that winning is not the only thing in this game; the team exists mainly to prepare players for the major league team so that sometimes a left-handed batter will start against a left-handed pitcher he has no hope of hitting, just to build character. Often a pitcher will be pulled from the game when he is doing well (once, when he was an inning away from a no-hitter) because the parent club has dictated how many pitches he will be allowed to throw. Triple-A fans know all this, so we are not as heartbroken when the team loses, not as annoyed when a player makes a mistake or a manager makes a decision we don't like. We are relaxed, not nearly as grouchy as the people two hours down the road at the Olympic Stadium.

Is there something Ottawa about this, this Triple-A mentality? Do we settle for too little, accept second-best too readily? This is not, as is well known, a city in which people are at their desks at 7:00 a.m. It is not a place where overweeningly ambitious people knock competitors out of their way with their briefcases. Which is one of the reasons I've always liked it.

On his drive through in 1963, Edward McCourt pronounced this "a sober, cautious, civil-service town of good taste, good manners, and a greyish atmosphere even when the sun shines." We have heard this many times since, of course, but McCourt has a nice way of phrasing it. "A Londoner carries an umbrella as a substitute swagger-stick, a Parisian as a weapon with which to play Cyrano de Bergerac, and an Ottawan to keep off the rain."

Yes, yes. On the other hand, Ottawa is a city in which people are taking some hard knocks. All those tough economic decisions that governments take such pride in making, tend to put real people out of work, right here.

Another thing that people don't know about Ottawa is that it is becoming a gambling capital. The notion that no one rolled dice after Brian Mulroney left town is wrong. There is a huge casino across the river in Hull, open since the spring, and people are flocking to it. No one is quite sure what the effects are. The gambling-addiction people are understandably worried. Some of Ottawa's politicians are annoyed that Hull got there first. The proprietors on Hull's notorious bar strip are worried that they will lose late-night business.

None of this fits in with the image of Canada's staid and dull capital. I decide to investigate, taking with me not Nancy, who hates casinos so much she doesn't want to know about them, but Brian Doyle, a writer and perceptive observer, who is also that rarest of creatures, an Ottawa native. Doyle has driven across the country too, and produced two fine and funny books about it, aimed at, but not exclusively for, a young adult audience: *Hey Dad* and *You Can Pick Me Up at Peggy's Cove*. Like me, he wouldn't be caught dead in a casino, except for research purposes.

So here we go. It is a Tuesday, about lunchtime. The casino has a majestically long approach with fountains in the middle, somewhat as if we were approaching the palace of Versailles. Uniformed people direct us into the parking lot, which has a fair number of cars. The building is big and white, some curved glass on the front, and resembles something – what? Perhaps an ocean-liner, perhaps one of the Expo '67 buildings. Something out of our normal world, anyway.

Once inside, we are met by a wall of trees, a large staircase, and guards at the entrance to the casino room, telling us to check our windbreakers. We do that, and then I remember that my notebook is in mine. To go back and retrieve the notebook would make me suspicious, I decide. I will have to rely on my magnificent memory. This is what I remember about the House Rules, which are posted at the entrance: Smoke only where permitted, check your coats, no photography. And the dress code – no shorts, no jeans, no bustiers, no clothing associated with groups of a violent nature. This may not refer to the armed forces.

The main hall is on the second floor. When we walk in I hear – what would you call it – a tone, a constant tone. The tone is made by thousands of slot machines, bonging away. It is like being inside a xylophone. Having just begun piano lessons, I listen carefully. I think all the machines are in thirds, a major triad: C, E, and G. I think of a new occupation for the nineties: Slot-machine tuner. "Good morning. I'm the slot-machine tuner. Where's the one that's making the augmented fifth?"

Perhaps being inside a xylophone is not the right analogy. It is more like being inside a pinball machine. There is a constant flash of colour and no noise other than tones. The deep blue carpet muffles footsteps. There is no conversation, no discernible muzak. Just tones. When we stop for lunch the waitress says she no longer hears them.

The room is as large as a football field, to use the first handy metaphor that comes to mind, although I don't pace it off. And it is full of machines, row upon row of them, 1,300 of them in all. The machines are gaudy and flashy. People sit at them with plastic buckets full of coins, feeding them into the machines and pushing buttons. No longer does one pull down a lever. The term one-armed bandit is a stranger in these parts. There is a bank here, and a bank machine. I take mental notes, which are the only kind available to me. There is a stream with bridges over it, and some trees. It is not too smoky. Just hugely artificial, the kind of unreal environment in which you could imagine that what was happening to you was not happening to you.

The colours are muted, browns and blues. Off to the side is a roulette wheel. Five Asian tourists are at it, and it is a relief to find them, since a massive influx of Asian tourists was one of the promises of the casino. (The promoters of casinos usually put out the line that the only people losing money will be Asian tourists and rich people in tuxedos and evening dresses.) For 2:00 p.m. on a Tuesday, there seem to be quite a lot of people here. They are ordinary-looking people. None of them are in tuxedos or evening dresses. Many of them are women. All of them are businesslike. There is no laughing or crying. If anyone is having fun, you would have a hard time proving it. People sit around a miniature track with what appear to be computer terminals in front of them. It looks like just another day at the office. Mechanical horses run around in front of them. Watching from above, it is impossible to tell the winners from the losers.

Doyle has brought twenty dollars to gamble. He finds a black-jack table and tries to hand his twenty dollars to the dealer. The dealer won't touch it until Doyle places it on the table, although he doesn't say so directly. There's probably a rule about this, but who would know? Then the dealer gives Doyle four chips. Other players at the table tell Doyle he has to bet two and where to put them. Doyle puts them there and is dealt 15. He hits it and gets 22. There goes ten dollars. He puts two more chips down and gets 17. He stays. The dealer gets 20. It took about a minute for the twenty dollars to be gone.

We have lunch in a restaurant on the third floor, overhanging the mechanical-horse table. We watch people not having any fun. Thousands will come this year to do this. Cards on our table invite us to play Keno while we wait for our food. If we knew how, maybe we would.

Another thing you don't think about when you think of Ottawa is the fact that it is a northern city. Not way north, not as far north as Flin Flon or Edmonton. Not even middling north, like North Bay.

But way north of Toronto, as far north as Huntsville or Parry Sound. What made the city was not government, but more northerly pursuits, mainly pulp and paper. Even today, when the wind is just right, you can smell the pulp mills from up the Ottawa River at Thurso. Some find it unpleasant. But on a cool fall day it is a welcome reminder that we are connected to the north, part of the wilderness.

Our weather connects us too, of course. There is all that snow and a considerable cold, although there are much colder places in the country. And every once in a while a moose wanders in from the outlying areas and causes excitement in a suburb. A few years ago a bear showed up on the steep hill down to the river behind Parliament Hill. Animal control officials captured it and carried it away, but a small and admiring crowd turned out to watch the capture and somehow it was nice to know that we live in a capital where a bear can walk behind the House of Commons. Try making that claim in London or Paris or Washington.

Although Ottawa is roughly the same size as Winnipeg, Calgary, or Edmonton, it is far different in spirit (he said, risking a journal-istic observation). Because it is warmer in the winter than in those places, it has more of an outdoor life in the winter time. That stunned me when I first came here from Brandon. Januarys in Brandon you sit inside on a Sunday afternoon and watch golf on television. In Ottawa you go out and ski or skate. It seems almost compulsory.

What Ottawa lacks that those cities have is community spirit. Perhaps it is because so much of our cultural life has been handed to us by the federal government – the galleries, the museums, the National Library, the National Arts Centre. Somehow we don't feel that these things are ours and so we have no loyalty to them. When the NAC comes under attack from the budget cutters, we don't feel that it is our community under attack and so we don't leap up yelling. In Winnipeg and Calgary and Edmonton, the culture is more or less homemade. People have a stake in it, a pride.

That pride also gives them a vigorous volunteer sector. Put on a Winter Olympics or Pan Am Games or Canada Games in one of those cities and watch the volunteers come out in droves, just to be involved. That would never happen here, and hasn't. We do come out in droves for the fall colours in the Gatineau, which no one has figured out a way to charge for yet.

You probably didn't know that the Sunday morning bicycle rides on the Ottawa River Parkway were commercially sponsored. But there you are. The age of privatization has hit everything, even a roadway owned by the National Capital Commission – which is to say, the taxpayers of Canada – and closed to automobile traffic on Sunday mornings so that people can ride, walk, and skate on it.

It is called Sunday Bike Day/ Velo Dimanche. The north lane of the parkway is closed to traffic. There is an in-line skate rental place at the downtown end. Signs list corporate sponsors, of whom there are many. This has all the worst aspects of commercialization with none of the best – where is the commercialized lemonade stand, for example?

Aside from that, it is the usual Ottawa Sunday look. Yellow carts being pulled behind cyclists. Invariably the little kids in the yellow carts wear bicycle helmets and the adults on the bicycles doing the pulling do not.

A little old lady on a three-speed rings her bell as she tries to pass walkers four abreast. There's a walkathon going on too. Why do they have to walk here, where people are trying to cycle? There is grass to the left, grass to the right, and they walk on the road. Their mothers are saying, "Did you get your tag punched?"

The unfortunate fact is that the nice outdoor activities in Ottawa are so nice that they draw a crowd, and in a crowd there are some inconsiderate people. If you think this is bad, you should try to drive across one of Ottawa's bridges into Quebec on a weekend when the leaves are turning in the Gatineau Hills or skate on the Rideau Canal when Winterlude is on. It's too bad. A nice activity like a Sunday morning bicycle ride shouldn't wind up pissing you off.

There is an organized feel to Sunday Bike Day, like skating on the canal. It should be free and formless but that doesn't happen here much. At a traffic light by one of the bridges to Quebec, barricades have been set up to ensure that bicycles come to a stop. A functionary stands there. "Keep to the right," she says when the light changes and the cyclists are forced to go through in single file. That seems to be her job, to say "Keep to the right." I think that even in Ottawa people should be trusted to figure out what a green light means.

People in Ottawa have become accustomed both to activities being free and activities being organized. Some of them even like it. When they opened the new arena, the Palladium (now the Corel Centre), last winter, thousands of people went out there and stood in line, in the middle of the winter, just for a free tour of an empty hockey arena.

Still, looking at Ottawa the way we would if we were driving through for the first time, it is a very pretty city. This was Mr. Gowland's view, back in 1957: "I think that Ottawa, with its wide, open spaces, tree-shaded driveways, canals and yachting lake, is one of the world's most beautiful cities," he wrote. And things have been added since then. There is lots of green, lots of water, and there is a terrific Sunday walk to be had through the market to the National Gallery. Away from the people, we can enjoy the river in the summer. At Remic Rapids, where cars turn off the parkway for a little belvedere, two dog owners meet and talk while their dogs make each other's acquaintance. The dogs aren't on leashes. They bark and chase. That's better. Birds sing, though a lot of them are seagulls.

There is a nice loopiness about Ottawa that is hidden by the Coma City stereotype. Here is one of my favourite Ottawa vignettes. A couple of years ago a store in the Rideau Centre, a shopping mall

downtown, had a party to celebrate the unveiling of the new Hugo
Boss line of clothes. A friend of mine, Sol Gunner, was hired to
play bass in the band. Sol, like many of the best musicians in town,
was a public servant by day. He called me. "You've gotta come
down and catch this," he said. This was because the rest of the band
was from Kingston, and included two musicians we knew from
university days, Murray ("Wink") Wilson and Paul Chabot.

So I drive down to the Rideau Centre on a Thursday night,
wearing jeans and an old windbreaker. Entering from the parking
garage, I hear bebop bouncing off the shopping centre walls. I
follow the sounds up to the top floor and find Sol and Wink and
Paul, playing away, good old fifties' jazz.

They are set up in the middle of one of Rideau Centre's aisles.
On one side of the aisle is the Harry Rosen store, where people
are walking around with wineglasses, and members of the Ottawa
Rough Riders, among others, are modelling the suits. The suits are
the kind that if you carry your phone in the inside pocket no one
will notice. On the other side of the aisle people walk by from the
movie theatre, which has just let out. A lot of them are Somalis.
And I'm thinking: If you had just arrived from Somalia, what
would you make of this, these aging hipsters playing jazz for young
guys with phones in their suits? And if you were inside the store,
looking out, how do you react to a bunch of people who are
clearly a lot worse off than you, staring through the windows?

And if you're Sol and Wink and Paul, what? Did you think,
when you first learned how to play "Lullaby of the Leaves," that
you would ever be playing it in circumstances quite like this? As
for me, I'm wondering whether people who talk about Canadian
diversity have *any idea* how far that term extends.

This Ottawa stay was originally going to be longer, but we need to
make up time and will have to move on more quickly than we
intended. It is a good opportunity to ponder the question: What
have we learned so far? Well, that it is a big and awfully diverse

country. Beautiful in many different ways, peaceful and challenging, foggy and sunny, hilly and flat. And the people? The people are almost without exception friendly and helpful. At least the people beside the road are. The stuff I've been reading at night while the car cools down shows that there are many worlds in these places and we are seeing the most pleasant aspects. Driving along beside the Saint John River, looking at covered bridges and lush fields, is one New Brunswick experience. Reading David Adams Richards' *Nights Below Station Street* is another.

We probably learn as much about ourselves as we learn about what we see. I'm learning that I like the road better when there are fewer people on it. I like a city better when I'm walking in it than when I'm driving. I'm learning that the details that obsess the journalists and politicians, and that would obsess me too if I were in Ottawa, have no impact at all for someone on the road. On the road, what matters is the road – what's that river, where do we stay tonight, where do we go tomorrow, when do we eat?

And that seems to be true, in a more practical way, for the people living beside the road. It is true that I did not play journalist and seek the opinions of people on the great issues of the day. But I did talk to them, and I didn't hear any of them changing the subject to Parliament Hill or Lucien Bouchard or the deficit. They have lives and their lives interest them. That's what they want to talk about.

If I wanted to make a serious Canadian statement about all that, I would say that Canada allows people to be different, to live different kinds of lives in different kinds of regions. Such differences would not be encouraged, or even permitted, in many other parts of the world. There: a serious Canadian statement. Time to get out of Ottawa again.

# IO

## Country Cats and City Cats

We depart late in the afternoon, heading west. That means we get what passes for rush-hour traffic in Ottawa, an annoying but not long-lasting phenomenon. The Queensway, the expressway leading out of the city, crawls along, but only until the outskirts of town are reached, at Kanata. Then everybody gets off and we have some room on the road. I am getting used to being with people on the road now and don't curse at them so much. Still, it is hard to see how a simple thing like a road going from three lanes to two can cause such complete paralysis. It happens all the time, and not just here. Trying to be Pollyanna on our first day back on the road (or perhaps Anne of Green Gables; how about Pollyanna of Green

Gables?) I announce that it is good we are having to drive in this stuff now so that we will appreciate it later when we don't have to. Nancy wisely refrains from comment, perhaps wondering who the strange man is who made the announcement.

Another thing you probably didn't know about Ottawa is that it hosts the Capital Classic Show Jumping Tournament. I didn't know that either until just now, when we pass a bunch of large tents north of the Queensway. This being Ottawa and this being the Nineties, there is a separate sign advertising the Capital Classic Show Jumping Tournament's website.

On we go, past the Corel Centre, which poses a mighty test for Pollyanna of Green Gables. Here it is, a modern hockey arena, out in the middle of nowhere, forcing thousands of people to drive on this godforsaken road, and contributing nothing to the surrounding area, which consists of empty fields, when, if it had been downtown, it could have revived the downtown economy, much as the SkyDome has helped revive and enliven a chunk of downtown Toronto. How did we let this happen?

Enough. We turn off the Queensway onto Highway 7. We are heading for the Thain family farm, Thainlea, where Nancy's father, Grant Thain, was born. It is south of Highway 7, near Marmora, about two hours down the road. As we drive, we will try to see Highway 7 as if for the first time. This will be difficult. Down Highway 7, past the farm, is Peterborough, where Nancy's sister, Mary Parker, lives, with Stuart and the two boys. Near Peterborough is Stony Lake, one of the Kawartha Lakes, where the Parkers have a cottage we often visit, also using Highway 7. And Highway 7 is one of several routes we take to Toronto, turning off it at any of several points to get down to the 401. So we know Highway 7 better than we would like.

Well, we see through our new eyes, it is a good old Ontario road. Lots of trees, some farms, a few old stone houses, a few of those standard Ontario brick farmhouses. I do a small meditation on the subject of old. Why do we equate beautiful with old?

Everything beautiful in Atlantic Canada is old. Can't new be beautiful? I resolve to look for beautiful new stuff.

Highway 7 crosses the Mississippi River twice. On neither crossing can you see off it. They've put those concrete dividers along the sides so that only a very tall person, half-standing in his seat, can see the view from the bridge. Is that what they wanted, these safety-conscious Ontario people, to cause only tall people to have accidents?

The towns go by: Carleton Place, Perth, Wemyss, Sharbot Lake, Kaladar, Madoc, Marmora. Before Kaladar are some unusual hills, with boulders resting on them. Thanks to the hard work that got me 50 per cent in first-year geology, I know that this hill has something to do with the glacier although I don't know exactly what, if I ever did.

Along this road, the restaurants and gas stations are always opening and closing and changing ownership. The motels are mostly closing. I haven't seen a new one open in years. I think the problem is that Ottawa is too close, or Peterborough is too close. A driver is never more than an hour and a half from a large community, so why stop for the night?

It doesn't take long for the feeling to return that the road is more real than so-called real life. As we drive we listen to a CBC afternoon show on which community leaders talk about something called the virtual community association, in which community people chat with each other and make decisions on the Internet. Imagine, well-educated people are talking seriously about a system to make decision-making easier for people who have home computers. More and more, I think that radio is the place to find people who need a life.

At Kaladar, the combined gas station, restaurant, and store is a big operation and I check the bulletin board there. There's a Miracle Service at Actinolite, George Fox is singing at Tamworth. There's a beef supper at Harlowe and a demolition derby at Madoc.

We turn off the highway at Marmora (slogan: UPPER CANADA'S PIONEER IRON TOWN), and drive to the Thainlea farm in time for supper. Jim Thain, Nancy's cousin, who was born in 1947, runs the place, a prosperous dairy operation begun by their grandfather, Jonathan, in 1908. Jim's father, Ernest, grew up here, along with his brother, Grant, and sister, Clara. Grant was the only one who left the farm, becoming a teacher, then a high school principal in Fort William. Jim grew up here with his two brothers, Harold and Linn. They both work in cities now. Jim went away for a while too, in the seventies, managing a Beaver Lumber in the Northern Ontario town of Blind River. But when his father's knees gave out and he could no longer look after the operation, Jim came back to join him and his mother, Gwelda. Ernest died nine years ago. Now Jim, who is divorced, and Gwelda rattle around in the big farmhouse, which was built in 1929. There is a hired man, Johnny Curtis, who lives elsewhere. There is also a lumpy black dog, Boner, who appeared as a stray six years ago, and the usual tribe of cats in the barn.

The layout is familiar – a long driveway between the front lawn and a field. The red brick house on the left, then across the driveway a building called the drive house, where tractors, trucks, and other machinery are kept. Straight ahead is the big red barn, beside it a concrete silo, and behind that a round metal storage building. Farms – at least growing ones – have this tendency to add structures. Over time, they scatter over the landscape in a haphazard way.

The farm milks fifty Holsteins. Corn and hay are grown. That much hasn't changed over the years. But the farm environment has. Jim talks about it after supper, sitting at the dining-room table under a large colourized aerial photograph of the farm in earlier times. Farmers can't exist on a hundred acres any more, he says. The required investment in machinery is too great. A few years ago, there were nine functioning farms on the Sixth Line, he says. Now there are three. For the others, farming has become a sideline for people who have pensions or other means of support. "Ninety per cent of our beef business today is run by people with two jobs," Jim says.

Jim just has the one. Farmers have to adjust, he says, and he has. His tractor is a big air-conditioned thing with a telephone inside. You could order a pizza from it, he jokes. He also has a hay baler, and brings in some revenue hiring it and himself out to neighbouring farmers.

Higher costs have also required more judicious use of fertilizer. "You've got to find the line where it's paying," he says. "I don't use as much fertilizer as Dad did." Gwelda adds, "The younger people can't believe how we farmed."

The people who settled this land were Scottish Presbyterians, Tories, Orangemen, traditional in the extreme. Jim's grandfather used to try to get the haying done by July 12, so he could go to the Orange Day parade in Campbellford. Now Jim is talking about the need to help Russia and the countries of the Third World so that there will be markets for Canadian farmers.

At dusk, I go for a stroll outside. By the pond beside the road you can hear three bullfrogs, loud as anything. The cows move silently, in that eerie way, on the other side of the fence. Cars can just be heard in the distance against the background of the soft round shapes of the hills and ridges and trees. "I like my life," Jim said. You can see why. Somewhere in the city, people are thinking about putting community groups on the Internet.

We are up at seven to watch the milking, which doesn't start as early as it used to. Nancy used to spend parts of her summer vacations here and can remember the chores and which were the hard ones. She shows me the field where she had to pick the stones. Most tellingly, she points out of the back door of the barn and says: "There's the field my father was stooking the day he decided he didn't want to be a farmer any more." Grant had to board in Campbellford to finish high school. Then he went to Queen's and became a teacher. Nancy and I met at Queen's, where she was influenced to go by her father. It is interesting to think that our joint presence in this barn today derives from the twin facts that Grant hated stooking and my father asked Frank Scott about Canadian universities.

There seem to be two cats. The dog wanders carefully through the barn, paying no attention to them, nor to the cows. It takes about five minutes to get the cows into the barn. Most of them learn quickly to go to the same stall every day. The milking takes another hour, the operation powered by a pump which produces a loud hum in the milk house. Upstairs in the barn round bales of hay – from "back north," Jim says – are stored, to be cut up with an electric chainsaw for the cows.

The barn is about as automated as it can be, even to having an automated manure system. I don't ask how that works. The milk goes from the cow up a tube into a pipe and down the pipe into a tank in the milk house, which is attached to the barn. Jim says to Nancy: "It's not like it used to be when we put it in a pail and the cats used to have a drink before we got it to the milk house." Every other day, the truck comes to take the milk away.

Breakfast is in the summer kitchen. In a corner of the summer kitchen is Jim's office: a desk, six file drawers, a calculator, no computer. We talk about country life, the way it is changing. Jim talks about the people who drive up from Toronto every fall to shoot rabbits. Johnny Curtis talks about the young people, who are leaving the area. There is nothing for them on the farms, unless they inherit one, and there are no jobs in town. We talk about Jim's farm, which is doing fine, because he is adapting.

## To Toronto, on Two Lanes

We're going to try another thing we always want to do but never have the time – get to Toronto without using the 401. We start by driving through Campbellford, the shopping place for the farm and the town where Jim's father bought his cars and trucks, and then down to Brighton on Highway 30 and under the 401 to Presqu'ile Provincial Park, where we stop for coffee. It has huge, flat beaches, islands offshore in the mist, a DESIGNATED BOARD SAILING AREA, and a bit of a beat-up look, for which I blame government cutbacks.

We continue along Highway 2, which used to be the way between Kingston and Toronto before the 401 was completed. The users of the 401 miss some beautiful places, including Colborne, Cobourg, and Port Hope, fine old Ontario towns. I am alert for signs of Orange Day parades, it being July the Glorious Twelfth and this being that part of the world. I don't see any. Port Hope's slogan is A RICH PAST, A GOLDEN FUTURE. I'm told that at one point it was THE TOWN THAT RADIATES HAPPINESS, until nuclear waste became a feature of Ontario life. We stop in Bowmanville for lunch, hoping for a parade, or at least a stroll through a stately old Ontario town. Somehow stateliness escapes Bowmanville.

Nearing Toronto with time to spare, we decide to do another thing we have never done, stop at the zoo. This requires us to get back on the 401, which probably is necessary for research purposes anyway. I hate this road, the ugly concrete divider down the middle, the three lanes on either side of it, the big trucks. It cuts a wide swath through Ontario, making more of it accessible, which is both good or bad, depending on where you live. We go through Oshawa, Whitby, Ajax, Pickering – places that have become bedroom communities. There is construction. Great: more lanes to put more people onto the Don Valley Parkway every morning, send more rabbit shooters onto Jim Thain's farm. The eastbound lanes, the ones moving out of Toronto, aren't moving. It is only 3:30 in the afternoon. People who live in Toronto adjust to this. I don't know whether this is good or bad either.

The Metro Toronto Zoo is fun, even without kids to take through it. In fact, we see lots of adults without children. Canada geese walk freely through, making intriguing juxtapositions with such creatures as the Great Indian rhino. The geese are also the subject of one of my favourite warnings (I think I am collecting warnings, beginning with the cliffs at the Plains of Abraham). This one comes from a guide on the Zoomobile, warning us not to feed any of the animals. "The geese, especially, have been known to be vicious," she says. I love that. Here we are, surrounded by some of the most dangerous critters in all of Africa and Asia and it's the Canada goose, our own Canada goose, that we're watching out for.

There are two gorgeous Sumatran tigers, an ugly Marabou stork, some fine wart hogs, three impressive polar bears. After the Atlantic provinces, which are ethnically homogeneous, the mixture of people at the zoo is quite impressive.

There is a healthy kind of commercialism. You can stop at an ice cream wagon, or a McDonald's. I'm just commenting favourably on this when we happen upon the Royal Bank Koalas. Can an animal be sponsored? Apparently. When we join a large crowd to see the animal in question, it is sitting in a tree, not doing much of anything. Serves the Royal Bank right.

On the way out we pass a sign pointing to the zoo composting area. The sign also tells us not to go there because there is heavy equipment there. And then: "For information about home composting, visit our Backyard Conservation Area, located next to the Education Centre." Toronto is so *nice*.

Actually, I am mellowing on Toronto. It used to be that just about anything could set me off on an anti-Toronto rant. Now I am more tolerant. Mary, our daughter, has moved there and has found lots to like and her judgement always influences me. The city seems to be over that eighties mentality, that hey-we're-better-than-New-York attitude that used to disgust Canadians from elsewhere. Toronto has had some hard times and that matures a city, just as it sometimes matures an individual. The real estate boom has ended, which means that you can go to a party in Toronto without hearing people talk about what they could get for their house. The Blue Jays have had some terrible seasons, which means that you don't have to listen to Torontonians talk about how they invented baseball (a special ordeal for Montreal Expos fans). And the sheer weight of the city has caught up with it, so that suddenly people living in other places are turning down opportunities to move to Toronto. It costs too much to live there, they say. It is possible, all of a sudden, to feel sorry for Toronto.

Which makes it easier to like. And there is a lot to like. Green spaces, an excellent public transit system, ethnic diversity, great museums and other public institutions. Above all, a tradition of politeness and civility that is often mocked – I just did – but which will probably make it possible for Toronto to be one North American city where people from different races and backgrounds are able to get along with each other.

### The Glorious Thirteenth

The next morning we take the subway from North York down to Queen's Park, where we are meeting Mary. The subway itself is full of little bits of niceness, from the Mind the Gap warnings at the edge of the tracks, to the pleasant little chimes that sound, instead of harsh whistles, when the doors are about to close, to the helpful posters announcing various attractions in the city. I do think that Toronto prides itself on this sort of thing, on being a place where people treat each other decently and don't get into the me-first mentality that has ruined so many other large cities. For a time, Torontonians seemed somewhat embarrassed when visitors told them, again and again, how clean and safe the city was. It was as if Toronto, by virtue of being clean and safe, was somehow not in the big leagues of citydom. Now being clean and safe is back in. Being polite goes with that, a bit of the old Toronto-the-Good legacy that is worth keeping.

I have never lived in Toronto but have spent enough time here to see it as a very livable place, under certain conditions. You have to be near the subway, so that you don't have to drive anywhere, particularly to work. And it helps to have money. It is frustrating to sit at home unable to afford the great stuff you see around you.

It also helps to love cities in the summertime. Toronto's greatest flaw is how hard it is to get out of it on a summer weekend. Torontonians regularly suffer the ordeal of driving four hours to lakes an hour and a half away, then spending the rest of the weekend psyching themselves up for the four-hour drive back. That can't be a good way to live and in the long run must do damage to the soul. Much better to decide to stay in town and enjoy what happens on the streets. The streets, of course, have the advantage of being uncrowded.

On the subway, we watch the panorama unfold. A younger guy eats, with a white plastic spoon, from a container of something, perhaps Baskin & Robbins. This is very much a big-city thing, how people make themselves at home on the subway no matter how short the ride, eating their food, taking out their work. A neophyte watches people, looks at the map and his watch.

Walking from the subway over to Queen's Park, I wonder how the legislative building of Ontario can be made so inaccessible to people. It is on a kind of island around which traffic flows rapidly with no light to stop it. So if you want to visit your MPP, as they are called here, you have to be prepared to sprint.

This is to be a continuation of the legislature tours. As a journalist, I have covered a few events at the Park, but I have never seen it the way a member of the public would. Walking up, we hear music, see people, and gradually come to the realization that what we are encountering is the forming up of the Toronto Orange Day Parade. I offer a small prayer of thanks. This is what we were looking for yesterday. Now here it is, a day late, in Toronto, coinciding with the Toronto Fringe Festival and the qualifying heats for the Molson Indy car races. What a city.

An accordion band is tuning up, if that is what you do with an accordion. There are thirty-five accordions, the people playing them dressed in black vests, red shirts and hat bands. It is not the only accordion band on the grounds. One is called the Ulster Accordion Band of Toronto. The accordions are small, not like the one your cousin tried to play "Lady of Spain" upon. The better to march with, I suppose. Marching with a full-size accordion you could get something caught. I think of Wilde, I believe it was, who defined a gentleman as someone who knows how to play an accordion but chooses not to. The Crown Defenders Flute Band is there. And so is King Billy, with a great red coat, long black hair and beard, riding a white horse. They pose for photographs.

There are many people, comprising the least multicultural crowd we are likely to see today. Many are elderly, but by no means all. I overhear someone saying something about no public washrooms in Mike Harris's Ontario. There is a marshal with a cell phone. When the parade is about to begin, flute players put their cigarettes out, and banners are lifted, one featuring a portrait of the Queen, waving. A flute band from Cambridge struts by playing "Red River Valley," followed by a white Grand-Am draped in a Union Jack.

One of the Orangemen says that Toronto is not the only parade. There are others, but they are not all held on the Glorious Twelfth any more. He is wearing an orange vest. I am wearing, I suddenly realize, a tee-shirt with the giant Salvador Dali horse on it, from the Beaverbrook Gallery in Fredericton. And I think *he* looks weird. A band from Brampton plays "Abide With Me" while we chase the Tecumseh Fife & Drum Band, the Temperance LOL Toronto, and the Sandhill Pipe Band up University Avenue and across to Yonge. Only one side of the street is blocked off and there are not many spectators. This is Toronto and so many other things are going on. I fall in with an older woman who has seen many Orange Day parades, always on the Twelfth in the years she remembers best, and is impressed by how small this one is. "Wait'll I tell my brother it was only fifteen minutes," she says.

We return to the legislature, a pink castlelike structure, full of curves. Romanesque, we are told. The first thing that greets us when we enter is a sign: NO PUBLIC WASHROOMS IN BUILDING. This is what those Orangemen were talking about. Interesting. It's *our* building, isn't it? To see how serious the government of Ontario is about this, we approach the desk and ask when the next tour is. It is half an hour away. We ask if there's a washroom we can use in the meantime. No, we are told. Fine. As we walk off I think of the Orangemen, some of whom had been out there getting ready for the parade for at least a couple of hours and some of whom may have had a drink or two in the process. It's all very well to keep *me* out, a CCFer in a Salvador Dali tee-shirt, but the Orangemen kept the Tory party in power for decades.

We decide to go somewhere for lunch. And a washroom. We walk through the pretty University of Toronto campus and see a photographer setting up a Chinese wedding photo. "One more," he is saying. We wind up in Yorkville, which I didn't know when it was the centre of hippiedom in the sixties, and couldn't stand when it was the centre of consumerism in the eighties. We find an upstairs patio and sit in the hot Saturday sun. It is the usual burger, taco, pizza, enchilada, salad, and Mexican-beer-with-a-lime-in-it kind of place. I continue my rant about Yorkville, always a highlight for my wife and daughter, until my plastic chair collapses underneath me, whereupon some law students sitting at the next table nicely inquire as to my well-being and ask if maybe my neck hurts.

We are late for the 3:30 Queen's Park tour but are told we can catch up. While the guide rushes us to where the tour is, he gives us a rundown on what we have missed. This is such considerate treatment. A genuine friendliness must be one of the requirements for any successful tour guide applicant anywhere in this country. It is amazing that people who won't even let the public use the can are able to hire so intelligently.

The chamber has blue seats, a red carpet, and ten chandeliers. There were originally four but six more were put in to add candle-power for the TV cameras. As in some of the other legislatures, the traditional look has been violated by digital clocks, necessary to keep orators from going on too long. The guide holds up a cardboard placard that has a picture of the mace on it. The real one is kept in a secret place in the building. An older version was stolen by the Americans when they burned the legislature down during the War of 1812. Franklin Roosevelt returned it in 1934 to help celebrate Toronto's one-hundredth birthday but clearly the Queen's Park powers-that-be, conscious of the level of American tourism, are taking no chances.

Muzakish sounds intrude upon the guide's discourse. He apologizes for this and says some glitch causes the music from the legislature's television channel to be piped through the building. One of the marble columns has a dinosaur fossil in it. This is too obvious even for me and I let it go. As we leave, we see another wedding being photographed.

Then it's down to Harbourfront, on our semi-aimless meanderings. Having seen the great things Saint John and Halifax have done with their waterfronts, Toronto's is a major disappointment. Of course, the city was playing catch-up from the start. With railway tracks and then the Gardiner Expressway blocking the city from Lake Ontario, the task of reclaiming it may have been impossible. And it didn't help that lakefront condominiums sprouted in the affluent eighties, further separating the lake from all but those who could afford it. Still, once you get down there it's not too bad. There is a long stretch of boardwalk, although not much of it is on boards, many boats for hire, and a ferry to Toronto Island. So far so good. There are street musicians, mostly amplified, and mostly playing the usual street musician repertoire. We hear "Amazing Grace" and, perhaps inevitably, Pachelbel's *Canon*. Tour boats and party boats go by playing rock music. For a scene that should be peaceful there is entirely too much artificial noise. Some rock musicians are tuning up at the Heinecken Summer Music stage, which doesn't bother me because at least they are musicians rather than somebody's recordings played on a sound system.

There are some large boats moored. Two of the biggest are from Florida. My warning sign collection expands magnificently with one I see at the water's edge: CAUTION: WATER'S EDGE, it says.

There are several restaurants with nautical motifs – Spinnaker's, The Boathouse. They seemed to be mostly staffed by Toronto actors, to hear Mary tell it.

When you look north and east, there is a great view of the Toronto skyline. It wasn't that long ago that the tallest building you'd see from here would be the Royal York. Now it, along with Union Station, is about all that is left of that part of Toronto. The rest is glass skyscrapers, and much of the commercial life has moved underground. This has happened, to a lesser extent, in Montreal. I don't think the historians of cities will regard it highly.

Enough. Tonight we are going to see John's one-man show at the Fringe Festival. Before that I want to catch another one, featuring and co-written by Mary's friend and George Brown classmate Pasha McKenley. I wander off on my own and grab a couple of streetcars, finding the Annex Theatre, at Bathurst near Bloor, almost by accident when the streetcar stops in front of it. The ticket taker yells "You've got forty seconds!" as I run across the street. I make it. Pasha has about twenty-five people to see her show, *The Diva Within*, which is a good crowd by Fringe standards. Pasha is terrific, funny and extravagant, alternating between island patois and grande dame gushiness. Having lived now for several years as a parent of actors, I often know the people who get up on the stage and become, most convincingly, something they're not. The process always amazes and impresses me. The show is confused but it does something that we are going to be seeing more and more of, I hope: it brings together the different ethnic sensibilities. The West Indians in the audience are killing themselves laughing at some of the language and cultural references. The WASPs are killing themselves at others. You could see this play, and its audience, as something Toronto makes possible.

The Toronto Fringe is one of nineteen such festivals across North America. Toronto's has seven stages, and more than eighty productions, running over a period of ten days. The performers, who are selected by lottery, pay an entry fee that covers the technical costs, then earn whatever comes in at the box office. Often it is not much. Fringe organizers expect 30,000 people to see the shows, which range from amateur to professional with some semi-pro in between. For the performers, it is a chance to perform, to be seen, perhaps discovered.

This theatre building, a former church, is also home to the Coalition for Lesbian and Gay Rights in Ontario and the Canadian Vegetarian Association. It is impressive to think of the range of Toronto encountered in one day – the opulence of Queen's Quay and Yorkville, a play for twenty-five people, many of them black, King Billy on the white horse, the Canadian Vegetarian Association, and a fossil in marble.

John, performing at a theatre just off the U of T campus, gets about twenty people to see his one-man show, *Slam*. About six of those twenty are his family and friends, so that's not too bad. I am learning that in this world if you can get half a dozen people you don't know personally to see your show, you're doing well. His play too is about a mixture of cultures – a white suburban basket-ball-playing kid admiring black culture and wanting to be part of it. When his show opened about a week ago, John had a backboard on the stage and incorporated a lot of layups and jump shots into his script. On the second night, the pole supporting it collapsed in the middle of the show. After trying unsuccessfully to put it back up, he finished the show, reblocking it on the spot, the basketball moves now stressing dribbling rather than shooting.

I knew he was a good basketball player. I didn't know he was a good writer, but the play tells me that. In the second part, his character becomes a twenty-six-year-old, still immersed in black culture, about to learn some lessons about trying to be something he is not, meanwhile striving mightily "to get the fuck out of my parents' basement." My mother, to whom he dedicates the play, might not appreciate the language (she always bugged Alison about the number of *shits* and *fucks* in her books) but she would laugh at the thought, as do others in the audience, not all of them knowing how accurate the line is.

After the show our gang, a multi-generational group of about ten, walks along Bloor West in search of a restaurant. The sidewalks are jammed but mellow. The traffic is barely moving, the people in the cars anything but mellow. This is a familiar city dichotomy – the laid-back sidewalk life contrasting with the tension where the cars are. The Lebanese restaurant where we wind up is loose and friendly, a reminder that you don't have to be in a small town to be treated warmly. When we come out, the sidewalk is still crowded, the drivers still have the veins knotted in their necks. We pass some young beggars who do not look badly off and some homeless people sleeping in doorways – another element in the Toronto equation.

# 11

## The Superior (and Only) Route

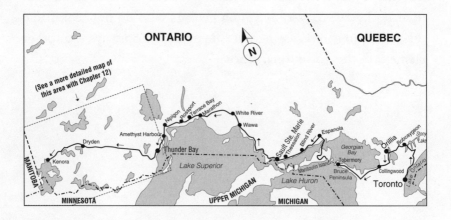

I think I'm trying to hit the *Guinness Book of World Records* in a new category: Smallest Community for Getting Lost In. Today it was Bobcaygeon, north and a bit west of Peterborough. It's a pretty little cottage town with lots of traffic. I've probably driven through three times and each time I come out on a different highway than the one I came in on. I drive to a gas station and ask, which really hurts, but I am able to report when I get back to the car that hundreds, well, lots, of people ask the same question – namely, where did Highway 8 go?

Nancy's sister, Mary Parker, is along on this leg of the trip, a guest star. We drove from Toronto to her cottage near Peterborough to pick her up. One reason for her presence is the fact that the cottage is under repair. Another is that she hasn't seen the north shore of Lake Superior in a long time. She can't be too impressed with the speed with which we're getting there. Especially when the road we think is taking us to Fenelon Falls actually takes us to Coboconk. But then it turns out we're still heading, perhaps accidentally, in the direction of Orillia, which is our first destination, so that's all right.

Today's eventual destination is Tobermory, at the tip of the Bruce Peninsula. Tomorrow we'll catch the ferry to Manitoulin Island, then pick up Highway 17 at Espanola. This route, which we have done before, cuts off Highway 69, a heavily travelled and scenically overrated route along Georgian Bay. Today we are taking little roads just to stay away from the Toronto cottage traffic, and because the little roads are pretty, and because we have time.

To get to Stephen Leacock's house in Orillia, you first must pass an ugly new subdivision called Leacock Point, about which Leacock might have had something to say. The Leacock house itself has a beautiful setting and is quite grand, a sprawling white frame building with two chimneys, set upon a large lawn. The whole operation is well looked after by a group of dedicated people in Orillia who make sure everything connected with Leacock's memory is treated professionally. We sit at a picnic table by the backyard, looking at the house and admiring Lake Couchiching. I tell tales of doing a reading on this lawn a few years ago and afterward getting a chance to shoot pool in the basement on Leacock's own table. I treated each shot quite reverentially, which is not to say that I made any of them, until one of my opponents, a top executive at the *Orillia Packet and Times*, missed a shot and said: "Goddamn drift!" And I thought, "Stephen Leacock's table has *drift*?"

Getting lost coming out of Orillia doesn't feel quite so bad, since it is a much larger place than Bobcaygeon. We are staying off Highway 11, one of the big cottage-country roads, by taking

County Road 11 which parallels it. But somehow we wind up
going north on 18. That's okay, I say to Mary, who is driving,
because we can catch 22, which is going exactly the way we want
to go. When we cross 22, however, it is called something else, the
Something Road, or something, and we drive on by, winding up
in a forty-five-minute meander, a Sunshine Sketch of a Little
Detour, and find ourselves back in Orillia where we, inexplicably,
land on the right road. How do you like it so far, Mary?

Then it gets better, particularly the part where we cross the 400
and watch all the suckers driving back to Toronto. We drive
against the traffic past Wasaga Beach and Collingwood, where rich
Torontonians come to visit their ski chalets. The road does not
give us much of a look at Georgian Bay and what we do see is
obscured by haze. There is a good sign, though: WIN HUNCHBACK
PRIZE PACK. This has to do with a movie, apparently. Otherwise it
would make you wonder. After Owen Sound, the road takes us
through Wiarton, which of course is the GROUND HOG CAPITAL
OF CANADA. Every February an alleged groundhog named
Wiarton Willy sticks his nose up and sees his shadow, or doesn't,
and the wire services dutifully report it. Every February I can't
believe that they are still doing it and we are all still putting it in
the paper.

Highway 6, which runs up the Bruce Peninsula, looks great on
the map. It has Lake Huron to the left and Georgian Bay to the
right, but you never see either of them. Thanks to getting lost here
and there, we don't have time to get off the highway and tootle.
There is great walking to be had on the peninsula, we know.
Something to add to the list for next time.

We check in at the Blue Bay Motel in downtown Tobermory,
which has okay rooms, a good location, and nice people. The
harbour is the reason for Tobermory. Pleasure boaters dock
here. Hundreds take the ferry, the *Chi-Cheemaun*, each day to
Manitoulin, with its four departures and four arrivals. The town
(slogan: THE DIVING CAPITAL OF CANADA) is also a launching place

for divers, who explore the dozens of wrecks off the peninsula and in an underwater provincial park. There are well laid-out walks along the harbour, using brick and treated wood, that get you away from the street and down by the water. I admire the town for making the effort to give the waterfront to the people. There are even public toilets in a couple of locations. Wait until Queen's Park hears about this.

A ten-minute stroll takes us to the Grandview Motel and Restaurant which is well named. One of the Top Ten sunsets appears along with some fine splake, a cross between lake trout and speckled trout. The sun is red and reflects in a narrow band across the water towards us. We walk in the dusk back into the town and stop at the Sweet Shop, which sells ice cream and must be a licence to print money in a town like this. At least it would be if I were here every day.

## Too Bad It's Not Nicer: Part Four

It is sunny on Monday, but we see fog out on the water. Uh-oh. This is such a pretty trip, too, or at least it was when we took it a few years ago. We drive onto the *Chi-Cheemaun* at 11:05 and walk up to the passenger decks and outside, where fog now surrounds us. People crowd to the bow as the ship leaves and we watch the nose of the ferry, through which we had driven on board, close up. Then everyone goes inside and crowds into the cafeteria, creating lineups that last the entire hour and three-quarters of the trip.

It's nice to be on a ferry again and this isn't a bad one, although not as roomy as the ones we saw in Atlantic Canada. It holds about half as many people as the *Caribou*, the ship that took us to Newfoundland. In one of the lounges there are information desks, with much useful travel information available. An information person says this to me about the fog: "It's not normal, really, but this year it's normal." Specifically, this means that the water is unusually cold this year, creating fog conditions when it meets the warm air.

With no scenery to see I concentrate on adding to my sign collection. One is on the door of the first-aid room. THIS ROOM CONTAINS NO DRUGS, it says. I don't want to think about this and turn to collecting Old Guys' Hats. In rapid succession I get COLLIE (with a picture of a dog); EVERGREEN; PUT-IN BAY, OHIO; MANI-TOBA HYDRO; WINSTON STEEL; and DOUG SIMMS SERVICE LTD. There is a knack to Old-Guys'-Hat collecting. With middle-aged eyes it is not easy to pick them up at a distance. So the person has to be approached fairly directly, with effort made to avoid anything that might be mistaken for eye contact.

We drive off at South Baymouth and turn off the main highway to do a loop around Manitoulin Island, something we've never had time to do before. Perhaps we don't go far enough – we don't get to the western tip (a blow to my obsession with getting to the end of things), instead turning up to Gore Bay, then back to Little Current – but what we see is not as impressive as we'd hoped, con-sidering that this is the largest freshwater island in the world. Much of our disappointment undoubtedly has to do with where the highway is placed. Two of the major lakes, Manitou and Mindemoya, are only glimpsed from the highway. There is a fine lookout at Gore Bay, high over the North Channel and looking down on the town, and Bridal Falls is nice, people swimming in quite warm water under the falls, and there is a good trail along the Kagawong River, which speeds its way down to the channel.

As we drive along the north side of the island, the vistas are better, as at McLean's Mountain, near Sucker Creek, from which we look across fields and the North Channel to the mainland. It is a hot clear day now. Heading for the mainland, we luck in on the swing bridge, which is open for us, and cross to Birch Island, where we begin to see boulders, more characteristic of Shield country. As we approach the turnoff to McGregor Bay, the landscape finally begins to resemble the Northern Ontario that Nancy and Mary love. We begin to see camps and resorts, then the big smokestacks at Espanola, which would carry the paper-mill stench to us if the wind were not blowing the other way. At 4:50, we are on Highway 17, the Trans-Canada.

It always amazes me that so few people take the Trans-Canada through Northern Ontario. The road is excellent, with a 90 km/h speed limit and so many passing lanes that you never get stuck behind a truck or trailer for very long. And the scenery is magnificent. Yet despite the fact that it is the Trans-Canada Highway, this part of the road is a well-kept secret. Most people don't drive west and many of those who do make the trip go through the States.

Never mind. We are thrilled to be on it. For Nancy and me it is an old friend. For Mary, it is a return to her childhood. We go through Webbwood (population 600), Massey, Spanish (slogan: GATEWAY TO THE NORTH CHANNEL), Serpent River, Spragge. These are not, for the most part, prosperous places. When you see motels advertising $34 rooms, you know that business is not booming. There are many closed roadside enterprises, motels and restaurants. But Blind River, where Jim Thain used to work, has new businesses, a wide main street, and all the chains. Northern Ontario towns are not picturesque, like Maritime towns, or stately, like Central Ontario towns. They stretch out along the highway and the tracks, serving the people who work on the railroad (or used to), in the forests or in the mills. There is nothing pretentious or artificial about such towns. I like to look at the ball diamond as a measure of the community. If it is well looked after, I figure that there is some life to it, some kids and some fun.

The place we always stop here is the Carolyn Beach Motel at Thessalon. It is a kind of throwback to roadside motels of the past – three long rows of rooms, each with a front and a back door, the front door opening onto a lawn beyond which is the North Channel of Lake Huron, the back door opening onto your car. The

rooms are basic motelish, the two narrow double beds, the TV set
with no remote, the ice machine whirring and groaning a short
walk down the row. The restaurant has a kind of forties decor,
carpeted, with picture windows, and the food is basic. You couldn't
get pasta there, although you could get spaghetti. The rest of the
menu runs to steaks and chops and fish cooked in the most basic
way. There is nothing trendy about this place, nor about its customers, who tend to be on the upper end of middle age, quiet,
experienced travellers. The menu even offers, in addition to a children's menu, something called Seniors' Portions. These people are
not going to be obnoxious in the restaurant and they won't keep
you up all night with their partying. All of this makes for a low-key
setting. It is the ideal roadside restaurant, all the more so for looking
right at a consistently terrific sunset. That's two in a row for us.

## A Great Lake

Nancy loves Lake Superior. Every time we drive this way, she gets
excited as we drive through Sault Ste. Marie and ecstatic as we hit
the first rise from which the lake can be seen. It is a beautiful lake,
to be sure, but this has as much to do with the spirit as the eye. It
has to do with growing up in Thunder Bay, beside the lake. There
is also something about Thunder Bay's isolation from the rest of
Ontario. Toronto is farther away than Winnipeg, especially attitu-
dinally. In their isolation, people who live in Thunder Bay form a
close-knit community. Away from home, they huddle together;
when two meet socially in another town, they find they have much
in common, even if they have never met before and are from
different generations.

The lake symbolizes that isolation and it also symbolizes home.
So it adds power as a metaphor to its visual power, which is considerable. I've tried to figure out why Lake Ontario, which is
awfully big too, has nowhere near that power. In fact, it is just a
lake. In Kingston, I lived beside it for years. In fall, it was a cold
grey thing. In winter, it was a frozen grey thing. In the spring and

summer it was fine, but there is little sense nowadays of Lake Ontario as an economic force, whereas in Thunder Bay the lake is *the* economic force, as well as an important recreational one.

The land at the edge of Superior is, for the most part, rugged, with steep hills and fast rivers emptying into the lake. The islands are large and high. Away from Toronto, Lake Ontario has few islands to gaze upon, and the landscape coming to the lakeshore is flat and relatively uninteresting. Prince Edward County, around Picton, is an exception and that seems to be one place where people feel a real affection toward Lake Ontario.

But nothing like the affection Nancy and Mary feel toward Lake Superior. After we pass through the Soo (HOME OF DR. ROBERTA BONDAR AND THE SOO GREYHOUNDS), the hills grow larger while the road stays low and close to the water. The sisters are in heaven. As we drive by Batchawana Bay, Mary wonders if people have camps here. Camps are what people from Thunder Bay call cottages. Just then a jetski whines by. They have camps.

We stop at an information place to pick up a Northwestern Ontario guidebook. Right there is a beautiful river, with falls and rapids. Also it is an important historic spot: the halfway point of the Trans-Canada Highway and site of a plaque, put up by the Ontario Motor League, honouring Dr. Perry E. Doolittle, "father of the Trans-Canada Highway." Inspired by all this, I suggest we stop here for coffee and am vigorously mocked for the suggestion: it is not beside Lake Superior. Would it have strengthened my case had I been able to produce the fruit of my subsequent researches and tell the sisters that Dr. Doolittle was an active nineteenth-century champion of good roads for bicyclists, the author, in fact, of the 1895 volume *Wheel Outings in Canada*? Or that he then – and this is what probably caught the Ontario Motor League's fancy – switched over to become an advocate for Ontario's automobile users?

No. It would have made no difference at all. On we go, with me muttering and grumbling – although the beach on Batchawana

Bay where we do stop is very nice and the lake looks terrific under a blue sky. This is a fairly peaceful part of the lake, the shore far from rugged.

My long-term revenge for this slight will be on the way back, when we take the more northerly Highway 11 and miss the lake entirely. Last year, driving back from Kenora, I persuaded Nancy to take a slight detour away from the lake, turning inland at Wawa for a bit, because a total stranger we met at a B&B said it was a nice road. And of course if a total stranger tells you something, it must be true. It didn't help matters that part of our drive was in the general direction of a forest fire that kept drifting smoke over the road. And it didn't help matters that another part of our drive was through a completely uninhabited area with the gas gauge nearing empty. We did find gas and *finally*, in the last sixty kilometres of the detour, found a beautiful river, the Mississagi, to drive beside. But that day's drive lives in family lore as "that awful drive through the forest fire." It's the price I pay for having left Lake Superior.

Nancy knows that it will be Highway 11 on the way back, knows it's "for the book," as I put it. Used sparingly, the phrase "it's for the book" allows me certain choices that no person in his or her right mind would make. So far I have been careful not to overuse it.

My short-term revenge is to force a stop at Wawa, to thoroughly research the Big Goose. It's for the book, I say. It is actually a pretty good big goose, when you see it up close, designed by Dick Vanderlift, constructed of Algoma Steel products, commemorating the last link of the Lake Superior section of the Trans-Canada and dedicated in 1960 by Premier Leslie Frost. After our weeks in the Maritimes, it is startling to see how new things are up here. The forest-fire hazard is low, a sign says, and suddenly it is rather cold, far colder than when we got up at Thessalon this morning.

The Wawa-to-Marathon section of Highway 17, although it leaves the lake for a couple of hours, is not dull. There are many small lakes and rivers. The problem with the rivers is that the bridges over them have been blocked off at the sides so that the rivers cannot be seen. We begin compiling a list of rivers that we can't see as we cross them – Goulais, Batchawana, Chippewa, Agawa, Black, White Lake Narrows, Pic, Prairie, Little Pic, Montreal, Sand, Barrett, Magpie. Also Wabikoba Creek, Cedar Creek, and Catfish Creek. To what do we owe this? Is it because it is cheaper to use solid walls of concrete for the bridge sides than metal railings? Or is it because someone in his wisdom decided that people in cars, allowed to gaze at a river, would immediately begin crashing into each other? Knowing what passes for wisdom these days, nothing would surprise me.

We pass the Green Gables Tavern and Restaurant, the new record-holder for being the farthest away from Anne's home, not counting Japan. At White River, we note that it no longer advertises itself as the Coldest Place in Canada, as it once did. Now it says: "See the Winnie the Pooh Statue." We all know that story now, thanks to public service messages on television, how the bear that became Winnie-the-Pooh was bought by a Canadian soldier during the First World War, how he named the bear Winnie, after Winnipeg, and left it at the London Zoo for safekeeping, where A. A. Milne's kid saw it. It was at the White River CPR station that the bear was bought, for twenty dollars. I don't know what Canadian soldiers were doing, hopping off trains to buy bears, but there you are. No passenger train stops at the CPR station any more, but there is a statue honouring its role in Pooh Bear history.

As for being the Coldest Place in Canada, White River now makes the statement in a rather oblique way. The big thermometer sign is still there, and if you look at it closely, you can see that the mercury is down in the bulb at the $-72°F$ mark, as it was recorded in 1936, but there is no longer any boasting about it being the coldest. Apparently, Moosonee bettered it, or worsed it, depending upon your point of view, so the sign was repainted to delete the Coldest Place reference. Sign or no sign, it still gets down to $-58°F$ and $-60°F$, they tell me at the gas station. Meanwhile,

White River adapts, and the big boast now is for Winnie's Hometown Festival in August, of which this is the eighth annual.

We pass the big Hemlo gold fields, with the three sprawling mine operations, which have been in production since 1985. As we approach Marathon, the lake re-emerges, along with fog, cloud, and a hint of rain. Marathon has a population of 5,500 and a bit of a pulpy smell, although the mill has been closed for the past few days. We leave the highway and enter the town, whose streets are named Ontario and Manitoba, etc., rather than King and Queen and George. It is another of the ways you differentiate the newer towns of the north from the older towns of Central and Eastern Ontario.

Cheryl and Ted Lake, Mary's friends, live on Manitoba Street. Cheryl is a former teacher. Ted is Superintendent of Schools. They have lived in the real north, the Northwest Territories, which they liked, but they found it difficult to establish roots there, what with "going out" every summer. They have roots in Marathon, grand-parents for their kids nearby. The town celebrated fifty years of existence last year; the nearby town of Terrace Bay has its half-century next year. Everybody knows everybody here, Ted says. Just ask where Ted's house is and someone will tell you.

Cheryl and Ted grew up in Thunder Bay and Ted frequently drives the three hundred kilometres to the city. He has what I think of as the Northern Ontario attitude to distance. "Two tapes to Thunder Bay," is how he sees the drive, and when he drives to Toronto or London or even Montreal, he does it in a day. None of this tootling along, stopping at motels along the way. This is an attitude we have seen in other of our Thunder Bay friends. When you travel the distance often enough, getting there becomes most important. To Nancy's horror, some of her friends even take the dread Highway 11, because it has less traffic and is faster.

There are pictures of northern scenes on the living-room wall and a delight in northern talk, the weather, the wildlife. "Did you see any moose?" Ted asks. We haven't, outside of Newfoundland.

Ted says he has seen lots lately, but mostly at twilight when they are tough to spot. He tells with great relish the story of the thaw in May when torrents took bridges out and washed away the highway. A truck driver, between Rossport and Nipigon, came down a steep hill and around a corner to find no bridge and decided his only chance was to jump the span. "He almost made it," Ted says, laughing. The truck flipped a few times but the driver wasn't hurt.

As White River has adapted, by adopting Winnie-the-Pooh, Marathon has adapted in a much larger way, from pulp-and-paper to gold. There was a three- or four-month span in 1984 where the entire community held its breath. First the mill shut down, then gold was discovered, then a buyer for the mill was found. Four hundred gold-mine workers live here. The mines have 27 per cent of all the gold in Canada. Some people got rich. Ted's school went from 370 to 800 pupils. "I guess I became rich too," Ted says. "I got more students and the school expanded."

As we get up to leave I see that the wall also has pictures of Quebec City on it. "My favourite city," Ted says.

Just after Terrace Bay, which has a big paper smell, pretty nice streets, and lots of birch trees (not to mention a slogan: THE GEM OF THE NORTH SHORE), we stop at Aguasabon River Gorge. One of the many advantages of knowing people along the way is getting their tips on what to see. It is not that the gorge is hidden away: signs point to it. But it is not visible from the highway and, since there are many signs pointing away from any highway, the tendency is to drive on. On Cheryl and Ted's recommendation, we stop, wander down a well-maintained boardwalk to the main lookout, from which we stare into a high and narrow waterfall, which drops into the Aguasabon River and boils down a steep-sided gorge lined with trees, into Lake Superior. We are high enough to see over the forest to where the river empties into the lake. Adding Mary to the nominating committee, we put it on the

list for Top Ten Belvedere honours. Somehow, on one of the walls
holding in the falls, Otis and Magnet and Dan and Kev have
managed to get their names painted on.

From the lookout, a nature trail heads off to Schreiber and to
Rossport, fifty-two kilometres away, another thing to do next time.
The spray from the gorge is so intense that the trees along the trail
are as wet as if it had just rained.

Schreiber itself is attractive, laid out around Walkers Lake.
Heading down a hill by Rainbow Falls Provincial Park, just east of
Rossport, we catch another Top Ten, the elements of which, seen
from up high, are Lake Superior, many islands, different shades of
blue in the late afternoon sun and haze.

At Rossport, we stay the night in an ancient hotel, the Rossport
Inn. It is more like a bed-and-breakfast, actually, with only seven
rooms in the main building, and shared baths. But it has a dining
room, serves dinner, and is therefore an inn. Rossport is a town of
only about a hundred people. From a hill, it looks like one of those
tiny fishing villages in the Maritimes. From the second-floor
balcony of the inn, you can see the large government dock, some
houses, and about twenty boats, at dock and at anchor. For many
years, fishing was the mainstay of the local economy. Two boxcar
loads of trout a week were coming out of Rossport. Then in the
1950s, the lamprey eel attacked the fish. The combination of that
and overfishing did in the fishing industry. Then railway and mill
layoffs hit the shift workers who live in the town.

Now tourism is helping Rossport come back. Ned Basher, who
owns the inn, says Rossport at one time "turned its back on the
highway and looked at the lake." Now it has to look at the highway
again. Since Ned bought the inn in 1982, another restaurant has
opened in competition. People are being drawn from the highway.
Ned and Shelagh, the kitchen manager and his wife of ten years,
have seen more people from Quebec this year than in the previous
ten. The general store is for sale and someone will buy it. "There'll
be cappuccino there for sure," Ned says.

I like the stories of how people got to be where they are. Ned tells his while eating spaghetti at a table in a large room off the dining room. His table has a command of the front door. Beside his plate of spaghetti is his portable phone and it rings occasionally. Ned is an American from Minnesota. He first saw Rossport on a sailing trip in 1971 and bought the inn in 1982, after it had been closed for three years, boarded up and with the windows all broken. A former air force pilot, Ned was "sort of between things" and "thought I'd buy myself a job," he says.

He reopened it in 1984, one hundred years after it was built. Originally it was the Oriental Hotel, and existed to serve passengers on the CPR, whose tracks run within a few metres of the hotel. "Tourists don't believe it will come by when they see how close the tracks are," Ned says. But it does, enough to give a thorough rattling to trackside guests a couple of times a night. The host doesn't apologize. "The train is kinda part of the place," he says.

There is no claim that this is a gourmet restaurant – "no fancy sauces, no French names on the menu," is how Ned puts it – but the combination of pleasant surroundings, the view of the lake, the service, and the lake trout must be a pleasant surprise to those who chance upon it.

The inn's lobby has a photograph of J.F.K. and one of the Queen. There are some jazz tapes and CDs for sale by a piano player named Steve Barta who is a friend of the Bashers. One of the tapes is called *Rossport*. Old newspaper clippings tell of the wreck of the *Gunilda*, a luxury yacht that went down in the waters off Rossport, and later, about the death of Reg Barrett, who died diving for the wreck. There are moose antlers, a mounted fish, maps of Lake Superior, and just the kind of idiosyncratic feel you would expect from a place that the train is kinda part of.

## Motor to the Paddle

We have a mission today, which is to find the place where Paddle-to-the-Sea was launched. This may be quite difficult, since

*Paddle-to-the-Sea*, a children's classic read to us all as children and read by us to ours, is a work of fiction. How do you find a fictional place? On the other hand, since it is a work of fiction, how can you prove that the place you are isn't it?

So onward. We know from the book that carved along Paddle, as the miniature canoe with the miniature paddler was known, were the words "I am Paddle to the Sea" and "Please put me back in water." We know he began his voyage where the Nipigon River flows out of Lake Nipigon and we can see on our map about where that is. So intent upon our mission are we that we barely slow down when we pass the spot where Ted Lake's fabled trucker tried his mighty leap of the Jackpine River. We do notice some fresh pavement where the pavement presumably wasn't, back in the spring.

In Nipigon, which has the slogan NESTLED IN NATURE, we buy some coffee and pastries with which to celebrate our triumphant discovery, then proceed to the town information centre to get directions. It is not that Nipigon is unaware of *Paddle-to-the-Sea*, even though it was published in 1941. The information centre actually displays a blow-up of a page from the book, but it is the wrong page for telling us where to look. And the staff don't know either. So we drive beside the river up Highway 585, which looks like it goes in the right direction. At the end of the highway, after forty-five kilometres, we find a gravel road and stop below a dam, watching the water coming over. The river runs fast and wide past us. We think this could be the spot, although we don't have the book with us. It's certainly quite a plausible place for a miniature canoe to begin a journey that will take it across the ocean to France. We can't be entirely realistic about this because Paddle started out life sitting on top of a snowbank, facing southward. "The time has come for you to sit on this snowbank and wait for the Sun Spirit to set you free," says Paddle's creator. "Then you will be a real Paddle Person, a real Paddle-to-the-Sea."

There are no snowbanks, and even if there were, we haven't got all day. We have our coffee and Persians, a Thunder Bay delicacy which is essentially a doughnut without a hole, but covered with pink icing. Everybody who grew up in Thunder Bay knows what a Persian is. Nobody east of Nipigon or west of Kenora has a clue. I keep telling Nancy and Mary that there may be a reason for this.

We also have fresh fruit and Mary accidentally drops a cherry into the river. "I am cherry to the sea," I say, caught up in the spirit of the thing. In the same spirit, I throw a stick into the river, launching it upon its epic journey. It hits the water and immediately goes the wrong way, caught in an eddy. By the time we leave, a few minutes later, it still hasn't turned around. Not everyone is cut out to be a Paddle Person, I suppose.

Back on the Trans-Canada, we begin to see signs advertising amethyst, which is the big gem in these parts. The drive today is not particularly ambitious. In fact, the entire Lake Superior stretch has not been exactly an endurance contest – three days to do 1,200 kilometres – but the idea is to see the lake, and that's what we're doing. From Marathon to here has been one spectacular vista after another. We are at the beginning of a section of the Trans-Canada known as the Terry Fox Courage Highway. Because it was near Thunder Bay that Fox was forced to give up his run in 1980, his name means a lot here and there is a fine monument to him closer to the city.

Our stop for the night, which we reach in mid-afternoon, is Amethyst, one of the many cottage communities that surround Thunder Bay. Nancy's childhood friend Sharon Robinson, a just-retired teacher, lives here, with her husband, Wayne, who has worked for lumber companies all his adult life. He is away, which is too bad, since he has a great deal of savvy about the region. Amethyst is a quiet little place, quite citified. People have lawns and decks and gardens. A street runs behind their cottages, many of which look more like houses. The more well-to-do residents,

down the road on Lambert Island, have fences and walls and ornamental lighting.

Some of the boats are quite large. There is a tennis court, baseball diamond, and basketball court. Amethyst is built around a sheltered harbour, so the wind stays off and the water is usually warm
enough to swim in. Although not today. We try, walking for miles
(or at least yards) in numbingly cold water and diving in for about
ten seconds.

People come here to be with other people, not to get away from
them. So as we go on our post-dinner walk, which begins at nine
because the sun sets so late, we keep bumping into people Sharon
knows. Many of them remember Nancy and Mary. This makes for
much chatting. My goal is Lambert Island, where the big houses
are, and a view I think is one of the loveliest in Canada. But the
light has to be just right and we are maybe three minutes too late.

It's still gorgeous though. From an opening in the bush, we walk
out onto flat rocks and look away from the sunset across to Caribou
Island and see the effect of the setting sun on the water and the
island. Caribou is a large and high island and the red the sun makes
on the exposed rockface is stunning. To the right of the island is
open water. There is a bit of wind and the waves lap in and you
know why people love Lake Superior.

The spot where we are standing has a certain small-scale
celebrity. In the Imax film *North of Superior*, there is a helicopter
shot of a wedding taking place at this very spot, the people waving
to the camera. As we are talking about this, the very bride and
groom appear, Tom Joseph and Margo Remus. A stronger word
than coincidence is called for. They show us where Margo entered,
at 2:00 p.m., twenty-six years ago, and where the organ was. The
organist was Paul Shaffer, who has gone on to greater fame, and he
would have been a young lad then.

Quite a day. We have found Paddle-to-the-Sea and an Imax
bride and groom. But we carry on, walking past some impressive
houses on Lambert Island, perhaps a bit more impressive than the

environment calls for. I find my least favourite sign of the trip – IF YOU DID NOT TELEPHONE, YOU'RE TRESPASSING. I am making the assumption that this does not belong to someone from Thunder Bay, whose people are notoriously friendly and welcoming. There is another sign that looks very odd on a fence in the middle of nowhere. NO SMOKING, it says. Not that I do any more, but aren't we *outside*? Has it come to that?

## Another Great Lake

On the way out, we see a fox, or at least the tail of one. We add that to our travelling bestiary – let's see, that's five whales, two moose, a bear, two eagles, a caribou, five rabbits, two Arctic hares, some chipmunks – and a fox.

Fog obscures the Sleeping Giant, a landmark peninsula, as we approach Thunder Bay, at the beginning of the sixth week of this undertaking. I like the story of how Thunder Bay got its name, upon the amalgamation of Port Arthur and Fort William in 1970. The residents were given the opportunity to choose a name for this new and more significant city and three names were put on the ballot. They were Thunder Bay, Lakehead, and The Lakehead. Understandably, Thunder Bay came up the middle and won.

Nancy and Mary have a visit to make and drop me in the centre of downtown Fort William to poke around. I go into a Coles in a shopping centre in the rather desolate downtown area and look for *Paddle-to-the-Sea* but it is not there. I head for the library.

The old railway hotel, the Royal Edward, is now offices and apartments. The church where we were married, St. Andrew's Presbyterian, is here, and so is the city hall, with a plaque honouring William McGillivray, 1764–1825, the fur trade merchant after whom Fort William was named. It is almost impossible to imagine what a jumping place this must have been back in McGillivray's day, when a couple of thousand traders and voyageurs convened here in the summers to trade and plot and perhaps have a drink or two. Relatively speaking, although Fort William and Port Arthur have always been robust places, things have been pretty quiet ever since. Old Fort William reconstructs things more or less as they were in 1816. I remember walking through it with Grant Thain, Nancy's father, and the kids, many years ago. I think I'd get more out of it now.

In the public library, the children's department easily finds *Paddle* for me. This is done in the modern way: a staff member scrolls through about five screens in a computer in the children's department, then takes ten steps to her right and pulls it off a shelf. "Far away," I read, "a river cut an icy path through the forest." That's the one.

On the way out of town, we drive around Shamrock Crescent, where Nancy and Mary used to live. There is new siding on the house, but still the same birch tree in front that Grant brought back from somebody's camp at Two Island Lake and put into the soil, probably forty years ago.

The drive out of town begins slowly on a congested residential road between Fort William and Kakabeka Falls. The town of Kakabeka Falls (NIAGARA OF THE NORTH) is a collection of road-side motels and a provincial park. The park is fine – magnificent falls dropping thirty-three metres, lots of treated wood, of course, with good wheelchair access, winding down the rockface on both sides of the Kaministiquia River, with interpretive boards giving both the geological and mythological history of the falls. We read of Greenmantle, an Ojibway princess, daughter of Ogama Eagle, the chief. Kidnapped by the invading Sioux, forced to lead captors in an ambush down the Kaministiquia River, she leaps out of her canoe and swims to shore just before all the invading canoes are swept over the falls. After that, she alerts her people who rout the remaining Sioux. And after that she marries a handsome warrior. That's sort of the Disney version, Anne of Greenmantle. Other versions state that she too was swept over the falls.

The boardwalk gives many fine views both of the falls and down the river from them. The view from the other side of the river gives you, in addition to spray in the face, a good look at the layering of the rock on the cliff. There is a waist-high fence and a relative absence of warning signs, although one says that you will be prosecuted if you put your boat into the water above the falls. Prosecuted is the least of it.

It is funny to think of these places, upon which we now look with wonder and awe, as they must have appeared to their discoverers, voyageurs in canoes, who were mostly preoccupied with getting up or down the river. "Oh, merde," you can hear them saying. "Another jeezly waterfall."

After the falls, the well-known dull section of Highway 17 begins. It doesn't matter. Just as Nancy and Mary were excited to see Lake Superior, today's my day, because we are on the way to Kenora and Lake of the Woods, where I have spent all but a couple of my fifty-five summers. It means a long and often dull drive of 500 kilometres, but that's fine. And when we get there, we'll sit still for a few days, a luxury we have not had for the past few weeks. The boring section is rather exaggerated in its length, since the scenery begins to pick up a bit east of Dryden and is great from there to Kenora. We are probably talking only 250 kilometres of boring highway. And there are little diversions along the way, such as the Arctic Watershed, from which all streams flow north into the Arctic Ocean. Think of that. Then there is the marker for the change to Central Time, at Savanne Portage, which also has a small river. And there is a sign welcoming us to Ontario Sunset Country.

What, exactly, is Ontario Sunset Country? Or, to put it another way, what's in a name? Just about every province is divided up, for the purpose of tourism, into regions, all of which have names like Sunset Country, names which are of absolutely no use to anybody in terms of figuring out where anything happens to be. Nova Scotia, for example, has the Lighthouse Route, Marine Drive, and Sunrise Trail. What would any of those be? Prince Edward Island has Ship to Shore, Hills & Harbours, and Bays & Dunes, among others. Ontario has, in addition to Sunset Country, Rainbow

Country. Is there anything essentially distasteful about using words like northwest and central and southeast? Have you ever heard a human being – other than someone who works in a tourism branch – describe himself as living in Rainbow Country or in Hills & Harbours? What about those sunsets we saw in Tobermory and Thessalon? We weren't in Sunset Country yet. Do they count?

Just into Sunset Country is my ideal roadside restaurant, Hansen's English River Resort. English River is a community so small it used to have a sign saying LOOKING FOR ENGLISH RIVER? THAT WAS IT. The windows at the back of the restaurant overlook a dock on the river, which is called a lake, Umber Lake. There are ten tables. Stuffed fish – pike, trout, pickerel – hang from the wall, along with a goose and the heads of a moose and a deer. This is the way a roadside restaurant should be. I don't know why, but it should have fish on the wall. The menu should have hamburgers and grilled cheese-and-bacon sandwiches. This one has something even more important – a Denver sandwich. Right here may be the mythical dividing line between East and West, the dividing line between the western sandwich, which you get in the East, and the Denver sandwich, which you get in the West. I don't know what you get in Denver.

Further evidence that we are on the dividing line is staring us in the face: despite the fact that we are now on Winnipeg time, the clock on the wall is an hour ahead, on Thunder Bay time. Many of the customers are truckers out of Thunder Bay, I am told, and this presumably makes them feel more at home, while they eat their western sandwiches.

We drive on, in our timeless way, with not much to look at. Around Ignace, a highway leads north to Pickle Lake, a name you always hear on Winnipeg weather forecasts. Signs advertising fishing camps dot the highway. People's names cover the rock faces. How does it work, writing on rocks? If you are a person who paints your name on rocks, do you carry a can of paint around with you at all times, in case the urge strikes you? Or do you race home to get your paint when you see a particularly attractive surface?

When we go through Dryden it is in the pouring rain. I ask for a stop just west of there at Egli's Wool and Sheepskin Shop. There is a statue of a giant sheep there. This is for the book. It is a huge store, with all sorts of woollen stuff. I buy a tee-shirt. Mary buys a leg of lamb, which seems sort of anti-sheep somehow.

The lakes come fast and furious now – Rae, Moth, Earngey, Island. It is rocky and there is much evidence of past forest fires. McCourt, in *The Road Across Canada*, has a perceptive passage about the right way to approach Lake of the Woods, a place I've approached so many times.

> It is a world of water and rock and forest, a well-balanced combination of the main elements of the Laurentian Shield. It is a world which is a microcosm of roughly one-third of all Canada, and it is better approached from the west than the east. For the visitor from the great plains, tall trees and great sheets of clear water exalt the spirit and accelerate the blood-flow because they are a combination seldom to be seen in his own land; but by the time the traveller from eastern Canada reaches Kenora he has seen so much rock and lake and forest – especially forest – that he may cast a cold eye on a world which deserves much more than a passing glance.

Those words take me back to my childhood. I remember arriving at Winnipeg with my parents and taking the train from there, east to Kenora. My father had a regular routine in which he would have us look for boulders as the train reached the end of the Prairies. Then we would look for rockfaces, then lakes. It was an agonizingly slow process. When we saw lakes we knew we were almost there and the excitement couldn't have been greater.

# 12

## *At the Cottage*

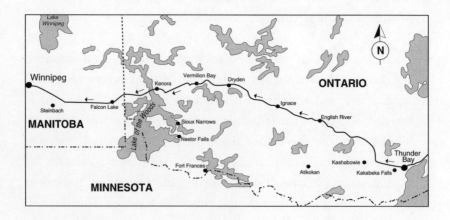

Everybody's cottage is unique. No other place on earth could possibly be the same, we all think. It is somehow disconcerting, then, to read cottage magazines and find articles on people who are exactly like us, have exactly the same problems, pretty much the same solutions, and definitely the same kitchenware. Paradoxically, at the same time as we think we are unique, we assume that the patterns we adopt at the cottage are adopted by everyone. When we grow up with some strange custom – throwing a fish down the hole in the outhouse at close-up time; scrubbing the cucumbers to get the poison out – we assume we are just doing what intelligent people do everywhere.

When I did a book tour for a book about cottages, people used to tell me about their cottage customs. Somebody told me about the custom at his cottage, which he assumed until he was much older was the custom at everybody's cottage, namely, to hang the toilet seat on a nail behind the wood stove. Anyone heading for the outhouse would automatically take the seat along, and it would be warm. Imagine how this person would have felt, the first time he visited someone else's cottage, looking all over for the toilet seat and finding it in the most unexpected place – namely, on the toilet. And cold.

So here we are at Lake of the Woods and an island our family calls Birkencraig, which is Scottish for birches and rocks. It is a large island my grandfather bought just after the turn of the century when the books were selling in large amounts. The house too is large, high on a hill and largely out of sight from the water. It has a verandah running around three sides, one side of which is screened. There are six bedrooms, although one is now used as a storage room, plus a two-storey octagonal annex, called the Lookout, which has two bedrooms. In the upper one, with a view down the lake, my grandfather wrote.

My grandfather had seven children. In the early days, they would bring their friends down and scatter across the island in tents. On the other side of the island was a beach, and a board tennis court upon which the young people would play (although my grandfather would play too; there are photographs of him in tennis whites). Now the boards are all gone, as is the money; the tennis court has reverted to dirt and we play badminton on it. But we still call it the Tennis Court, just as we call the area behind it The Garden, although nothing has grown there for years.

In more recent years, as the generations began to pile up, several of us have put up our own sleeping cabins, most of them near the main house. We all eat at the main house, in the large screened-in dining room with the table that can seat fourteen or fifteen.

All of that seems quite unique to us, although it probably isn't. We don't have electricity and there is little likelihood of getting it.

Honouring the strong views of my grandfather, who died in 1937, we don't, at least officially, have liquor on the island. He was such a dedicated temperance man that he entered into political campaigns to support the party that seemed least likely to support the liquor interests. Unofficially, there is drinking on the island, but only within the last twenty-five years or so, and not at the main house.

Perhaps what makes us most unusual, we think, is that we get along. We are into the fourth generation now, with a fifth just beginning (the children of my generation's children) and almost all of us keep coming back. There are some who move some distance away and get to the island less frequently, but the place has stayed together. The biggest group of us is in Winnipeg, just two hours down the highway and an easy commute on weekends. The rest of us come for longer periods from farther away, mostly Ottawa and Toronto, but sometimes Carvers from Nova Scotia too.

We keep pretty much to ourselves. Away from the lake, when we encounter people who know Kenora they ask us if we know so-and-so. We never do. We don't go to the yacht club, we don't socialize, we just stay on the island. It has always been that way and even today, eyebrows are raised when any of our campers, usually the teenaged ones, spend much time with people who aren't at the island. We all enjoy each other, obviously, but the island and the lake have a strong pull, as well as the legacy of my grandfather. Only two members of my father's generation are alive now and only one member of my generation was born when my grandfather was alive. But the traditions live on, the stories continue to be told even by people who weren't yet born when they were new, and the history is in no danger of being lost.

The nature of work has changed. Chainsaws have made the woodcutting faster, as well as less pleasant and less communal. Sawing and chopping for stove wood once involved most of the camp on a morning. The little kids would saw, while their parents told them to pull, not push, and the grownups, men and women, and the older boys would chop. The little kids not sawing would pile and carry. It was part of the daily routine. Now with the chainsaw two men can do a week's work in the morning, but it is work.

One of the links with the past is the paths. There is one straight across the island, called the Beach Path, one halfway around, intersecting with the main path, and another that goes around the northern side of the island, beginning behind the tennis court. The path that goes most of the way around the island is called the Ladies' Path, because it was made by my grandmother and a couple of her friends, apparently just to prove they could do it, which they certainly proved. It is an up-and-down trail, taking probably twenty minutes to walk, and a route that doesn't always take the line of least resistance.

There are stories on the paths, places where bears were spotted, where hornets inflicted stings, knees were permanently injured, or a bumper crop of Saskatoon berries appeared. There is the place where you get poison ivy, the point at which the only jackpines on the island are located, the huge white pine with the notch on it that the turn-of-century loggers somehow failed to fell. More recently, there are the places we associate with the departed, places they loved to sit and look out at the water. In some cases, such as my father's and now my mother's, their ashes are there. There is a beautifully engraved stone honouring my father's sister Mary, who married Humphrey Carver, the stone brought there by Humphrey, some thirty years after her death.

The paths are a form of immortality. We walk along them and join those who walked before us. Here is Mrs. Fisher's rock. Here are Ellie's and Annie's trees. Here is Strothers' Slide, here is King's Climb, here is Sunset Hill. Not many years ago, by Birkencraig standards, my father and his cousin Charley, called Chili, decided that the island needed a new path, one that would go from the middle of the Beach Path and join the Ladies' Path. My father and Chili grew up together on the island. They were about the same age which, when they began on the new path, was about seventy-five.

They hadn't gone more than fifty yards, with their axes and clippers, when they had a difference of opinion over the direction the path should take. So they split up, my father turning west, down into a valley and up the side of a steep hill, Chili staying south, taking a more gentle route. They did the work themselves, and quite successfully. The paths still stand. In subsequent years, my father would ask me to come along to help clear his path. Now, I take along one of my kids, if they are at the island, so that they can connect with their grandfather. And they do. It is fascinating to walk along a path, moving the trees and branches that have fallen over the winter, clipping the bushes that have grown up, and imagining the choices a man made while he walked it for the first time. Would he go up this steep hill for that lookout on the lake, or would he head down into the shadow where the footing is surer? My father, arthritic hips and all, always went up the hill. Chili, a quiet, enigmatic man, wound his path through the woods on level ground.

Because he has no descendants on the island, Chili's path fell into disuse until about three years ago when Nancy and I and some friends decided to find it. It is not easy to locate a path that no one has walked for ten years, and at times we found ourselves improvising. But a path has a way of revealing itself if you look hard enough and think of the person who made it. Now it is back.

## A Rainbow with the Purple

We stay at the island four days. John flies out from Toronto to join us, after the run of his play in Toronto. The number at the camp peaks at twenty-one on the weekend. It can go as high as thirty, on the August long weekend when we hold our annual meeting. I spend some of my time, until the computer's battery wears out, typing notes, wondering (while Nancy and Mary go off to clear King's Path) if my grandfather ever used the excuse of writing to beg off some physical chore. I suspect not. It is more likely that he used the chores as an excuse not to write.

We get all kinds of weather. On the Sunday there is one of those great Lake of the Woods days, with several rainstorms, some thunderstorms, and two instances of double rainbows. Rainbows always seem to happen when we are at the dinner table, which means that we have to race around the verandah to the other side and gaze down the lake to the south. My cousin-in-law Bill Millar is a United Church minister and perhaps because of that, perhaps despite it, a connoisseur of rainbows. "Is there purple in it?" he asks, upon being informed of the rainbow. "Oh, okay, I'll look." To be a good rainbow it has to have purple in it, apparently. I never knew that.

Earlier that same day, Bill conducts an informal little service in honour of my mother. We have it right by the front steps, and Bill stands near the spot where she liked to look for a four-leaf clover. It was something she did, successfully, every summer. The things we bring to the island are the things others take away. Bill talks quietly and eloquently, as he always does, about the rocks and the birches, the rocks remaining, the birches being replaced, the new ones growing from the old. I think about the birches outside Nancy's former home in Fort William. That's how they grew, from a birch log found lying on the ground at Two Island Lake.

Saturday we went for a paddle around the island. It takes half an hour, if you are not in too much of a hurry and make sure to notice what's around you. In this case it is three pelicans, two beaver, and two heron, as well as the usual assortment of loons. There is lots of growth on the island this year, from lots of rain. An expedition goes out to pick Saskatoon berries, enough for two pies. The purple berries are sweet, nicer in a pie than blueberries, in my opinion, which is heretical.

There is giggling, there are stupid games. There is a rummy tournament (a rummy tournament?), which I win (for the record) and which involves much shouting. I would not want to live near our island, the way noise carries on the lake. We justify this to ourselves in that arrogant Gordon way we have, something to do with the fact that we have always done this. It helps that we are not pumping amplified music out into the night air.

There is a trip into town, as we call Kenora. Anybody want anything in town? Town is now a ten-minute boat trip. It used to be much longer, although less congested, with slower boats, an expedition for the children, at the end of which would be a milkshake or a sundae. We park at the Safeway dock or the Laundromat dock or, now, the Harbourfront dock, an expanded and quite spiffy new addition to the town's facilities, with car- as well as boat-parking and a number of shops and restaurants. The town looks about the same as I remember it from childhood, small houses with bright and neat little gardens I somehow associate with what you used to see around railway stations. But it is quite different. The cottage people used to have a much greater impact on the town than they do now. I think progress has much to do with this. It is easier to get to and from Winnipeg, so people are less dependent upon the Kenora merchants. Therefore the Kenora merchants have made themselves less dependent upon the cottage people. The relationship is not as close.

To take another example, boats now have more efficient and reliable engines and larger gas tanks so there is not the same need for places to buy gas or get a boat fixed. I can remember when there were at least three places to buy gas in Kenora harbour (they were not called marinas then). Now there is one, and if you want to get your boat fixed, you have to take it to one of several locations away from the harbour. These days the prime waterfront space is taken up with boutiques, real estate and law offices.

Still, enough of the old stuff remains to make Kenora a town of contrasts. On this expedition, my three cousins and I visit the propane place to see if we can get a tank fixed, as well as to idly investigate the latest solar stuff, which we are idly pondering. (I, for example, don't want to see television on the island, but wouldn't mind having a solar panel that would keep a laptop computer charged.) I find a great item, for $44.95, a solar baseball cap billed as "the hat with the built-in breeze." It has two solar panels on the top and a fan on the front. I ponder the idea of wearing a solar baseball cap while collecting wood for the stove. Then it's on to Fife Hardware on Main Street where a cousin challenges me to identify the $135 blue-painted metal thing that looks like a shovel with teeth. I can't and it turns out to be for shaving blocks of ice. Somewhere on the lake people still do that, chop the ice out of the lake and store it under sawdust for use the rest of the year. And Fife Hardware has the tools for it. In its beautifully organized and neat basement, Fife also has handles for billhooks, and on the stairs are little bottles called Mink Special and Fox Special, $4.95, for spraying onto your trap.

Like Rossport, but on a larger scale, Kenora looks less to the lake, and more to the highway, more to the tourists. The town has begun worrying about how it looks to tourists. There are no people hanging around the bus terminal on Main Street any more because the bus terminal has been moved down the highway to Norman. This is a massive inconvenience to many residents, not to mention cottagers, but never mind. Main Street looks better to the tourists. There are no people hanging around the liquor store on Main Street any more because the liquor store has been moved several blocks away, hidden away behind the shopping centre. The boutiques have arrived and at the new Harbourfront are many events aimed at tourists. Harbourfest, one is called. A big one is the Kenora Bass International, bringing in professional fishermen (imagine: professional fishermen) from all over North America. Husky the Muskie, the giant fish that greets motorists from the West, has just been renovated for the new season, if renovate is what you do with a giant fish.

When we drive by it on a Monday morning, heading for Winnipeg, we have no time to stop, since we have to get Mary Parker and John to the Winnipeg airport and I have daringly allowed only three and a half hours for the trip, which is only one hour more than it takes. We pass more lakes – Berman, Rice, Moth,

Royal, Lyons. Fifty-seven kilometres along the road we are in
Manitoba, which begins with a gaudy four-lane section I have
always admired; the gaudy four-lane section disappears after a kilometre or two. After Falcon Lake, the four lanes resume and will
carry us almost to the Saskatchewan border. As the Shield recedes
behind us, the highway becomes straight and boring, reminiscent
of 417 between Montreal and Ottawa. We lose the lakes, then the
rockfaces, then the boulders. I try to pinpoint the spot where the
prairie begins. I think it is around Lilac, just before the Steinbach
turnoff, 166 kilometres west of Kenora. You come over a slight –
very slight – rise and the scruffy landscape gives way to magnificent
prairie, with the fabled big sky. It really is a big sky.

# 13

## Old Home Week

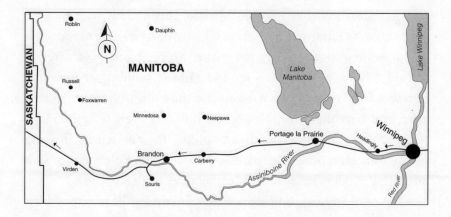

Winnipeg gives the impression of constantly changing. The old neighbourhoods remain, many of the houses going back to the time when my father was growing up here. But different people live in them. A part of town that was once middle class is now called rough. Another part of town is gentrified and becomes expensive. Portage Avenue and Main Street, once the axes of the city's commercial economy, are in a constant state of flux. Money is poured into Main Street, then onto the north side of Portage, where people had stopped going, even though it is just the other side of the street. Mind you, it is an awfully wide street. Then the north-of-Portage development, which seems to consist of turning the whole street into a mall, is deemed not to be working and attention turns elsewhere. Money is poured into The Forks, an area at the junction of the Red and Assiniboine rivers, just east of Main Street. Osborne Street develops a certain cachet, becomes the hip place to shop and dine. Then Corydon Avenue, one of a number of lookalike commercial streets south of the Assiniboine, becomes trendy. In a four-block area you are suddenly surrounded by young people, coffee bars, and Italian restaurants. There are a couple of street musicians but no beggars, something that strikes me after Toronto. I'm told that they are elsewhere in the city – for example, on Portage and on Main.

After dinner with my cousin Michael Cox and his wife, Sandra, they show us around The Forks, which we have never seen. It is an impressive spot, given what it used to be, namely 56 acres of nothing. Now old warehouses and railway buildings have been renovated and turned into markets and museums. There are restaurants and bars that are doing good business even on a Monday night. Even after dark the area is pretty, the two rivers flowing gently into each other, the paths nicely lit up and pleasant to walk around. Patrollers tour the area on bicycles to make sure.

One of the fascinating aspects of our trip has been to see how cities adapt, how they try to stay livable, and how they attempt to maintain their individuality in the face of continent-wide economic pressure that drives them to be the same. The harbour developments in the Atlantic provinces are one form of reaction. This is another. Tinkering with the downtown business core hasn't seemed to do much. The big office buildings have a dehumanizing effect. Along the arterial roads, the shopping centres are filled with the same old (and new) chain stores and restaurants and you wouldn't know what city you are in. But away from the glass towers, the city's personality has a chance to assert itself. When you look at the economic blows Winnipeg has suffered in recent years, coupled with the Jets leaving town and the Blue Bombers consistently walking a financial tightrope, it is so encouraging to see the way the city has adopted Plan B and how well it seems to be working. Plan B, it is true, is yuppification, and will necessitate Plan C, which is to deal with those areas that are left behind. That is a sobering thought. Another one, which is related, is that the massive public investment that made The Forks development possible could not happen in today's repressive climate, even though it has not been that many years since The Forks development was put together. But Winnipeg has, I think, all the good old civic virtues, such as civic pride and a kind of self-sufficiency. This may just be Pollyanna of Green Gables talking, or it may just be because my father was brought up here and so many of my cousins live here.

But I don't think so. Look at Winnipeg's cultural institutions – the art gallery, the Royal Winnipeg Ballet, the Manitoba Folk Festival, the Manitoba Theatre Centre, the Museum of Man and Nature, and the list grows: the Prairie Theatre Exchange, the Mol Sculpture Garden. Look at the pride people take in them, and contrast that with, say, Ottawa. It should tell you that Winnipeggers have a big emotional stake in their city's survival.

## The Four-Hour Winnipeg

54 Westgate is the place my grandfather built when the books were selling, literally in the millions. The three-storey brick house sits on a quiet street, on the banks of the Assiniboine just a bit west of The Forks. A plaque dated 1948 from the government of Canada notes that my grandfather was pastor of St. Stephen's Broadway from 1894 to 1924. "As a churchman and ardent Canadian nationalist, he worked for such social causes as temperance and aid to immigrants. His optimism and his advocacy of good Christian charity reflected the views of many native-born Canadians in the opening decades of the Twentieth century."

After the money went, in bad investments while he was overseas during the First World War, the house and the island were all he had, and after he died the house was sold for back taxes. The University Women's Club bought it in 1945 and maintains it beautifully, renting out two apartments upstairs, and using the rest of the house for luncheons and cultural events, renting it out for receptions and meetings. We introduce ourselves and are given the freedom of the place.

A pamphlet put out by the University Women's Club tells me – I should know all this stuff, of course – that the house was built in 1913–14 and that the architect, George Northwood, was instructed to built an Elizabethan house appropriate for an English gentleman (presumably an English gentleman with seven children). He did that, for $50,000. The house has a circular driveway and an exterior described as Jacobean. There are six rooms on the ground floor, in addition to the kitchen. There are leaded glass windows, beamed ceilings, oak panelling, wide staircases and landings. There are two fireplaces upstairs. Now that I think of it, I am reminded of the rather grand house that became the Winterholme Heritage Inn in St. John's.

The room that was my grandfather's office has been maintained as the Ralph Connor Room, and contains a collection of his works and other memorabilia, including the remarkable edition of the *Winnipeg Free Press* in which his obituary ran to three pages. Winnipeg, it said, had lost "its most famous citizen." The fireplace tiles in that room are decorated with biblical scenes.

Our family maintains a peripheral connection with the house. Offhand I can count one family wedding and five family wedding receptions that have been held there in recent years. Inevitably, while the wedding photographs are taken and guests mill about sipping their wine (for, indeed, alcoholic beverages are allowed on the premises), some of the Gordons who were too young to have lived here, explore the house, somewhat bug-eyed. Sometimes we will enlist the help of one of the senior members, such as our aunt Lois, who will show us where the children kept their boots, and other significant historical details. At the last reception, a year ago, I walked into the office and announced that I was a Gordon and we would like to have our house back now. This was treated as a joke.

## Thirty-Nine Steps Up from the Skating Buffalo

Outside the legislature, the first thing we notice is how many of the statues have no connection with British kings and queens. We are in the West now, where that stuff counts for less. Queen Victoria is inescapable, of course. Standing on the legislature steps and gazing down Memorial Boulevard over the gardens, we see her back. Wolfe is around too, and the Lords Dufferin and Selkirk. But also on the grounds are Louis Riel, Robert Burns, Jacques Cartier, a Kwakiutl totem pole, Taras Shevchenko, the Ukrainian poet, patriot, and painter, and Jón Sigurdsson, the Icelandic patriot and man of letters. Up on top is the Golden Boy, a Greek messenger carrying a torch and a sheaf of wheat, cast by a Frenchman in 1918.

The whole building, in fact, is characterized by a goofy and endearing sort of eclecticism. In the rotunda is a mural by a Liverpudlian and the floor uses Greek symbols in its design. There are Corinthian columns, Roman and Egyptian symbols. And the steps leading up to the rotunda number thirty-nine, in three flights of thirteen, to ward off bad luck.

This is not the first thing you see inside the building. The first thing you see inside the building is a sign telling you where the public washrooms are.

Under the rotunda is a room that showcases Manitoba art. The display is changed each month. This was done in Newfoundland too, a helpful affirmation that the legislative building is a showcase for more than the government.

We get a guide all to ourselves again, a University of Manitoba student who has to decide, that very day, between economics and business. How can she find the concentration to tell us that the Golden Boy is thirteen and a half feet high and weighs 10,000 pounds? By now I recognize that such numbers, such facts, are the staple of the legislature tour, no matter in which province it takes place. I don't know why, exactly. Are many tourists demanding to know exactly how many tons of marble are in the columns, how much gold is in the lieutenant-governor's jacket? Have people been interrupting the guides to say: "Excuse me, you wouldn't happen to know exactly how many rolls of wallpaper were required to cover the walls of the legislative chamber would you?" or "Just how much do the front steps of the building weigh?"

The other thing that beats me is the obsession with the mace. At every legislature the mace is on display (or, as in Ontario, a cardboard replica of it is trotted out) as if it mattered. I mean, what happens to the mace when the legislature is in session is they bring it in and they lay it down and it sits there. Then they put it away. Yet it is assumed, in every province, that there is some frenzied public fascination about it, as if travel agents in Dallas and Kansas City and Berlin and Yokohama were lining up Mace Tours of Canada.

Now, when the guides are really interested in their work and get a chance to get away from the statistics, some fascinating stories come out. My favourite so far is the one about how they got the two life-size bronze buffalo statues that flank the thirty-nine steps into the building. The buffalo, as you might have suspected, weigh 2 ¼ tonnes or 2 ½ tons each and were cast by the same guy who did the Golden Boy, and there was a justified fear that they might scratch the floor. So what they did is this: they flooded the floor in the winter, left the doors open until the water froze, and then slid the buffalo in over the ice. What a nice Winnipeg touch that is.

The other thing worth noting about the Manitoba legislature is how big it is. Begun in 1913 and not finished until 1920, it is by far the largest such building we have seen. The chamber, which has an unusual horseshoe shape, is far larger than it needs to be for the fifty-seven members. Our guide explains that the building was planned at the turn of the century when it was thought that Manitoba would have, very soon, a population of three million. So it is a building born of optimism, a spirit of expansion. It is interesting to contrast it with the Nova Scotia legislature, shoe-horned into a small corner of Halifax. It is not just the sky that is bigger out here.

We go back to The Forks in the daytime, looking for lunch. We walk through the Forks Market Building, which has a light-coloured brick interior and is oddly reminiscent of the Old City Market in Saint John. The stores are mostly crafty and touristy but there are fruits and vegetables and cheeses too. Perhaps this is a stage all these places have to go through – get past the boutiquiness and into selling things that people can actually use. It looks like it may happen here.

We go to another building, the Johnston Terminal, which also has stores, and find a restaurant. A big table full of tourists from China is nearby. In the adjoining bar are those video gambling games that are all over the province now. VLTs. People play them, joylessly, helping Premier Filmon's budget surplus. Who are the players? I ask a greeter at the restaurant. "During the day it's mostly, like, addicts," she says.

There is a good Manitoba tourism office with displays on all the main regions. Around the Western Manitoba area, an East Indian woman turns to her friends and points to a display about Neepawa, the home of Margaret Laurence. "She's one of our best authors," the woman says. I like this. Some day I want to overhear a white Canadian make the same kind of remark to another white Canadian about Rohinton Mistry.

Gradually, we work our way west, driving along Wellington Crescent, one of Canada's loveliest residential streets, into Assiniboine Park and the Leo Mol Sculpture Garden. This is another example of going where the locals – in this case Michael and Sandra – point you. I know Mol's work a bit. I was there in Ottawa when his statue of John Diefenbaker was unveiled on

Parliament Hill. Dief looks resolute, standing, facing in the general direction of the American embassy, holding his Bill of Rights.

Mol, who graduated from the Academy of Art in St. Petersburg, is now eighty-one. The sculptures, of animals, nudes, and well-known people – the Pope, Andrei Sakharov, Riel, A. J. Casson, Shevchenko – cover a time period from the sixties through the nineties. They are arranged along grassy walks, often lined by hedges. Plaques list corporate and individual sponsors, sometimes families but often familiar local institutions: Great-West, Richardson, Wawanesa Mutual. Despite the light rain there are quite a few visitors in the Mol garden and the adjacent English garden, which is also an impressive sight. Here is another sign that Winnipeg is different from Toronto, the sign being a sign: ENGLISH GARDEN, it says. NO PETS, NO WEDDING PICTURES.

The English garden includes a statue of Queen Victoria. A young boy stops in front of it and reads the inscription, then he runs from it to his parents, shouting: "Queen Victoria *died*?"

On the way out we accidentally find a shortcut that lands us on Highway 1 at Headingly, from which we begin the extremely familiar drive to Brandon, a drive that we must have done a hundred times or more in the ten years we lived there in the sixties and seventies. There are two curves, I think, maybe a couple more since the bypass around Portage la Prairie went in. And the landscape is basic prairie, with a bit of diversity around Carberry (GATEWAY TO SPRUCE WOODS PROVINCIAL PARK). It is an easy drive now, four lanes all the way, two hours from Winnipeg, but everyone who lives in Brandon has a horror story to tell about it. It could be "highway hypnosis" – a phrase you never hear except on the Prairies, for the simple reason that other highways have curves and trees to give the eye something to do. It could be a whiteout, the snow blowing right up into your face along the Winnipeg to Portage section. It could be slippery roads, or even wind. Our first car was a Volkswagen beetle and I can remember walking around for ages with one shoulder higher than the other after a couple of hours spent holding the car against the constant gale. And then there's simple cold. The Prairie driver carries a blanket and a candle in the trunk, just in case.

We have developed a radio-listening pattern. At five minutes to the hour, on the digital clock, one of us hits the button that turns the radio on to the CBC and we find out if Canada has won any Olympic medals in Atlanta. Then we listen to the news and the weather. As soon as we hear somebody chatting, we turn the radio off. For some reason, although we have dozens of tapes in the car, we haven't listened to any. I think it's for the same reason we don't listen to the chat. We don't want to be distracted from what we are seeing, we don't want old songs to intrude on new sights.

Although we have visited Brandon in each of the past two years, the excitement of returning comes back as we come down the North Hill from the Trans-Canada. From this height Brandon looks the same as it did when I first came down this hill in 1964, the McKenzie Seeds building looming over the valley and the CPR tracks. Although there has been a bit of suburban sprawl and some shopping centre development on the outskirts of town, the core of Brandon is reassuringly unchanged. We cross the Assiniboine River, for the fifth time today, and the tracks, and turn west onto Rosser Avenue, past the first house we lived in. The house cost less than the car we are driving now. Not that I feel old. Renovation has taken place, and the house has changed beyond recognition and been painted a light purply colour. Perhaps someone from the Gaspé lives there now.

We are staying with Terry and Colleen Mitchell, friends with whom we have been many places. They were in Brandon when we lived there, then they lived in Ottawa briefly. We even bumped into them on a trip to Africa and toured Kenya together. Over dinner with other friends, we talk about the university, where Terry is the librarian, about Rosser Avenue and about old friends. I ask about Lew Whitehead, former owner and publisher of the *Brandon Sun*, who gave me my first job. About ten years ago he sold the paper. He has not been well and no one has seen him lately.

When I was taking graduate work at Queen's, I got a letter out of the blue asking if I wanted to work as an editorial writer at the *Brandon Sun*, a newspaper of which I had never heard. The *Sun* knew about me because I had applied to the *Kingston Whig-Standard* and the *Whig* had passed my clippings on. The publisher of the *Sun*, Lewis D. Whitehead, wrote asking me to meet him for dinner in Montreal at the Queen Elizabeth Hotel. It was the fall of 1964. I remember a lot of things about that dinner, especially how proud Lew was of the paper he owned, which had come down through his family, and the aspirations he had for it. I don't know if he told me that night, but he was an admirer of William Allen White, proprietor of the equally small but incredibly influential Kansas paper the *Emporia Gazette*. Lew was also terribly proud of Brandon, which he hoped was on the verge of becoming a prosperous and modern community. It was then, as now, a city that served the surrounding farming communities and was dependent upon them. I think what I remember best about that dinner was what Lew said upon seeing a bearded man walk across the Montreal restaurant. "There's a guy with a beard in Brandon," he said.

Sure enough there was. He turned out to be Les Paine, the best jazz musician in town and the manager of a bookstore bankrolled by Lew because he thought Brandon should have a good bookstore. I agreed to go out to Brandon to have a look. I arrived on a weekday afternoon at the CPR station after taking the train from Winnipeg. Lew, who was then in his late thirties but seemed fairly middle-aged to me, met me and took me to the *Sun*, which was just up from the station on Tenth Street. The World Series was on, Yankees against the Cardinals, and the game was on a TV set in the cramped newsroom. The room seemed to consist of one giant desk, with a few cubicles off to the side. The paper still had a final edition that came out about 3:00 p.m., and the news editor, Charlie

MacFarlane, who was a newspaper legend, although I didn't know it at the time, was watching the game and updating page one to get the latest score in. I was completely and utterly hooked.

Later, I went with one of the reporters, Paul Minvielle, to the Prince Edward Hotel where some touring trade commissioners were meeting the media. We went in and talked to the trade commissioners, one of whom turned out to be an old Queen's classmate, and they gave us Scotch to drink. Years later the rules would change and it would no longer·be appropriate to accept drinks of Scotch from news sources, but on this day, at twenty-three years of age and just off the train, I thought this was pretty good. You become a newsman and you go places and people give you Scotch.

That night I sat in the bar of the Prince Edward Hotel and wrote Nancy, to whom I was on the verge of getting engaged, a letter, telling her that I was taking the job. "A newsman!" I wrote, marvelling at and revelling in the new description I would have.

This probably happens to everybody, but almost as soon as I began I discovered that I was coming in precisely at the end of a golden age of newspapering. I kept hearing about the colourful characters who had just left, the great stunts that nobody pulled any more. But there was still some romance in it. There was hot metal in the composing room, which was down several flights of stairs and our copy and our layouts went down there by dumb-waiter. My layouts in the early days would come up with notes saying that they didn't fit. My first editorial was written on U.S. election night. It said it was a good thing that Lyndon Johnson had defeated Barry Goldwater. It never occurred to me that I should have a little more experience of the world before I began making authoritative pronouncements on the affairs of other people. It turned out that I was not just an editorial writer, but the only editorial writer. I was also the editorial page editor, which meant I did the layout, handled the letters to the editor, and wrote four editorials a day. That wasn't any trouble. I was twenty-three years old, almost twenty-four, right out of graduate school, and there wasn't much I didn't know.

When I left, almost ten years later, I knew a lot less. In a small city you are always coming face to face with the people you are covering, and that can have a humbling affect. I had become, by that time, managing editor and was, at the ripe old age of thirty-three, weary of dealing with unhappy people – unhappy that we had not taken a photograph of a little league team, angry that we had not run a story about the ribbon-cutting at a new hotel. A couple of days before we left for Ottawa, a woman telephoned me at home in a panic. She was at her parents' fiftieth-anniversary party and the *Sun* photographer was not there. The guests hadn't had their cake yet. I said he would be along, and why didn't she just give the guests their cake. She said her parents couldn't cut the cake until the photographer got there. When I hung up, I said: "I'm glad I'm not the managing editor any more."

## The Same Old Rosser Avenue

Brandon hasn't changed in any of the important ways. It is still a place where you can put dimes and nickels into the parking meter and someone brings you a second cup of coffee without you asking for it. The businessmen on Rosser Avenue, as they always did, worry about parking. This kills me, as I feed dimes into a meter right on the main drag, but it is the way merchants have always thought. Don Gardner, who has had a clothing store on Rosser for as long as I can remember, tells me a parking lot was put up off-street for merchants' cars. But many of them still insist on parking in front of the store. I like that. I know I shouldn't.

Like Thunder Bay and Winnipeg, Brandon has tried to fight the suburban malls by malling part of downtown. The mall is hidden away behind the Eaton's store, which forms part of it. The fact that it is largely invisible from the street is a plus from where I stand, but maybe a minus for the businesses in it. People may be inclined to ignore a mall when it doesn't loom over several acres of parking lot. The other problem with malls is that they are dominated by chain stores, which are owned elsewhere. Thus the city loses some of its economic independence.

Don Gardner is a kind of touchstone for me. I drop in every time I am back and find out what's happening, which he tells me, after we bring each other up to date on guys we played basketball with in the sixties and seventies. His store used to be part of a chain, but he made it independent and distinctive. He now specializes in Western clothes. The fact that his is one of only three or four stores on Rosser that I remember from twenty years ago tells me that doing something distinctive is a key to survival. Aping the chains is, at least in the long run, doom. In every town we visit I keep finding examples of people surviving by adapting. Don's block now has some good-looking restaurants and coffee places, a start at the kind of niche marketing that could help save downtown, since it is something the malls won't attempt to match.

It comes and goes on Rosser, with people always worrying about it, always proposing new solutions. Rosser Avenue is not synonymous with Brandon any more, just as the main street of most cities is no longer as dominant as it once was. But it is not irrelevant. People still go there, people still worry about it. Don Gardner, who has seen it all, or most of it, is typically philosophical. "There's good times and there's bad times and it's the same as it always was," he says. "It all depends on how the farmer's doing."

## The Only Columnist on a Swinging Bridge

On the way west the next day, it looks like the farmer is doing fine. The fields are ablaze with canola, which may be the most brilliant yellow in nature, short of the odd tropical fish. There are lakes of blue flax. Where the two combine, it is clear that a great vista, a Top Ten Belvedere, need not have water, need not even have height.

We spent part of yesterday figuring out our route, and where we will spend the next couple of nights, and Nancy has been busy on the phone. Now, when we finally have it figured out, we take an impulsive detour south off Highway 1 to Souris, home of Canada's longest swinging bridge. The road to Souris is straight and flat, running between the fields, from which birds fly up and across the road. Souris is an attractive small Prairie town of 1,700, nicely treed, with the Manitoba Pool elevator, the legion, the old Avalon theatre building with a mall built into it, the wide main street, the diagonal parking. We get lost. It appears that the smaller the community, the greater our chance of getting lost in it. The town has one river and one swinging bridge over it, a long one at that. How hard can it be to find it? I attribute this tendency to get lost in small towns to hubris. Because the town is small we (or, more properly, I) figure it is impossible to get lost in it. Consequently we (or I) don't pay any attention to such details as street names. Then if a wrong turn should happen to be taken, it is difficult to find our way back to where we were.

Eventually we find the bridge, which is 582 feet long. A plaque tells us that it was built in 1904 by the town's founder, Squire William Sowden, "as a convenience to allow him access to his property across the river." It was damaged by a cable break in 1961, swept away by floods in 1976 (which would be after we saw it last), and then rebuilt. Now it has new treated wood. We bounce over to the other side, and are halfway back when we encounter a boy who has discovered a large snapping turtle in the muddy water under the bridge. The boy, Robert Hillyer, says you should pick up a snapping turtle by its tail, otherwise it will scratch or bite you. "I know this from experience," he says. His mother, Brenda, asks us if we are from Nepean. We aren't, but the place we bought our car is, which is where she got the idea. It turns out she and her husband, Steve, Robert and his sister, Eleanor, are from Renfrew, just up the Valley from Ottawa. They are also from Brandon, having lived there in the early eighties when Steve was the Baptist minister there. More small world. Brenda and Steve are *Ottawa Citizen* readers and Steve says something I like when he is introduced to me. "Glory Hallelujah," he says. There is something to be said for being the only newspaper columnist on a swinging bridge.

We exchange travel stories. They have been to the West Coast, then to a wedding in Red Deer. They rave about Long Beach on Vancouver Island. We make a mental note of that and head west again, up to the highway, past Virden, beginning to see the donkey pumps, about one to a field, that indicate the presence of oil in the ground. The four-lane highway ends and signs saying REMEMBER TWO-WAY TRAFFIC appear. Perhaps this is not being too cautious. As we near the Saskatchewan border, we see a storm awaiting us.

# 14

## *Only in Saskatchewan*

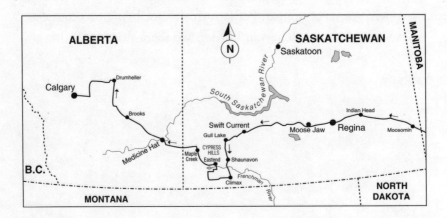

Time is one of Bruce Penton's pet themes. He is co-publisher, with his wife, Barb, of the *Moosomin World-Spectator*, the weekly newspaper he has owned since 1991 after working there for ten years. In that time he has been a persistent campaigner for Saskatchewan to adopt Daylight Saving Time. "I don't like to brag," he says, "but I'm the Daylight Saving Time spokesman in Saskatchewan." At the moment, Saskatchewan is with Alberta in the summer and with Manitoba in the winter. That causes spirited discussion about twice a year. Whenever the media rediscover the issue, which would be about twice a year, Bruce's is the name that pops up in reporters' Rolodexes and he is called for a quote. Some of the motivation for his crusade may come from his love of golf, at which he is proficient and which he could play later into the evening if only Saskatchewan would wise up. Some of it may have come from his upbringing in Brandon, which featured both golf and the clocks being moved ahead an hour in the spring, as nature intended.

The campaign has ruffled some feathers in a province where tradition is valued and opposition to daylight time is defence of the status quo. But it doesn't seem to have hurt Bruce, whose paper averages thirty-two pages a week and has a circulation of 3,400 (more people than there are in the town), reaching forty miles in each direction. He has pagination equipment, e-mail, and even a web site. The paper's successes are not just financial. A few years ago, the *World-Spectator* was nominated for a Michener Award, the prestigious journalism prize for which only the big boys are usually considered.

Bruce and Barb show us around the paper. It is in its 114th year, beginning as the *World*. For its name alone – a paper in a town of 2,500 called the *World-Spectator* – the paper is worth visiting. Bruce and I go back to *Brandon Sun* days, where he got his start as a sports writer. After that, he went to New Westminster, to work for the *Columbian*, a paper that is no longer with us. On the August day in 1980 when the *Winnipeg Tribune* and the *Ottawa Journal* were shut down, in what their respective owners claimed was a coincidence, Bruce decided that the daily newspaper business was the wrong line of work for him. If the *Trib* could be shut down, so could the *Columbian*. He turned out to be right, although he was long gone by then. He looked for a weekly to get involved in and found it in Moosomin.

We look at some back issues. This year's New Year's baby didn't show up until the January 16 paper. Bruce comes out with what may be the only weekly newspaper joke I've ever heard. "In some small towns, the New Year's baby for 1977 just arrived."

In Moosomin, Bruce and Barb also found a good place to raise three children. "In the time we've been here, fifteen years, there's been one armed robbery," Bruce says as we walk to a restaurant. Then he corrects himself. "Pardon me," he says. "There's been two." Apparently somebody from out of town robbed the Kentucky Fried Chicken.

At Tino's Family Restaurant the waitress brings the four of us coffee automatically before we order. She then refills the coffee every time she goes by. We are talking about this and that and I ask about the controversy about the Canadian Wheat Board, the demand by some farmers that they be allowed to market their grain outside the board. Bruce discusses the political ins and outs of the issue and we move on to another topic, which we are discussing when a man in a nearby booth says, "I heard you talking about the Wheat Board," and launches into a spirited defence of it. He is an older man, from Manitoba, it turns out.

"These guys weren't around in the thirties, the end of the thirties, and I was," he says. Then an older woman wanders over from another table. She is Betty Gordon, known to Bruce as a Wheat Board supporter. "They're out to destroy the Canadian Wheat Board," she says. The discussion rages, as I take notes. The Inner Journalist seems to have put a notebook into my hands.

"This is why I go home for lunch," Bruce says, after the various participants have returned to their seats. Did this happen because you're the publisher of the paper or because it's Saskatchewan, I ask. "It's Saskatchewan," Bruce says. As we settle up our bill, the fellow from Manitoba walks by our table. "It's greed for money and when there's a greed for money there's corruption," he says. Then I am approached by Les Gordon, Betty's husband. "There's an old saying," he says. "If it ain't broke, don't fix it."

We step outside and shake our heads. I can't imagine any other province in Canada where this little event could have taken place.

There are other stops along the Trans-Canada to make today, one of them being Indian Head, which my sister Alison has just selected as the home town for Kate Henry, the heroine of her detective novels. The selection of Indian Head came from a scouting trip last year. Part of the reason was the church, St. Andrew's United. Kate's father is a United Church minister. Alison looked it over and then found out, almost by accident, that our grandfather had preached there. So that was it. Kate had to be from Indian Head. As Kate's honorary older brother I have to see for myself.

We find a pretty town – slogan: A PROGRESSIVE PRAIRIE TOWN – with a *really* wide main street, called Grand Street. The church, a red brick structure at the corner of Eden and Buxton streets, is closed, but a woman washing windows at the side says we can go in and wander around. The trust you find in Canada's small communities never ceases to amaze and please me. We walk through all the rooms of the church, looking for traces of Ralph Connor, but without any luck. Still, we figure any place that lets two strangers inside with no questions asked is a good place for Kate to have hung around as a kid.

Between Indian Head and Regina, the landscape is much as Easterners imagine it, and as most of the prairie isn't – namely, billiard-table flat. "It struck me," wrote Mr. J. S. Gowland in 1957, "that a person suddenly transported from one section of prairie to another 100 miles away without knowing it would remain unaware of the change unless he had an intimate knowledge of the lay of the land." It was dry when Mr. Gowland made that comment. Now it is far from that. The crops give the land colour and it is neither desolate nor monotonous. We reach Regina around five with no reservation and not a very clear idea of where we are going. It's strange that having lived so long within 220 miles of here this should be unfamiliar territory, but it is. We find a small and not terribly expensive downtown hotel and park the car in a nearby parking garage. On the way there I almost get smashed into because what a green arrow means to me is not the same thing as what a green arrow means to people here. I think it means I can turn left and have the right of way. They think it means I can turn left if nobody is coming. I wonder if this is one of the little differences of opinion the provinces could get together and solve some day, for people like me who like to drive in more than one province.

In the hotel, we work the phones. I call ahead to locate friends to visit. Nancy continues a telephonic mission she began in Brandon, to get us a reservation on the British Columbia ferry from Port Hardy to Prince Rupert, the Inland Passage, the praises of which were sung to me by my cousin Peter Carver during our stopover at Kenora. Nancy called from Brandon and was told there was no space, but to keep trying. So she keeps trying and there is still no space and still more encouragement to keep trying. Then we ponder what to do in Regina, where we know no one.

In fact, Regina is familiar to me, but only in a . . . call it mythological sense, through the writings of and about the late, great and arguably imaginary poet, Sarah Binks. In his critical biography, published in 1947, Paul Hiebert spends almost nine pages on Regina, so great is the city's importance to the poet. In 1926, when Sarah went there with Henry Welkin – "aesthete, patron of the arts and letters, and travelling salesman" – Regina was "the Athens of Saskatchewan" and it was Henry's task to show Sarah "the real Regina behind its polish, its sophistication and its long rows of box cars." The estimates of the experts (notably, the scholars Professor Horace P. Marrowfat, Miss Rosalind Drool, and Dr. Taj Mahal) vary as to the length of their stay, but it must have been somewhere between one and three weeks. We know Sarah and Henry went to the opera twice, rode again and again on Regina's streetcar, frequented the cafés, Chinatown, the Botanical Gardens. "He took her to the aquarium and to the public library," Sarah's biographer writes, "and together they studied what fish and what manuscripts were available at those places." They visited the department stores, the groceterias, the implement warehouse of the firm Henry represented. They visited the Union Station and perhaps they visited too much in too short a time, for Sarah grew irritable, in ways that will be discussed later, and this may have affected the course of Saskatchewan literature, her biographer thinks. At any rate, these landmarks, although we can't find most of them, seem even more real to us, travelling around the city, than Paddle-to-the-Sea's launching place. Especially the Union Station, which I decide we must visit.

What would Sarah have made of the fact that Union Station has become a casino? Perhaps it was with the thought of gambling heartbreak that she wrote, soon after she returned to her little town of Willows

> Come crush, harsh world, and snuff this life,
> And bid my sorrows cease,
> Rejected and dejected I
> But long for my decease.

Perhaps not. At any rate, it is just down the street. I try the "it's for the book" gambit once more, and it works again. Each time may be the last. Reluctantly, Nancy accompanies me on a stroll down Rose Street to the old CPR station, which is at least as busy now as it ever was when the trains stopped here. The place is all spiffed up, colourful, carpeted and full of machines. As we walk from room to room, we can vaguely make out the architecture and layout of a train station. At one end is a restaurant, called Van Horne's (another specious evocation of CPR lore). At the other end is a gift shop where you can buy coffee mugs and the usual souvenir stuff, as well as a Casino Regina tee-shirt just the right size for your baby. Three things strike us (aside from the absolute and total immorality of the thing; remember, we have just come from Kate Henry's father's church). The three things that strike us are, first, the tone: that same inside-the-xylophone sound I heard at the casino in Hull. This one comes from five hundred slot machines. Once there was passenger rail service to Regina. Now, in the same spot, are five hundred slot machines.

The second thing that strikes me is the total niceness of the staff. They are young and clean-cut and smiling. Innocent. This is how you fight the sinister connotations of a gambling den in the middle of the province that lives by the social gospel: Be nice. It must be good, clean fun if the people working there are so nice.

The third thing you notice is much more striking: the age of the customers. They are old. You've never seen so many old people in one place. They are old and they are from the farms and the small towns. These are not big-spending tourists from the Far East and they are not sophisticated high-rollers in tuxes and evening gowns. They are people off the tour bus from Melfort and Indian Head and Melville, home of a hockey team called the Melville Millionaires – and perhaps from Willows too.

Fortunately for them, and for us, there is no dress code. We wander about in our jeans and lose eight dollars in loonies just to see how things work. I think my Inner Journalist has popped up again, so fascinated by the scene that he forgets to disapprove. Nancy has no Inner Journalist. She just wants to get out of there and somehow fails to appreciate the Inner Journalist's little lecture on why people put money into machines. It is (now that you ask) because the machine, if it takes your money, never looks at you like you're stupid, never laughs at you, never bluffs you out of a pot. There is no ego loss in losing to a machine.

### What Have You Done with the Regina Manifesto?

Today we have both a deadline and a mission. The deadline is to be in Gull Lake in time for dinner. That's about a three-hour drive away. The mission is to find the Regina Manifesto. I know it was signed here in 1933 at the founding convention of the CCF but not where. I have searched all the books I can find on the subject. None of them says where the Regina convention was held. I figure we have about four hours to find the Regina Manifesto before we have to hit the road for Gull Lake.

The Regina Manifesto has a connection to Lake of the Woods, at least in Gordon lore. The way my father told it, he and Eugene Forsey and someone else, perhaps Joe Parkinson, were driving to Regina for the convention and stopped at the island. They had the Manifesto with them, which had been written by Frank Underhill. Upon looking it over, they decided it needed a punchier ending. "How about this," one of them said. "'No CCF government will rest content until it has eradicated capitalism and put into operation the full programme of socialized planning which will lead to the establishment in Canada of the Co-operative Commonwealth.'" Great, they all agreed, and in it went, the phrase that would haunt the party forever, as a symbol of its radicalism and scary intentions.

Whether the story is true or not, I'm fond of it. We begin by driving to the Wascana Centre, the huge park south of the downtown area. The park is vast and impressive. It contains the Saskatchewan legislative building, the University of Regina, the Mackenzie Art Gallery, the Diefenbaker homestead, and much more. There is a lake that failed to impress Sarah Binks, who might have been away from Willows a bit too long at this point. She called Wascana Lake "a mean little puddle; I could spit across it." But it looks fine to us, as do the trees around it. The view from the legislature steps, where we start, is of a formal garden and hedges, to a lake and across it to downtown and its bank towers.

With a mind to what makes one legislature different from another, we ask a guard why workmen are putting rough logs and burlap around the security desk. "We're building a corral," he says. Of course. This would be for Buffalo Days, a local celebration which is coming up.

There is another touch we haven't noticed in other legislatures, a series of memorials to Saskatchewan civil servants who died in the wars. Then the tour begins. Again we have a guide to ourselves and he tells us that the legislative building is the largest in the country. Saskatchewan, like Manitoba, thought it would be a much bigger province than it turned out to be. This building is very much on the Manitoba model: lots of marble, a rotunda with balustrade. The marble comes from Ireland, Italy, Sweden, Quebec, and Cyprus. "There's not enough marble in the world to replace what we have here," he says.

We go into the library, which was once the legislative chamber, and I see my chance to find the Regina Manifesto. The guide is patient while I make my inquiry. The librarian does not ask me for my I.D. or tell me to fill out this form or come back tomorrow. She just tries to answer my question. Not only does she not think I'm crazy, she knows where to find the Regina Manifesto. Namely, on the Internet. The Manifesto, she was told just the other day, is now on-line. She calls it up on her computer. There it is, but not even the Internet can tell us exactly where in Regina it was signed.

There is some consultation with other librarians, all of whom seem rather interested in the challenge. Eventually they suggest I go downtown to Tommy Douglas House, which is the headquarters of the NDP, successor to the CCF.

Good. The tour continues. It is somehow incongruous to see all this grandeur, all this marble, in what we often think of Canada's most unassuming province. The guide blames Saskatchewan's first premier, Thomas Walter Scott. One of the things he did was change the building's original brick design to tyndal limestone. Another thing he did was put a red carpet in the legislative chamber, even though red is the traditional colour of upper houses, because "he decided that he was going to make his chamber better than any other lower house in Canada," according to the guide.

The building departs from tradition in many ways. There is a statue of John Diefenbaker in the rotunda, even though he never held provincial office. His nose is shinier than the rest of him and the guide explains that this is because he was polished with brass cleaner even though he is bronze. After the nose, the cleaner realized a mistake had been made and switched to something else.

Diefenbaker, of course, was a politician who kept his nose clean anyway.

In the basement are portraits of former premiers. Scott, who is clearly not a favourite of the guide, poses with a cigar. The guide points out that he has been painted larger than life. Another premier, W. R. Martin, has those trick eyes that follow you around the room. Ross Thatcher never posed for his portrait, so what we are seeing is his head superimposed upon the body of the self-effacing person who did pose. Allan Blakeney's portrait, done in a more contemporary style, is controversial. Some people don't like his suit, which is good old NDP corduroy, although in blue.

Other displays include portraits of all the Indian chiefs at the time the legislature was built. There are also photographs of each year's appointees to the Saskatchewan Order of Merit. To a greater extent than any legislature we have seen, Saskatchewan's represents the modern life of the province.

We move on to the Mackenzie Art Gallery, a fine (and free) museum, built in 1990, that shares a building with the Department of Health. Featured now is an exhibit of Ivan Eyre's work, which we quite enjoy but which gets mixed reviews in the guest book. Four days ago someone wrote: "His work seems very passionate, allows for contemplation and personal reflection. It was wonderful." But just yesterday another visitor wrote: "Ivan Eyre's works are of group sex, self-indulgence, and dark-evil things (perhaps even satanism and sadistic things)." That would have been an interesting time to be in the gallery, when this fellow walked through.

Then there was the entry by someone who felt he had to write something but didn't know what. "It was okay. Thanks."

Just inside the door at Tommy Douglas House is a statue of Douglas done by Joe Fafard, which is much smaller than life, which was small anyway. Once again I am surprised pleasantly by having my Regina Manifesto question taken seriously. No one says "Why do you want to know?" They just think it's an interesting question. One person drops her other duties to look through files. Among the things she comes up with is a list of guests at the fiftieth-anniversary celebration in 1983. Representing the 1933 Montreal delegation are Frank Scott, Eugene Forsey, and my father, all since gone. There is still no indication where that first convention was held. "Call Pemrose. She'd know," a woman suggests. So they call Pemrose Whelan, whose husband Ed was Tommy Douglas's campaign manager. Pemrose says the convention was held at the old city hall. Oh, I say, that's where we had dinner last night. It was a nice Italian restaurant whose pasta was made "with Saskatchewan-grown durum flour," according to the menu. But no, it's not *that* old city hall. It's another old city hall, where the Galleria, a shopping centre, is now. The Galleria is where the car has been parked. Perfect. I hope the car appreciated it and am glad that it was not eradicated.

It is warm and we see mirages on the Trans-Canada Highway, imaginary puddles of water. The land is flat and looks lush, with beautiful canola and flax. We stop in Moose Jaw (THE FRIENDLY CITY) for lunch. Moose Jaw's main street is extremely wide and the city looks prosperous, more so, at least downtown, than Brandon, which is roughly the same size. It may, again, be a question of adapting and adjusting. A snazzy new spa opened here only a month ago, called the Temple Gardens Mineral Spa Resort Hotel. We have lunch in the restaurant, although we decline to take the waters. The hot geo-thermal waters are said to be similar to those at Radium Hot Springs and Bath in England. Federal, provincial, and city money is involved, and there has been quite a bit of promotion, drawing people to the city, which seems quite excited about it. A newspaper supplement carries congratulatory messages from the mayor, the MP, and the MLAs.

All around the hotel are people in wheelchairs and on crutches and walkers. Visitors like us walk through the muted pink-and-green art deco lobby and take the elevator up to the fourth floor where the pool is flanked by an outdoor patio and an indoor snack bar. The pool itself looks just like a regular big-hotel swimming pool, except that no one in it is swimming.

Back on the highway, we watch the land curving gently, the slightest rise giving a commanding view of the land for miles around. Bales of hay dot the distant landscape. One sweep of the eye produces a farmer irrigating, a truck driving down a dirt road, somebody burning stubble, some Charolais cattle standing around. The farmhouses are set inside rings of dark green caragana trees, a typical and attractive Prairie sight.

A few years ago someone in the town decided that Gull Lake needed a big-time system for numbering houses. Some say the Boy Scouts were selling numbers and persuaded someone that bigger addresses would mean more sales. Whatever the reason, Vern and Nettie Small have a street number in the 5000s on Kings Avenue, and they sometimes have trouble remembering what it is. When I challenge each of them to tell me what their number is, Vern gets it right, after thinking about it for a moment, but Nettie misses by quite a bit. The system is puzzling for a town of 1,095 people. "We see a place for sale in the paper," Vern says, "and it's 3,000 numbers away and it's only two blocks away." Besides that, if you get lost, you ask anyone where Vern and Nettie's place is and they'll tell you.

Sitting on the deck of the blue-painted bungalow, which they built in 1968 with an eye to retirement, we see pock marks on the north wall from a hail storm last August 15. The kind of town it is can be best illustrated by what happened when Vern built that deck. A fellow strolled over from city hall bringing an application for a building permit, in case Vern had neglected to get one, which he had.

Nancy and I get into Vern's truck for the drive to the family farm, twelve miles to the east, which is now run by one of his three sons, Steve. Another son is Doug, a close Ottawa friend and the journalist famous for airing the news of the leaked Michael Wilson budget in 1989. Just about every August Doug and Brenda come out to help with the harvest. As we drive, I ask Vern where he stands on the Wheat Board issue. He says farmers have the best of both worlds: they can sell canola or lentils or other crops on the open market if they want, and wheat and barley through the Wheat Board.

"Hard wheat is the crop in the Prairies," he says, "because it's the easiest thing to do." But farming in this part of the world has changed. Like the farms in Eastern Ontario, the farms in Saskatchewan have grown larger, but the math is different. "You couldn't possibly make a living on a section any more," Vern says, which reminds me of what Jim Thain said back in Hastings County. Except that a *quarter*-section is 160 acres. When Jim Thain talked about the size of farm you couldn't live on in Ontario, he talked about 100 acres. So the size of farm you can't live on in Saskatchewan – 640 acres – is about six times the size of farm you can't live on in Ontario. Here, two sections is a small farm. Steve has ten quarters, but he and his wife Shannon work off the farm. Another key, in addition to size, is technology, the whys and wherefores of weed sprays and fertilizers.

Still another key is diversity. "I farmed in a fairly simple way," Vern says, as did his father who homesteaded it in 1906. Steve, on the other hand, has durum wheat, hard spring wheat, field peas, canola, Limousin cattle, and malting barley. Farmers now are always looking for a new crop, something with which to spread the risk around, perhaps bring a high price some year. A neighbour is trying Oriental mustard.

As we drive east, we are climbing continuously, although it doesn't feel like it. We stop to examine the canola bloom up close. The longer it blooms the better, Vern says, but it's usually from ten days to two weeks. The colour is just past the peak. "Three days ago that would just hurt your eyes, it was so beautiful."

As we look at the canola and some lentils, we see movement in the distance. It may be deer or coyotes bounding over the fields, looking almost like kangaroos. Whatever they are, they are a long way away. Near the farm we pass a field of hard spring wheat that was late getting planted. Now frost is on the horizon: "It's a nail-biter," Vern says.

At the farm, we find a beautiful house, with carefully planted trees and a dugout for the kids to swim in. Vern and Nettie's kids and the kids of the kids come back to the farm for holidays, from British Columbia and Northern Saskatchewan as well as from Ottawa. As we walk around we see the inevitable cats – I count twenty of them – and all kinds of machinery: a combine, an automatic bale wagon, and an air-conditioned tractor on which the seat adjusts seven different ways. Wandering around the property, you never know where you are going to encounter a piece of machinery. In the city you get used to the idea that everything has to be put neatly away every night, the car in the drive, the lawnmower and the bicycles in the garage. On the farm the stuff is left where it will be used, a much more functional, not to mention relaxed, way of looking at it.

In 1937, when he was eighteen, Vern spent some time away from Saskatchewan and when he got his first look at the prairies on his return, he thought: "My God, why would I ever leave this?" On a day like this, the air soft, the wind light, the grass sweet, the birds and animals all around, you see what he means. I'd be a Saskatchewan farmer in a minute, if it wasn't for the farming.

## The Perfection of Eastend

After breakfast we drive around Gull Lake before leaving. We see the North Gate Family Restaurant (a Chinese restaurant run by a Vietnamese), the Clarendon Hotel, the Co-Op, the Recycle Depot, a law office, and several oil-related businesses. Over takeout from the North Gate last night, Vern talked about how the implement dealers have left town but their places have been taken by the thriving oil-well supply business, which has created employment in the town providing parts for the rigs and pumps that are on so many farms, servicing the wells and storage containers, trucking the oil. That's one of the ways the town has changed, even though the population hasn't. There is also an increase in the number of retired farmers.

The road to Eastend, where we will visit Sharon Butala, is not long, so we decide to drive the long way around. We drive south, crossing the Frenchman River, to Climax (the bride's fourth major disappointment), then find Highway 18 and drive west on it. We are near the U.S. border and out of the hills and there is nothing, the effect of desolation heightened by a horrible highway full of holes. In three and a half hours' driving we see five cars. We also see two groundhogs and a coyote. Some friends said it would be fun to take this highway all the way from the Manitoba border and we are very glad we didn't.

When we turn north and then east toward Eastend we begin climbing, almost imperceptibly, except that we notice the car working harder. We cross the Frenchman River again, the weathered clay walls of the valley giving it the look of a flat-topped canyon, a badlands look, but green and pretty. Eastend is a very western-looking town, the population 641, the main street twenty-nine paces wide, by actual pace. The town was the boyhood home of Wallace Stegner, whose book *Wolf Willow* is very much about the area and whose house has been turned into a retreat for writers. Eastend is also home to the Eastend Fossil Research Station, which houses a small museum demonstrating the reconstruction of a Tyrannosaurus Rex skeleton known as Scotty found near here. A downpour begins just as we hit the main street and we dash into Jack's Café for lunch. Jack's is very much a fish-on-the-wall, wood-panel-and-Denver-sandwich kind of place. A pike is on the wall, also a salmon, or perhaps a trout, and three perch. I always thought you threw perch back. They bring you coffee as soon as you sit down. Good place.

The rain stops just as we leave and it is sunny and hot by the time we get to Sharon Butala's place, which is reached by another excellent set of directions, involving tracks, a deep coulee, a yellow farmhouse, a broad deep valley, a wooden bridge and a Texas gate – the latter being a kind of grate stuck into the road, the strips of metal spaced so that cows can't walk across.

Sharon is a writer, author of a surprisingly big-selling book, *The Perfection of the Morning*, published in 1994, which is about this place and the ranch to the west of it, about how she moved here to marry Peter and how she came to know the land. It is a very quiet book and it somehow struck a nerve with Canadians. There is something in us, it seems, that wants to get in touch with nature and responds to someone who has. I met Sharon once in Ottawa and, at the urging of my sister, who knows her well, phoned from Regina. She warmly invited us down to see the place.

The place is two places. There is the hay farm, where the house is, and there is the ranch, which is about forty miles away. I notice we are thinking in miles again. The house, with other farm buildings, is set among poplar trees, in the middle of a valley, hills to all sides. A poplar tree blew over in a high wind – a plough wind, it is called – the other day. The Frenchman River runs by the property, narrow, but not a creek by any means. There are old cars off to the side, including a fifties-vintage Studebaker. The house is modest but has good views, west and north.

We load up the truck and get in. Every time the driver's seat is folded forward to put something or somebody in the back seat, the horn honks. Peter, a big and quiet man, is oblivious to it, and the physical isolation of the place is suddenly brought home to me. Who cares if the horn honks? In town, the honking of a horn is a source of irritation, sometimes a sign of aggression. Here it's just a noise nobody will hear.

On the drive, much of it over well-maintained gravel roads, we see antelope, a group of them. Imagine being in a place where you drive by antelope. I notice later in Sharon's book her description of an encounter with an animal she had watched bounding, kangaroo-like, over the land, and which turned out to be a bobcat. I wonder now if that was what we saw yesterday.

Peter talks about the different farms as we pass them. He has been here all his life and knows the agricultural history. He points out a piece of machinery that might cost $200,000, speaks of the stress that kind of investment puts on farmers. He doesn't like pasture land being "broken up," as he puts it, ploughed and put into crops. He talks about farmers who put too much into wheat. But he can understand the appeal: "No fences to fix, nothing gets away on you," an interesting echo of what Vern Small, a wheat farmer, said yesterday.

Sharon and Peter have great eyes. At one point he stops the truck. "What's that black animal?" he asks. Somewhere, it must be miles away, is a dot on the landscape. But to Peter, it is something that doesn't belong. Perhaps a cow that has strayed. It reminds me of a guide picking out wild animals on the plains of Africa. The same kind of horizon is involved, the same strength of sight.

I would not begin to describe the land, since Sharon's book does it so eloquently. Except to say that it is magnificent – high, short-grassed, full of colour and birds (sparrows and horned larks), bees and butterflies. The sun is strong, the sky clear, and there is a powerful quiet accented by a bit of wind. It goes without saying that you can see for miles.

Some of our driving is overland now, off the road on tracks and trails, but done with great care and an awareness of the sensitive parts of this vast acreage. There is a coyote den, for example, to which we are taken. We find the den but not the coyotes. Nancy asks what damage they do and Peter says it is mostly to rabbits and mice. Some farmers blame them for killing calves but he thinks the coyotes only feed on the carcasses after the calves die of other things. Sharon and Peter keep finding things to show us as the truck takes us slowly over the rolling land. Distance and time become unimportant until Sharon suddenly notices the time and says we might as well stay the night with them because there's no way we're going to get to Medicine Hat tonight. That's fine with us. This is magic out here.

At the ranch is the old farmhouse, where Peter grew up. There are parts of other homesteads around. This is something else you notice in the West. Things are left where they are. History is always there, leaning a bit. The homesteads go back to 1913–15 when the country started to be opened up. This house is where Sharon wrote *The Perfection of the Morning*, before they moved to the house on the hay farm.

There is a bush rabbit around and lots of dung. Peter is concerned about cattle being in the field in front, where they shouldn't be. There must be something wrong with the fence. With us in the truck, he begins herding the cows out, driving the truck towards them and honking the horn. Reluctantly, they move.

We go looking for a burrowing owl's burrow. The burrowing owl is an endangered species. It doesn't really burrow, but sets up shop in burrows made by badgers and other creatures. As we approach on foot, one flies up and comes down in nearby grass. We watch him through binoculars and keep our distance from the burrow.

Peter has made a gift of his land to the nature conservancy. It is called the Old Man on His Back Shortgrass Prairie and Heritage Preserve and there is a plaque on the wall back at the house commemorating the occasion. On the ranch we stop at the remains of a sweat lodge that was constructed out of sticks for a ceremony involving some of the tribes in the area. The idea of the gift is to make sure the land remains as it is, which seems to us an excellent idea.

Back at the hay farm we have dinner, barbecued steak, and watch the sun go down over the hills, giving the scene a Top Ten Belvedere nomination. It may not be the brightest sunset we have seen, but it is the widest.

## Fossil Stand at a Miniature Canyon

The next morning is, as someone once said, perfect. Sharon and
Peter have given us a shortcut over to the Cypress Hills, a gravel
road that runs beside the Frenchman River and crosses it several
times. It is gorgeous at the valley bottom early in the morning.
When a bluebird flies across the road I wonder if all this has
somehow been staged. As we climb out of the valley we look down
on fields of wheat and canola. There has been almost no traffic,
three trucks perhaps, each slowing down so as not to throw stones
at us.

A paved highway takes us into Cypress Hills Provincial Park.
This is the first place we see lodgepole pines, tall and thin, like red
pines, clear of underbrush, but not red. It is also a place with a
magnificent view. The Cypress Hills have the highest altitude
between Newfoundland and the Rockies, which you wouldn't
suspect until you get to Lookout Point, near the top. We are at
1,275 metres, looking down at the tops of the poplar trees growing
on the side of the hill and beyond them mile after mile of fields.
My Prairie fiction-reading is Guy Vanderhaeghe's *The Englishman's
Boy*, which concerns the events leading up to and the myths surrounding the Cypress Hills Massacre in 1881. Following the trail of
the wolfers who attacked the Assiniboines here, he drove back and
forth through the area several times researching the book, and you
can see the impact it would have on a storyteller.

Nancy is driving as we leave the park and head north for
Highway 1, the Trans-Canada, and I find it is all I can do to keep
from hauling out the Alberta maps and brochures. Some days on a
trip are looking-ahead days. We have had a great run in Saskatchewan and now it is on to the next. It begins to get hilly as we
near Alberta, which we enter at 11:40 in the morning. We are now
on a four-lane road with a speed limit of 110, which tends to put
one in driving mode. So we don't stop at the WORLD'S TALLEST
TEPEE at Medicine Hat and we go right by Redcliff, GREENHOUSE

CAPITAL OF THE PRAIRIES. Perhaps all this is getting to me. I make a couple of turnoffs that don't result in a decent place to have lunch and we wind up at the A&W in Brooks. Then I leave some maps and one of my many pairs of glasses on the table and we have to go back to get them. Maybe we were not meant to leave Saskatchewan.

On the Trans-Canada, the landscape is mostly flat and colourless. Saskatchewan was flat too, along the highway, but the crops added colour, and there were some rises to give vistas. In search of a vista we turn north toward Drumheller. The great thing about driving on the prairies is how far ahead you can see, so we enjoy ourselves looking for the first sight of the badlands. What we see is a sign saying that trucks should check their equipment and suddenly we're looking down a steep road into the Red Deer River valley, the steep rise on the other side harsher and uglier than the valley walls at Eastend, but the same idea. There is a suspension bridge at Wayne, the Star Mine Suspension Bridge, not as long as the Souris one and all metal, with high sides. The fact that you can see through the metal floor down into the water doesn't compensate. Souris wins the swinging bridge competition.

This bridge also has considerably more traffic. We are suddenly in a more touristy part of the world. The river is muddy and moving. The scene, with the dry, crumbly, and rugged banks, has a very western-movie feel to it. Robert Mitchum and Marilyn Monroe should be floating by on a raft any minute.

At Drumheller we turn southwest toward Calgary, then stop at the top of Horseshoe Canyon, a kind of privatized lookout, which is quite spectacular. The canyon is a miniaturized Grand Canyon, only a kilometre and a half across, but looking far larger because of tricks of perspective. The opening scene of the movie *Quest for Fire* was shot here. It is only when you look way down at the people walking across the canyon bottom that you realize they are not very far down at all, only a hundred feet or so. At the top, a guy is selling fossils out of a booth. Another guy has a chipwagon (with no poutine, I note, and not even the thought of a Persian). I see an Old Guy's Hat: WORLD'S GREATEST AUTHORITY. We push on to Calgary and grab a roadside motel. We're tired after 627 kilometres of driving and I need time to put three days' worth of notes into the computer. We're going to wind up missing the big city nightlife, but then we mostly do.

# 15

## A Canadian in the Rockies

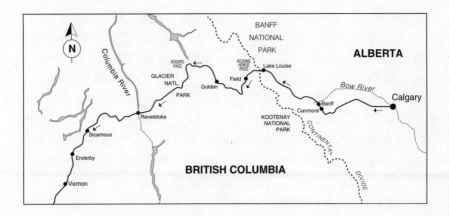

At breakfast, we share a table with another couple, francophones, and we don't exchange a word. You know how it works: if you don't say something early, it gets harder and harder to break the ice and eventually you both decide it's not worth it. I don't know if they're being unfriendly or we are, but I can't imagine it happening in Prince Edward Island. Come to think of it, I can't imagine it happening in Calgary. It reminds me of a story I heard the last time I was here, which was about fifteen years ago. It was about the residents of a street who all complained to a social service that their neighbours were unfriendly, that no one knew their neighbours and so on. It turned out that everyone on the street was from the East.

That was around 1981 when Calgary was booming and widely perceived, by the rest of Canada, to be in a greed-head phase. I came out to spend a week and write about all this. Expecting the worst, I was quite taken with the city. People were indeed friendly. They talked to you in elevators. In Ottawa people who talked on elevators were thought to be perverts. Calgary, it is true, did have a coldly impersonal downtown, full of glass towers and not much else, aside from a pedestrian mall that was going the way of head shops and second-hand comic stores. But it also had interesting neighbourhoods, a fine museum, some nice little galleries, and an attractive setting. The people I talked to were pleased to be in a city that was growing and changing so rapidly. Their pride in it could reach unimagined heights. One friend told me that Calgary's dry climate meant it didn't take as long to dry off after a shower. I picture him now, writing interpretive boards for Parks Canada.

I remember going up the Calgary Tower and counting the cranes. The boom was supposed to be winding down, but there were still ten new building projects visible from up there. Today we go up again, the elevator giving us a readout of our altitude, stopping at 160 metres. The crane count is zero.

But the city looks pretty good from 160 metres, plenty of trees, the Bow River and Prince's Island Park. There may be an answer here to the question I was asking myself in the Maritimes: Can we find beauty in things that are not old? Here, yes. The Olympic Plaza has the look of a relaxing urban oasis. The new Calgary Municipal Building, multilayered in blue glass, is quite handsome, with the old city hall preserved beside it. All of this is helpfully presented with the aid of labelled photo blow-ups at each viewpoint, showing us what we are looking at. The distractions don't matter much – except that I find myself wondering: Why must there always be video games? I know: To make money. But why do people put money in? Looking out the window is free. I imagine the conversation: "Let's spend $4.95 each and ride up the elevator to the top of the Calgary Tower, 160 metres up, and then play video games."

Having said all that, I should also say that no one should be put off a ride up the tower by the commercial nature of the operation. It is an excellent way, perhaps the best, to get a feel for the layout and overall look of a city. In Calgary's case, there is also a chance to get a preview of the mountains, appearing in faint outline on the southwestern horizon.

We're doing the Four-Hour City again today, with a view to arriving in Banff with some daylight left. The Glenbow Museum, easily one of the most interesting in Canada, has an exhibit that could have been designed with us in mind. It's called "A Hiker's Guide to the Art of the Canadian Rockies," featuring the art of Walter J. Phillips, Peter and Catharine Whyte, A. C. Leighton, Lawren Harris, A. Y. Jackson, J. E. H. MacDonald, Charles Comfort, and even Sir Frederick Banting – a good name for a painter, just as Comfort is a good name for a doctor. In addition to their paintings there are some good photographs of them working beneath the peaks. Once again we find a way to extend our family into a hitherto unknown area. When Nancy's mother, Betty Thain, was attending the University of Manitoba, she worked summers at the Banff Springs and Château Lake Louise and she met Lawren Harris, who was probably working on one of these very paintings.

Looking at the exhibit, you can see the magic the mountains had for artists. You can also see that, to some eastern eyes, one mountain is very much like another. A. Y. Jackson, for example, is quoted in the exhibition materials as saying "This country is less paintable than Northern Ontario." It doesn't appear that Harris would agree.

There is also an exhibition of William Armstrong, a Brit who painted Northern and Northwestern Ontario in watercolours, mostly before the turn of the century. Some of the paintings we examine are of places we have just been – Little Current on Manitoulin Island, Nipigon (*Indians in a Canoe, Nipigon River*, an 1867 precursor of *Paddle-to-the-Sea*), Kakabeka Falls, Fort William. The Glenbow resembles the New Brunswick Museum of Saint

John in combining natural history and art in one building. New Brunswick's is better organized, Calgary's is grander, with full-size tepees and a range of artifacts of pioneer life in the West, including a reconstruction of an old CPR station. In addition to crediting corporate and private sponsors at every opportunity, the Glenbow also gives prominent photo credits to the designers of each exhibit, a thoughtful touch we have not seen elsewhere.

Many of Calgary's large downtown buildings, with their internal shopping centres, are connected by above-ground pedestrian walkways called plus-fifteens, for their height, in feet, above the ground. For the book, I decide it might be a fascinating exercise to plus-fifteen it all over the downtown. The notion founders completely when, upon entering one glassy structure, we hear an amplified voice ordering us to do something unintelligible, urgently, then see five yellow firetrucks through the glass. So we go outside and carry on the Four-Hour City in the traditional way, feet on pavement. The Eighth Avenue Mall, which I remember as being seedy, still looks a bit scruffy at its eastern end, but turns rapidly upscale as we head west. It resembles Ottawa's Sparks Street Mall a bit, although it appears healthier.

There are some street musicians. The Book Company, now part of the Chapters chain, has an impressive store. Although I am partial to independent bookstores, I can be won over through such high-powered sales techniques as having one of my books on display. I find one. "This is a quality bookstore," I announce to Nancy and she, having been through many bookstores with me, immediately understands what I mean. I then announce to a store person that I would be glad to sign the copies they have. I can't believe that I, a card-carrying introvert, have done this, and I'm beginning to suspect that I am becoming like my father, who battled what some said was a severe case of shyness, although you could have fooled me, by striking up public conversations with strangers in situations that seemed calculated to provide maximum embarrassment for his children. The tendency for a man to become his father accelerates, I am sure, when the father dies. It could be that when my mother died it tipped me right over the edge.

Anyway, here I am in a bookstore in a city I don't know, talking to bookstore employees who don't know me, and trying to see if Nancy is sidling away, which is what I used to do when my father did this sort of thing. They say sure, sign the books, and I say, ha-ha, that means you can't send them back and they say, ha-ha, yes we can. Oh. Then I ask them to recommend some Alberta fiction I can read while I'm here and they sit me down and bring me a great selection – Aritha van Herk, James Hilles, Thomas Wharton, Darlene Barry Quaife, and Peter Oliva. I'm impressed and heartened to find a bookstore, especially in a chain, that seems to take its responsibility to the writing community seriously and enjoy it too.

Encouraged, we resume our plus-fifteening, noticing what seems to me to be an inordinate number of young men in dark suits. None of them loosens a tie, I notice, even though it's lunchtime. The funny thing about walking around indoors, from building to building, shopping centre to shopping centre, is that you lose all connection with where you would be if you were outside on the street. So it is a bit like being in the country and not having an address. I imagine, then, how you would give directions: Second jewellery store past the Coles, up an escalator, three stores beyond the GrabbaJava and opposite the fountain, but not the one with the chairs around it. You can't miss it.

We have lunch in a hole-in-the-wall sandwich place, then get some coffee and take it up to the Devonian Gardens, which I remember from my last time here. It's two and a half acres of enclosed garden on the top floor of the Toronto Dominion Square. There are shrubs and trees and statues, walkways and benches, artificial and natural light, fountains. Many people bring their lunches and coffee up here and it is easy to see why. It is the indoor equivalent of those little city parks that provide respite from the traffic. Even indoors you have to get away from the traffic.

We cross the Bow River twice on the way out of Calgary and join the crowd headed for Banff. It is a crowd, too, although it is only 2:00 p.m. on a Monday. It is cloudy and at first the mountains are only a shadowy promise, then the land begins to roll and the mountains take shape. Thinking of McCourt and his notion of the best direction from which to approach a place, I think this is a pretty good one. We see the mountains in the distance and gradually are in them. The element of surprise may be lacking, but the sense of anticipation more than makes up for it.

The sense of anticipation seems to be a bit more than some of our fellow drivers can handle. Although the speed limit is 110, they go zooming by anyone going even close to that. Why is it, I wonder out loud, that people drive faster in the mountains than on the prairies, where the roads are better, or at least straighter. Nancy thinks it's because the speed limit is higher but I want a theory with some heft to it. I propose this: that prairie makes you peaceful and unhurried; mountain makes you edgy and rushed. Either that or there is a big shortage of something in Banff and everybody is racing to get there first.

The road between Canmore and Banff is ugly, six lanes with a concrete divider down the middle. As we approach the park gate, we see a board with urgent messages for four people to contact the RCMP. You don't want your name to be there. We buy a seventy-dollar pass that will get us into all the western parks for a year and enter the park, where the road is more pleasant. Rain begins.

We check in at our B&B, which is unassuming-looking on the outside, but has nice rooms. It is right downtown, which may be noisy but also means we don't have to drive in the town. I will like that. George Baptist, who runs the Banff Holiday Lodge, is a pro. He's been in the business longer than anyone we've seen, seven years, and knows the town inside out. One of the good things he does is his own little restaurant guide, which tells you not only what kind of food to expect in each restaurant but what kind of crowd. "The Germans love it," he says of one restaurant popular with the tourists.

We take off on foot in the rain, and find most of the business area is under overhangs or in malls, so we needn't get too wet. We find a Japanese restaurant that isn't on George's list and go in. It is very Japanese, with the specials written on the board in Japanese, not English, and the serving people weak in our language. The cooks and the bartenders bellow at each other, in the Japanese manner. Undoubtedly, this makes the Japanese tourists feel at home. The peculiar effect is to make us feel like foreigners.

It isn't something that bothers me particularly. When I was in high school, we lived two years in Japan and I can't think of any time I enjoyed more. The food is fine, just presented out of order. As we are leaving we see a nice bicultural touch, Banff style. An old Japanese guy emerges from his private booth, and steps into his shoes, which are among those piled outside the rice-paper door. His shoes are brand new Nike Airs, that he might have bought at Athletes World in the Cascade Plaza.

As we stroll a bit in the town, we begin to notice more signs of Banff's peculiarly exotic flavour – for example, a Japanese Old Guy's Hat: SEOUL KOREA 1988 OLYMPICS. And a table in the Cascade Plaza, staffed by two women. It is labelled Refund Service Inc. and it's where you go to get your GST back. There is much to be said for being Japanese.

### Banff Without Tears

I'm up early, not having slept too well last night. We had the window open and heard lots of chatter in the street as the movies and bars let out. City noises take some getting used to. I go out for a paper and walk past a big lineup at a car rental place. It is cloudy, with some fog to the north. The Cascade Coin Laundry is in the Provincial Court Building. This is the extent of my observations.

Back at the Holiday Lodge, we have breakfast with a mother and daughter who turn out to be from Brandon, but who did not have this place recommended to them by the same people who recommended it to us. So it is a small world, but not that small.

We discuss trails. There is also a couple from Kelowna. They and the Brandon couple have a mutual friend, it quickly turns out. It never ceases to amaze me how rapidly you can establish connections in this country, if you try. Later, getting something out of the car, I encounter the Kelowna people again and they offer advice on the different routes to Vancouver. There is very fast, very scenic, and a sort of compromise. As always, I value this advice, coming as it does from people I have never seen before and will never see again. There is something about the jungle telegraph on the highway. People love to pass on tips and share experiences, and I think they are almost always more valuable than what is in the guidebooks. Good as the guidebooks are, they are written with a general audience in mind and don't allow for follow-up questions.

We wander over to the Banff Visitor Centre and pick up a good pamphlet on the trails for a dollar. That's nice. But didn't we just pay a substantial amount to get into the park? How many times do we get nicked in this new pay-as-you-go society?

Enough. We walk along the Fenland Trail, an easy one along the valley floor, featuring spruces and ferns and Echo Creek, which is a nice slate-green colour. The trail description promises us elk, beaver, muskrat, and waterfowl. We don't see any of those. I, of course, am grateful that we don't see any grizzly bears. The park puts out literature that is guaranteed to scare you to death about every local animal, including the apparently tame elk that wander through the streets. We have to watch out for the males in the mating season, females in the calving season. Apart from the most blatantly obvious signs, how are we going to know which season it is? We are having enough trouble with the time zones. Chipmunks seem to be safe enough and we do see some of them, as well as a woodpecker, which sits very quietly, posing a danger only to the tree, while a man with a camera shoots from four or five feet away. It is a lovely, quiet trail, full of big trees and good smells.

We have a good lunch in town, chatting with an Australian waiter who has been here since last November and leaves in a month or so to tour the States before going back. There are many Australians here. In fact, the more we look around, the more we think that Canadians are in the minority. On the way to Tunnel Mountain, which is the walkable mountain around here, we see elk poking around the back lanes and in the parking lot of the Banff Centre. I think if they knew they were dangerous they would stay out of parking lots. In fact, if they knew how danger-ous parking lots are they would stay in the forest.

Tunnel Mountain takes about forty-five minutes to walk up, thirty-five to walk down, and has many Top Ten Belvedere oppor-tunities. About two-thirds of the way up there's a view westward over the town, down into the valley, with mountains all around, some snow-capped. It is spectacular, flawed somewhat by the steady hum of traffic from the town and the nearby highway. Near the top, there is a view to the south that brings in the Mount Rundle range and the Bow River. In the middle of the vista is the Banff Springs Golf Course, which would be pretty if you were on it, but is just another piece of civilization from up high. Perhaps I feel this way because I know how many golf courses humans would put up around here if there were no one to stop them.

The top is identifiable by people having written their names on the rocks there. It is rocky and the edges are steep, but at least there are no signs saying CAUTION: DON'T FALL OFF MOUNTAIN. This is not a mountain you would even brag about climbing, but the views are terrific and it is probably a good test of your fitness level if you are not sure how much hiking you want to do. If you do this one fairly easily, then on to the next. Otherwise, take it easy.

Back in town, we stop at the Grizzly House, a well-known tourist attraction that has a kind of "Northern Exposure" feel to it. We sit outside and watch people go by. Banff is great for that. I am surprising myself by sort of enjoying the place. Yes, Banff is over-commercialized, crowded, and full of tourists. But we're staying right downtown so I don't have to drive in it; if I was driving in Banff I would really hate it. Also, I like Japanese people, so the pro-liferation of them doesn't bother me. The relentlessly upscale com-mercial scene, with its Benettons and Hard Rock Cafés, Spirit of Christmas and Ralph Lauren, should be nauseating, but I find it fascinating. I think this is the Inner Journalist, sensing the presence of Subject Matter.

The waitress tells us the average stay for people is two days, which will be ours, four at the most. Then it gets to be too much for them. It also gets to be too much for the locals, who walk the back lanes (with the elk) to avoid the pedestrian traffic. The con-ventional tourist season slows in September, but conventions keep it going. There are many skiers in the winter, but they mostly stick to their hotels. "We like winter," she says. This echoes what George Baptist has said, back at the B&B. In the summer, he says, you have no idea when the weekend is. If anything, weekends are less busy because Albertans, fearing weekend crowds, stay away. Not much of Banff's traffic is from Alberta anyway. George talks of a won-derful week just before Christmas when the town is all lit up and mostly empty.

Before dinner we go for a major walk around the town. I want to see every restaurant before we decide on the one that we decided upon right at the beginning. Nancy is humouring me, either because "it's for the book" or because she sees me liking Banff and thinks I'm starting to crack. For some reason, I am finding it difficult to be offended, even by the lineups at the fancier restaurants. We are not in that fancy a mood anyway. We wind up at a place called Earls (there are no apostrophes in Alberta, another sign of its secret kinship with Quebec), which is loud, garish, and very cheerful. The place, part of a chain, is jammed but the waiters stay friendly. "Hi, gang, how's it going?" they say to everyone. It is so relentlessly young that you wonder how older people react. I think it's fine and our pizzas are good. And I think it's funny when somebody – probably an American but possibly from B.C. – asks: "Do you know if there's a Starbucks in town?" No. But there are places you can get coffee.

## Our Third World and Welcome to It

By working at it, of course, I can get up a bit of a sense of outrage at the Banff syndrome. It surprised me, at first, how upmarket Banff is. I assumed that all this designer-label stuff is available, just as cheaply, in Japan and Germany. But I guess it's not. What seems to be happening is that our low-valued dollar is luring affluent people from more crowded climes (including the United States) to places like Banff partly because they can get stuff cheap. This is Canada as Third World and it doesn't feel good, just as it can't feel good for the people in Africa and Asia to have relatively wealthy North Americans treat their countries as flea markets.

With this mentality comes the kind of arrogance we usually associate with ourselves in other countries. There is a story about a German tour operator who tried to get the maître d' at a Rockies resort to clear customers from the window seats so that the people on his tour could have them. And there are statistics showing that 94 per cent of tourists at Banff never get more than three metres away from the beaten track, however that is defined. Roughly it means, get on the bus, get off at the scenic lookout, take a picture, get back on the bus.

The up-side of this is that some of the fears about crazed hikers churning up the countryside, trampling all the cinquefoil that grows wild here, may be misplaced, since most visitors never set foot on it.

We will see more of this at Canmore, which is less spoiled but clearly heading that way. On the way, we stop on Wolf Street, so that Nancy can take a picture of Tunnel Mountain, trying to make it look taller. The drive east to Canmore is pleasant, into the haze of the sun, mountains on all sides. Could we get to love mountains? Do people who live with them all year become indifferent to them? In Canmore, when you step out of your house, you see a mountain, no matter which direction you turn. What does that do to you? During our time living in the Prairies, I can remember talking to people who felt claustrophobic in the mountains. I don't feel claustrophobic, but the mountains do stir rather than calm you.

We have a map and good instructions and easily find the B&B, which is called Hogs and Quiches, so help me. Just the name put me off, but George Baptist recommended it, and that's good enough for us. We are learning that B&B people don't make bad recommendations. Hogs and Quiches is on a quiet residential street, with a sign that is more art than advertising. There is a reason for this, according to Brenda Martin, who runs the place with her husband, Tom: Canmore wants $225 for an advertising sign. On top of that, B&B owners, a rapidly increasing breed, want to keep a low profile in their neighbourhoods.

Tom and Brenda have had this operation for three years, with the maximum two B&B rooms allowed by the town. It's interesting how the regulations are different in each community. Although there have always been B&Bs, the field is rapidly expanding. Some towns see this as an opportunity, others as a problem, and the regulations reflect the two points of view. Tom and Brenda's house is new, with a huge, high-ceilinged kitchen/dining room/living room set-up. When Brenda makes breakfast, she looks at the Three Sisters out the kitchen window, which must be inspiring.

You can think of Canmore as Banff for Canadians. It may have begun as a kind of overflow for Banff but it now has its own appeal, even its own tour buses. The town is developing rapidly (population 3,000 in 1978, 8,000 now, and there is a plan for 25,000 not long into the next century), but it does not have the up-market glitz of Banff. But there are several fine restaurants and the carrot-and-orange curry soup on the patio at Sinclairs is as good as any carrot-and-orange curry soup you're going to have on a patio anywhere, probably.

That's the good side of growth. The bad side is that suburban development to the east is up to the fourth bench, as the residents put it, looking at the mountainside. Development has interfered with the corridors normally travelled by game. "As soon as the animals come into town we get cross," says Mary Smith, a friend and local resident. "I lost my tulips to an elk this spring."

We tend to think of how unspoiled a town is when we see or hear of animals on the streets, but it can also mean that the animals have been driven by development into dangerous places. There was a grizzly bear on the same street as our B&B just a few days ago, apparently lured by garbage. So it is perhaps less a question of unspoiled town than of spoiled habitat. Some of the blame is put on so-called weekenders, people from the city whose big new homes are their second or third, and who put out their garbage several days before it can be collected.

Whatever the reason for the animal visits, they seem to have presented a revenue opportunity. A pharmacy has something called Mad Bear pepper spray. Called "a Red Pepper defensive product," it is $55 for an aerosol can the size of a shaving-cream container. The spray, says its advertising, "is incapacitating, causing the bear to cease further aggressive activity." There is a cheaper spray for use on dogs.

The B&B operators are in the middle of the development-versus-habitat argument. They want more tourists but they don't want to lose what attracts them. Many of the people who live in the Rockies, like Tom Martin, are naturalists. They are mountaineers and hikers as well as business people and they know what is at stake. Depending on who is telling you, there were as many as twelve new golf courses being proposed for the area at one point. Now one is being built and the pressure has eased, at least temporarily.

"This is such a nice town," I say to Mary Smith at one point, bowled over by one vista or another.

"Well," she says. "We have our fingers crossed for it."

I know Mary Smith because she is the historian of the local United Church, which happens to be called the Ralph Connor Memorial United Church. A few years ago, when it was having its one-hundredth anniversary, we corresponded. Now she is going to take us through the church.

It is on Eighth Street, one door away from the Northwest Mounted Police Barracks. The church was opened in 1891, the barracks in 1893. They are two of the three oldest buildings in town. The oldest is the Canmore Hotel, opened a year before the church. That seems a logical progression. First the hotel, then the church, then the police. Right across the street in today's Canmore is the Grizzly Paw Pub, about which my grandfather might have had a thing or two to say.

The plaque outside the church, put up by the United Church in 1942, when the church was renamed in his honour, says: IN MEMORIAM REV. C. W. GORDON DD, PIONEER PRESBYTERIAN MISSIONARY, CANADIAN AUTHOR, MINISTER OF THIS CHURCH WHEN BUILT 1890. It is a white frame building with a bell tower and a Canadian flag. In 1984, the church was restored and moved off its rotting foundation a few feet to the west. The province put up some money, which the church matched with the labour of its members. Unlike the church at Glengarry, this one functions the year round. The congregation is active and there is a need to grow, but the church can't really expand any more than it has. Some thought is being given to running two services each Sunday.

Inside, it would be hard to recognize the old church. The pot-bellied stove is gone. The pews are not the originals. There is a piano and an electric organ, instead of the pump organ donated by my grandfather's brother Gilbert. The pulpit furniture and the stained glass windows came after the Second World War. But the members have done a great job of keeping up the history. There are no photographs of Ralph while he was at the church, but photos taken in 1887 and 1895 are on display in the narthex. And there is a wonderful shot of him speaking to a huge crowd on the golf course in Banff. He is standing on a raft in the water hazard of the eighth hole during the Highland Games.

They still have Highland Games in Canmore. Twice today I hear bagpipes in the distance. This would not be my imagination. I don't even like bagpipes.

Other artifacts on display in the church hall include a crucifix of square nails from the original church, made by Ed Scott in 1991. Also under glass is a stick cross which Ralph had made on the Flanders Front for a dying Roman Catholic soldier who had no crucifix. "I see it. I see it," he said, before dying.

The church bell is not the original. It is an old CPR bell. (The CPR, I'm told, used to give ministers free passage to the West.) Mary Smith asks if I'd like to ring the bell, so I do, feeling a sense of family obligation. It takes a strong tug. Then we go to her house for tea and a look at some scrapbooks that contain more church history. There is a photo from 1895 that shows no steeple (this from a post-card made by an itinerant photographer; people had enterprising ways of paying down the deficit even in the last century). There is a photo from 1910 showing the church with a steeple. People have donated old wedding photos, all in the interest of helping to compile a church history, showing how the interior changed. Most interesting to me is a photograph taken at the unveiling in 1942. It shows Chili, my father's cousin, in uniform. Just a few days ago we were looking at his path across the family island.

The Smiths' back deck looks north, out on a backyard full of lodgepole pines, and behind them, of course, mountains. Walking back to the B&B, we drop in on the Canmore Public Library and Art Gallery, where there is a good collection of local art, including photographs by both Mary Smith and her husband, Bob. Close to the Hogs and Quiches, around where the grizzly showed up, we pass workers and a sign announcing that luxury chalets and condominiums are going up.

### Extras in a Home Video

We are sitting at breakfast Thursday morning, looking at mountains, when we hear voices coming up the stairs. Heather Camargo is talking to Brenda Martin and Heather's husband, Juan Pablo, is talking to the video camera he is carrying. Heather and Juan Pablo are on their honeymoon and they are recording it for posterity.

As they enter the room, Juan Pablo announces to us that we are about to be part of the video. "What's my motivation?" I say, ever the ready wit. There is no laugh at all and I suddenly flash forward a year, to the 127th time Juan Pablo and Heather are showing their wedding trip to their friends back in Miami. "Here's where the Canadian says that dumb thing," one of them says, as the camera mounts the stairs in the Canmore B&B.

Well, nothing I can do about it. I can hardly ask them to edit me out. We just met.

There is a guest book, into which some of our predecessors have put rather emotional words about their strong feelings about mountains and Canmore and breakfast and whatnot. Some of them seem to have had their lives changed. Mind you, few of them are Canadians. Even if their lives *had* changed, Canadians wouldn't share that fact with strangers. Brenda Martin says that hardly any of her guests are Canadians. Most are Americans and Germans. "Great breakfast," I write, feeling as if I am letting the side down.

The Camargos will have lots to put in the book. Heather, an artist in Miami, saw a television show about the Canadian Rockies and decided this was the place for her honeymoon. Her sister, who works for an airline, arranged the whole trip. She and Juan Pablo, who just graduated in industrial engineering, got married on Saturday. They flew to Dallas, then to Calgary, and here they are. Already they've been whitewater rafting, seen Moraine Lake, which "seemed less commercialized" than Lake Louise, had lunch on the terrace of the Banff Springs Hotel, peeked into some of the rooms to see how fancy they are, and taken in the Ride 'n Dine Dinner and Theatre at Lake Louise, getting a meal that was better than they expected and a performance of *Romeo and Juliet* that was very professional. They want to canoe and hike some more.

I think of the Camargos a few miles down the road, west of Banff, when we meet a throng of people who couldn't be less enthusiastic about anything. This is at Johnston Canyon, on the way to Lake Louise. Someone warned us about construction on Highway 1, so we take 1A, the best detour we may ever see. Highway 1A runs through the forest, the trees so close and high that you sometimes lose sight of the mountains. It is the kind of road that when you are forced to slow down behind a trailer you consider yourself lucky. During one such lucky incident we catch sight of a big bull moose in the woods.

Seeing Johnston Canyon, we pull off, remembering that one of our B&B confrères at Banff had said it was beautiful. A little hike will be nice, we think, as we pull off into a big parking lot that is as crowded as a shopping centre two Saturdays before Christmas. Cars are circling, waiting for other cars to back out. This is the most dramatic evidence yet that we are in another phase of the trip.

But we must be brave. Finding a parking space we set out on a short walk to the lower falls, 1.1 kilometres. The setting is not exactly primitive, a paved catwalk, carefully fenced along the entire route, but the canyon is terrific, a fast-flowing stream of jade-coloured water through a towering forest, Top Ten Belvedere candidates all along. The accompanying signage is a bit melodramatic, making me think of the Parks Canada copywriter we encountered back at the Cabot Trail, the one who made the other trees sneer at the little jack pine. The one here verges on suicidal. "Some day it will be gone," he writes of the canyon, after tracing its history. And later: "Nothing lasts forever, not cliffs, not creeks, not canyons."

Perhaps it is these expressions of melancholy that have depressed our fellow travellers, because they could not be a gloomier lot.

There are hundreds of them and they trudge solemnly along, eyes down, never pausing to say "Wow!", looking as if they are trying to decide if they are getting their money's worth. Among those we pass is a candidate for Top Ten Rottenest Mother. She has two boys with her, one of whom has to go get something. "I've got an idea. I'll time you and if you're not back, you're in the car. I give you one of these," she says, in an eastern seaboard American accent, waving an umpire's thumb, "you're in the car." I wonder if this is just a function of stress caused by overcrowding and whether similar stuff is going on right now on the Cabot Trail.

Despite all this, I'm having a good time here, because the canyon is so thrilling. I want to cheer these people up, make them feel welcome. I want to say: Look at this, this is Canada, look how great it is. Enjoy it. I don't, of course. We settle for trying to be Canadian goodwill ambassadors, smiling and saying hello to people as we pass them on the path. But it is impossible to achieve even eye contact, much less a smile in return. It's like walking in the city. A grizzly bear would be the sentimental favourite in this crowd.

I am cheered by seeing an Old Guy's Hat – CONFEDERATE AIR FORCE – and I see a cute little girl nose to nose with a chipmunk – or at least what she thinks is a chipmunk. It could be a ground squirrel. If it is, that's one. And as we walk back from the falls, I hear the following comment from a ten-year-old boy to his friend, standing over a beautiful pool: "They have a bit longer fangs than the cobra."

So I am still in a good frame of mind when we reach Château Lake Louise. This is to be another big blowout for us, justified partly by the desire to check out another big railway hotel "for the book," and also by the fact that Nancy's mother worked here about sixty years ago. She will be delighted to know that we are here.

The lobby is a good one, with a substantial bell-captain's desk, a big double staircase leading up to the mezzanine. Our room is small but classy, with the usual heavy doors and that stupid big piece of furniture that hides the TV set. I begin to think approvingly of some of the rural homes we've seen in the last few weeks: a great big television set put prominently in the living room where everyone can look at it. That's more honest. A notice by this TV tells us how to get pizza, which speaks to the democratization of the premises.

The view is not bad. (Not bad? Someone who had not been exposed to non-stop mountains for the last four days would call it spectacular.) It is not a lake view. It is called a mountain view, and it is that. To get to the mountains, your eye must first travel over the parking lot. We are not going to let the fact that the room costs $279 bother us. For $219 we would have faced in on the courtyard. And a lake view would have cost $359.

Never mind. We make a reservation in one of three dining rooms for dinner, then find, in this vast hotel complex, yet another restaurant, called Poppy's, and have lunch. Lunch is fine and there are bright orange and yellow poppies out the window, green grass, blue sky, the lake beyond. The highlight of the lunch is an announcement over the PA system of a fire test about which we should not worry. So we don't. More worried are the waiters and waitresses whose function it is to stand at something like attention and not serve anyone until the non-emergency passes. All announcements are made in two languages: English and Japanese.

So far so good. The hotel is fun to prowl around. It has the same kind of upscale stores (with Japanese staff) as downtown Banff, including the Spirit of Christmas. This is yet another of the many phenomena I don't understand. Why would you shop for Christmas stuff in July in a hotel in Lake Louise? There is also a tiny but very good bookstore, Mountain Lights, which is full of Canadian books. I talk briefly to the manager, George Tutt, who says visitors want to read Canadian books and he makes a point of pushing them.

I am having a tough time figuring out how I feel about this place. There is beauty and elegance. And there is also a kind of weirdness that I find fascinating – the completely numbed looks on the faces of the people who get off the buses and stand in the lobby, waiting for someone to tell them what to do; the sign announcing a performance of Sebastian at the Zither, making me think of Horatio at the Bridge; the official group photograph place, by the poppies, where a photographer assembles tour groups, and how would you like that job? Weirdest of all is the spectacle of hundreds of people standing, just standing, at the spot beside the lake from which the lake looks just like the lake on all the photographs of the lake. Some of them take still pictures of the lake looking just like the pictures of the lake. Some of them take videos. I think we are extras in hundreds of amateur videos. We will be seen in living rooms in many countries of the world, although not, I suspect, in Canada.

We walk by, trying not to wave at the cameras, and go to the canoe rental place. There is no point being at Lake Louise without paddling down to the end of it. The only trouble is that it costs $22 an hour for a rather tublike canoe. This too is part of the equation of conflicting emotions at this Canadian landmark: the feeling of being ripped off. If you pay more than $200 a night for a hotel room, couldn't they throw in a crummy canoe ride? (At Manoir Hovey they do, I remember.)

But off we go. That nice blue-green water is murky when you're on it but the paddle is peaceful, the only sound being the chatter of people on the hiking trails around the lake. There must be a lot of them. Out on the lake, with the mountains looming overhead and the glacier down at the end, you would have to be very hard-hearted not to be impressed.

On the way back to the hotel we read a plaque about Tom Wilson, the first white man to see this lake, on August 24, 1882. This was less than ten years before my grandfather arrived on the scene. In the lobby I count the number of tours listed on a board: sixteen. Talking to different hotel people, we get varying percentages of how many guests are on tours. They start at 80 per cent and go much higher. You can look at that two ways, depending on your state of grouchiness: either ordinary Canadians paying full price are subsidizing the Americans and Germans and Japanese; or else the Germans, Japanese, and Americans are helping to keep open a Canadian landmark that otherwise would go under for lack of paying guests.

Before we go to dinner, we phone Betty, Nancy's mother, in Peterborough. She is delighted that we are at Lake Louise, but disappointed that we are not on the lake side. She tells us that when she worked here, the lakeside rooms were $17 and the mountain view rooms were $15.

In the Tom Wilson dining room on the seventh floor, we pay more than we have paid for any other meal on the trip ($103.16) for a dinner that is good, but not that good, in fact nowhere as good as the meal we had last night in a tiny restaurant in Canmore. We have a window seat overlooking the lake, and the waitress, who is from Quebec, is nice. But we have to listen to some Americans from a tour who complain constantly about the service. I suspect they may have no idea where they are. Perhaps they are used to having the food on the table when they sit down. The mixed emotions come in again: I want to defend this Canadian institution from unfair foreign attacks; and I want the institution to be worth defending.

To top off my confusing day, I strike up a conversation, in the manner of my father, with some Japanese in the elevator. Japan has just defeated the United States at baseball in the Olympics and I say something congratulatory about that to the man standing beside me. He stares uncomprehendingly at me. A woman chimes in helpfully that she doesn't follow baseball, but knows Nomo, the Japanese pitcher for the Los Angeles Dodgers. I smile to cover my shock over the sudden realization that this man can travel to Canada and tour the Rockies, probably the entire country, without having to understand our language. My outrage lasts about as long as it takes me to realize that he is only doing in our country what we do in his.

### Up to Lake Agnes, Without Even a Sapling

One of the things Betty said last night on the phone was that we must make sure to walk up to Lake Agnes. We set out at 8:30, perhaps expecting an easy climb because Nancy's mother recommended it. We forget that Nancy's mother was probably thirty years younger than we are now when she last did the walk. It is a tough uphill climb that takes a solid hour. On the plus side, it affords a great high view of Lake Louise, and of Mirror Lake, which we encounter near the top. Also, we get completely out of range of our fellow guests, who don't seem to have this one on their tour agendas. Lake Agnes, when we get there, is clearer than Lake Louise, and a more conventional colour. The tea house is closed, but we rest a bit, looking at old photographs showing climbers from the twenties, I would guess, men in ties, women in long skirts, having tea.

It reminds me of a story by my grandfather I just read, contained in an anthology someone recommended to me called *Tales from the Canadian Rockies*. His story, called "How We Climbed Cascade," was published in the *Canadian Alpine Journal* in 1907. Cascade is a real mountain, a nasty-looking rocky thing dominating the view to the north from Banff, not at all like the little things we walked up, and he did his climb in 1891, before hiking boots with air cushions and gel in the heels were invented. There were six of them, three women. "Without trail, without guide, but knowing that the top was up there somewhere, we set out, water-bottles and brandy-flasks – in case of accident – and lunch baskets slung at the belts of the male members of the party, the sole shred of mountaineering equipment being the trunk of a sapling in the hand of each ambitious climber."

The climb, up and back, takes four days. Some of the long skirts have been torn to make bandages. "There are no words to paint these peaks," my grandfather wrote, upon achieving the top. Upon achieving the bottom, he wrote: "It takes us a full week, the greater part of it spent in bed, to realize that mountain-climbing, *sans* guides, *sans* mountaineering boots, *plus* petticoats, is a pastime for angels perhaps, but not for fools."

Up here, at Lake Agnes, I ask a Japanese couple if they have ever climbed Mount Fuji, and which is higher. They say they have, and that this is higher. Later we see the same couple at breakfast back at the hotel. With true pioneering spirit, we have not waited for the tea house to open but have flung ourselves back down the mountain, without even a sapling.

Over breakfast, I thumb through the newspaper. It is different now to look at a newspaper and see echoes of where you have been, even when they are unpleasant echoes, an elevator fire at Brooks, a mass shooting at Gore Bay. While Nancy checks out, and gives a little pep talk to the hotel, I wait for the car and look for Old Guy's Hats. I am rewarded with ALEXANDER GRAHAM BELL MUSEUM, taking us back to Cape Breton, which is not bad.

We drive to Moraine Lake, another shopping-centre parking-lot situation, but we are getting used to it now, grudgingly consenting to share the road. The lake itself is amazing, a deep blue-green quite unlike Lake Louise, clearer, and, to my mind, more beautiful. There is a sound like traffic, but I think it is the wind, along with the fall of an outflowing stream.

I am fascinated now by the interpretive panel-writer's art. This may be the same writer who did Johnston Canyon. "What about the future?" he writes. "Will glaciers scour the valley again? Will the mountains crumble and wash away? Only time will tell." I picture him, depressed and perhaps with a hangover, trying to finish Moraine Lake before lunch.

We drive back to the Trans-Canada, admiring the wild flowers, which are getting almost as much attention as chipmunks (or maybe ground squirrels) from the amateur photographers. We are out of Lake Louise at 1:15 and into British Columbia seven

minutes later, across the Continental Divide and into Kicking
Horse Pass, where the descent is felt in the ears. The road is fine,
but you tend to do the corners at the speed you are advised to. This
is not always easy with a guy from Alberta (they are always from
Alberta, I am starting to notice) tailgating you.

Around Field, we leave the highway for a thirteen-kilometre
drive to Takakkaw Falls, which is billed as Canada's largest unin-
terrupted drop. We stop at the Meeting of the Rivers, where the
silty Yoho joins the clear Kicking Horse and silt wins the day. This
is all new to us and quite wonderful. Nancy is driving when we
encounter our first serious switchback, which is done very carefully, the turn being so severe that you look behind you to see if
anyone is coming towards you. On the way back we will see a tour
bus and wonder what it would be like to meet it in the middle of
the switchback. Is it time to do something about tour buses, or is
it just me?

The falls, which we walk quite a distance to see, along with
many others, including our Japanese friends from Lake Agnes, are
spectacular and will get you wet if you walk too close, which we
do. They pour down a 254-metre cliff, making a noise that sounds,
in the middle distance, like a jet plane passing overhead.

Onward we go, not knowing exactly where we will be tonight,
thinking of heading in the direction of the Okanagan and aiming
for somewhere around Revelstoke, maybe. We have three days to
reach Vancouver and are in no hurry, mostly concerned with
adjusting our notion of what constitutes a Top Ten Belvedere.
Whereas a big-time vista really sticks out in Ontario or Quebec,
it's like a scenery machine around here. If there isn't a mountain,
there's a river, or a lake, and often there's a mountain *and* a river
*and* a lake. Plus, at regular intervals, thin and high waterfalls down
the side of every mountain.

As if to keep drivers from getting too happy about all this, the
highway keeps up a steady nag of warnings. Look out for moose,

look out for mountain goats, look out for construction, look out for avalanches. We are already looking out for the guy from Alberta. The standard sequence begins with a sign telling trucks that warning signs are coming up, then the warning signs tell the trucks (and eavesdropping cars) that a steep downgrade is ahead and there is a spot ahead for them to pull off and test their brakes. Then, as we start down the hill, another sign says there's a runaway lane ahead, the runaway lane being what you turn onto, if you can, when your brakes don't work.

All it takes, after a while, is the sign saying TRUCK NOTICE AHEAD to start that sinking feeling.

We stop at the beginning of the Rogers Pass for coffee from the Thermos, pondering how it must have looked to A. B. Rogers when he first hit it in 1881. It was only four years later that the first railway went over it. That process would take much longer now, what with all the politicians saying we can't afford it. Soon we travel through snowsheds, which look like tunnels from the inside, but are really just roofs over the road to keep the avalanches off, which I don't resent at all. A bighorn sheep is standing beside the road, with his back to us. We cross the Columbia River several times, thinking about how the road goes, the decisions that had to be made, which side of the river to be on. At one point, we drop down and are driving along the valley floor beside the river and I catch myself thinking: That's better. I think this is my proper relationship to mountains. Me down here with the river. The mountain up there.

Because we are in our own little time bubble, we have forgotten that we are driving on the Friday of another long weekend, although the heavy traffic should tell us. So we pass on some vacancies at Revelstoke, only to encounter NO VACANCY signs further on at Sicamous. Oops. Since we are psychologically incapable of turning back, we are thinking of Vernon, another eighty kilometres down the less-travelled 97A. It is not late, especially given the time change, but we are spooked now. We've never been in B.C. on the August long weekend. Maybe there's no such thing as a motel room.

Ah, but the spirit of Pollyanna of Green Gables is with us, and causes us to notice a B&B sign, just ten kilometres south of Sicamous. We find the Swansea Point Bed and Breakfast, and there is a room, a comfortable modern room with a big comfy chair right next to the three-prong plug for the computer. Never in doubt, as they used to say when the Expos won in fifteen innings.

Michaela and Allan Husband are friendly, their house is spotless, and they direct us on a nice walk through the drizzle to a roadside restaurant called The Bears Den, which has a bear motif. I have the perogy special and it is just right. I have never ordered perogies in a restaurant before. It must have something to do with being in B.C.

# 16

‒‒‒‒‒‒‒‒‒‒‒‒‒‒‒‒‒‒‒‒‒‒‒‒‒‒‒‒‒‒‒‒‒‒

## *Talk about Distinct*

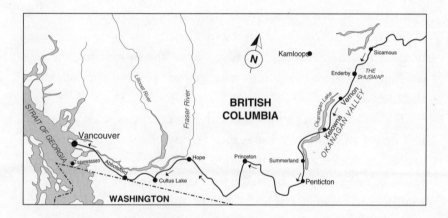

Now we have to learn about B.C. But there are so many different parts of B.C. and they are all so different that the Inner Journalist is worried. Here in the Shuswap, at the edge of the Okanagan, we hear talk of ginseng, the newest cash crop. Allan and Michaela Husband are talking about it over breakfast. It is lucrative, takes four years to produce, is grown under dark plastic and may in the long run damage the soil. But people are trying it out. We should watch for it. If we see a field that looks like it's covered in green garbage bags, that's it.

Allan and Michaela have had this place for five years. At one point it was the only B&B in a twelve-mile (they talk in miles here too) stretch of highway. Now there are nine. The Husbands rent out two rooms. Their guests are from all over, many of them from Germany.

Allan says his friends warned him about getting ripped off when he first went into business, but he has nothing but warm thoughts about his guests. "The kinds of people who go to bed-and-breakfasts are really first-rate," he says. "We've never lost a face cloth." He accepts personal cheques, as opposed to credit cards, and has never had a problem with that. It is nice to be where people trust each other.

We leave around 10:00 a.m., heading south, probably for Penticton. We drive along Mara Lake, in a light rain. This is supposed to be the houseboat capital of Canada but this is not house-boating weather. Although we are out of the mountains, the hills are high and there is cloud in patches over parts of the valley and the lake.

The most striking thing about the landscape is what grows on it. I begin to compile a list – apricots, peaches, Colorado spruce, apples, ginseng – as we drive along a fairly narrow two-lane road. Just south of Enderby, the traffic jams up, then stops. Way down the road there is police activity. We wait and finally a policewoman drives back from the front and talks to the drivers in the line. "You'll have to turn around and I'll show you a little detour around the accident." This is thoughtful, but imagine an entire highway doing a U-turn. It takes quite a time. While we're sitting there, we watch alpacas and llamas in the field next to us. So alpacas and llamas grow here too. As we edge along, we watch horses running through a field and birds fly up out of it. Since we are not in a hurry, we can enjoy the scene, disturbed only by a guy from Alberta sneaking by on the shoulder. Eventually we get on the detour and see ginseng, cows, and ostriches. This is some valley.

The road takes us down the main street of Vernon, then past Kalamalka Lake. It is a beautiful drive and I'm having my usual difficulty absorbing it all – for example, the fact that yesterday we were in the Rogers Pass and today we're in a valley surrounded by fruits and vegetables. Maybe the problem is thinking about writing what we are seeing instead of just looking at it. We talked last night, after learning that we are not on the Port Hardy ferry yet, about maybe finding a nice place and just staying a couple of days in which I wouldn't write and think, just read and goof off. Vancouver Island might be the place for this.

Kelowna's billboard and junk food strip seems to last forever, the longest I can recall seeing, but eventually we cross Okanagan Lake on Canada's longest floating bridge. Then we see a sign that says this is where Ogopogo, Canada's longest floating sea monster, hangs his or her hat. They just keep trotting this stuff out for us.

We pass Peachland, an accurate name, incredibly, then stop for lunch at Summerland, which seems accurate also. We reach Penticton in mid-afternoon and luck into a room at the Riordan House, a place that goes back to 1921. Just ten minutes ago they had a cancellation. The room, one of the biggest we've had, is just stuffed with period furniture and art. The proprietor, John Ortiz, collects a kind of art called gesso, the word defined as "gypsum or plaster of Paris prepared with glue for use as a surface for painting." Some of the paintings resemble the work of Maxfield Parrish, definitely an acquired taste. John's collection ranges from 1887 to 1936.

Nancy takes the car and the laundry and I walk downtown. Penticton is like Canmore in that everywhere you look there's scenery, with a lake to the north, another to the south. When you gaze down Orchard Avenue you're looking down the valley. I stop at a place on Main Street and have an iced cappuccino, just to mark the fact that I'm in B.C. It is one of at least five coffee places I see, which seems like quite a few for a city of 27,000. It is certainly a different culture. There is a place called Bubblee's Cold Beer and Wine, which is a long way from the Liquor Control Board of Ontario. With the ghost of Ralph hovering over me, I can't say in which direction it is a long way.

Penticton's downtown seems to go on forever, which I admire. It is as if the big suburban mall either hasn't arrived or has been vanquished. The streets are quite busy too, for a Saturday afternoon, with many cruising kids. Later I am told that this is almost an official weekend for that – cruising in cars. People come from miles around to Penticton on the August long weekend and drive up and down in cars. "Be careful out there tonight," the waitress tells us at the restaurant where we have dinner. So we're careful. We go home and go to sleep. Mind you, that's what we would have done if we *weren't* being careful.

The restaurant, recommended to us by John Ortiz, is called Granny Bogner's and it is very good, a stately old house, tastefully decorated, with friendly and competent waitresses, excellent food, and Bill Evans playing on the muzak. It is not expensive either, just a bit more than half of what we paid at Château Lake Louise. In the afternoon we watched Canada beat the United States in the 4x100 relay race at the Olympics. It has put everyone in the restaurant in a festive mood.

This is one more illustration of the absolute necessity of accepting the advice of your host. In Canmore the other night we went, at the recommendation of Brenda Martin, to a Swiss/German place called the Peppermill and it was excellent, a bit less fancy than this one, but with a nice ease and informality. We start compiling, on this the forty-ninth day, a list of the best meals we've had. So far, they've all been in small places – Trout River, North Hatley, Tobermory, Canmore, Penticton.

## A Highway Called Hope

Here is the perfect example of why people who like to meet people like bed-and-breakfasts. At one big table in the Riordan House are:

1. A middle-aged couple from Ottawa driving across the country;

2. A young couple from England taking five weeks to do B.C. on the cheap;

3. A teacher who leads tours from Japan;

4. A middle-aged couple from Surrey, B.C., in town for a square-dance competition.

Over the course of a pleasant half-hour breakfast, we learn that Penticton is a square-dance capital. We learn that some tour leaders ask to be seated away from their tours on the plane. We learn that if you know what you are doing, you can find rooms for the night on university campuses. We learn that if we are driving into Vancouver on the Monday of the August long weekend, good luck to us.

Today, Sunday, we are going to rest up for that by stopping at Cultus Lake, not too far from Vancouver. The road out of Penticton, once we find it, takes us past Lake Skaha, where jetskis buzz around and people are jammed together with their trucks, campers, cars, and selves.

We turn southwest onto 3A and then 3, the so-called Hope–Princeton Highway. There are several different routes to Vancouver. Good friends in Brandon boosted the new Coquihalla Highway. Relatives preached a more northerly route, through Lillooet and down the Fraser River. So of course, I chose a route given to us by people we'd just met in a B&B parking lot in Banff. Such is the kinship of the road.

And it turns out to be a pleasant and interesting route, first with ranches and orchards, then hills and rivers, the hills having a distinctly parched look to them. We stop at a fruit stand, marvelling at the range of stuff available. I buy an apricot. I spot salmon jerky for sale and don't buy it, but add it to my collection of things that distinguish B.C. from other provinces, filed next to paintball, for which we have seen three facilities in two days. The Inner Journalist wants it to mean something that people charge around shooting paint pellets at each other in British Columbia. But it's just as likely these courses (ranges? battlefields?) won't exist in a year. They'll be replaced by ginseng ranches, the paintball moving to Prince Edward Island where Inner Journalists will posit a theory about the Fixed Link bringing simulated violence to the island.

For a time we have sage and mountains to the right and the clear, fast, and pebbly Similkameen River to our left. We stop at Bromley Rock Provincial Park where the narrow river is deep green in colour, fast, and perhaps four feet deep in the middle. I have my apricot and enjoy the scene, the moment being spoiled by yet another example of a little kid being threatened. This one, a cute little blonde girl, is being told that if she doesn't behave it will be "the truck." Isn't it a bit counterproductive to make the kid fear the truck, since she's got to spend her days in it whether she's good or not? "If you don't behave you're going to have to get into the truck . . . Now get into the truck." Something about being cooped up makes people stupid. Not us, though.

Lunch is in a fish-on-the-wall kind of place called Eastgate Lodge just east of Manning Provincial Park, on the way to Hope. There are no actual fish on the wall, but it has that feeling, also poutine on the menu, which I never eat, but am always glad to see for the feeling of biculturalism in cholesterol it signifies. There are people at five tables and the occupants of one begin chatting with the occupants of another about where they are from, and the cold winters. Turns out they are both from the Prairies, one from Reston, Manitoba, near Brandon. A woman at a third table interrupts: "I'm from the coldest place: southern Saskatchewan." She has a Brandon connection, too, and she and the Reston man begin discussing Simpson-Sears. It turns out they both worked for the company. Then a woman at the fourth table chips in that she also lived in Brandon and the conversation gathers momentum. The waitress laughs, and so do we, watching it all unfold. Finally, I volunteer that it is unanimous: that everybody in the restaurant is, in one way or another, from Brandon. This is followed by a lengthy who-do-you-know? conversation. As we pay our bills and prepare to head west or east, we all wish each other well. What if we were all from Ontario? Would there even have been a conversation?

In the park, we stop in what is now heavy rain to take a little stroll at Sumallo Grove, on the west side of the Allison Pass, which features old growth. To our unspoiled eyes, it is a marvel – hemlock and cedar, four, five, and six feet across. We are in B.C. for sure. We walk in the rain and read some interpretive panels telling us what all these huge things are. Part of that nice smell seems to be wild ginger.

As we drive on, we are back in mountains now, as well as back in the fog. Out of the park we stop at the Hope Slide Viewpoint, where four people died and Outram Lake was buried on January 9, 1965. Not thinking of that as very long ago, I have a suspicious look at the hills. Even history is young out here. For some reason there is a sign saying PLEASE LIMIT YOUR STAY TO EIGHT HOURS. Don't worry.

The roads are steep and curvy and a Jeep from Alberta passes while we're doing 110. Is it Ralph Klein causing all that? We see another Alberta vehicle, a truck pulling a camper with four bicycles on top. The camper and RV world out here is rather overwhelming. So is the rain. So is the traffic. After Hope we join the Trans-Canada and Nancy is trying to keep up with it, while I keep my foot firmly on the brake on the passenger side. Finally, I make a helpful suggestion, something along the lines of "For Christ's sake, slow down!" This does not make the ride any more pleasant during the next stage of the drive, which consists of getting lost in Cultus Lake. Cultus Lake is tiny and impossible to get lost in, unless you drive along the wrong side of the lake.

All bad things come to an end, eventually, though, and we have a good fried-chicken dinner at the Aquadel Golf Course restaurant with our friend Evelyn Kipp. She is eighty-one, spry and quick-witted. Over the din of the Olympic Games' closing ceremonies on the television set, she talks about having lived here fifty years, the last twelve of it by herself. Cultus Lake is a pretty cottage community with some permanent houses, surrounded by provincial campgrounds, with stores out by the road. But the isolation can be troubling, as in last winter when a huge storm knocked over some trees. On the other hand, the way the community is changing makes isolation look better all the time: there are more permanent houses and more traffic, more influence of the city, which is only an hour away. There is a tiny house, a cross between a bungalow and a shack, down by the water that is for sale for $200,000.

On the way back to Evelyn's house, we take a nice loop up into the hills, looking down onto the lake, then past dairy farms, down into old growth woods, then out and along the Washington border. At one point, the border is carved into a hill, a wide straight strip with no trees. That's attractive.

## The Wrong Way into Vancouver

From Cultus Lake to Vancouver is almost as much north as west. Initially the road takes us through dense brush and signs advertising rabbits, horses, ducks and geese, hogs, blueberries and strawberries. Yarrow has a very postwar look and houses with blue hydrangeas. Highway 1 is encountered at Abbotsford. It is already crowded at 10:30 but the traffic moves along and there seems to be as much coming out as going in. The highway is divided, attractively, with trees on both sides, which hide the scenery but also probably hide the sprawl. Haze begins to appear as we near the city, crossing the Fraser River which is gentle and wide. We pass Port Coquitlam, Burnaby, and enter the city quite easily. There is something I might call the Law of Apprehension that accompanies me when I travel. If I fuss about traffic or missing a plane, it never happens, which is the up side. The down side is that one develops a certain reputation.

I remember, as we drive in, that the flashing green, which you see at many intersections in the approach to downtown, doesn't mean what it means in the East, namely, that you can turn left across the traffic. It also doesn't mean what it means in Regina, whatever that is. What it means here I can't remember either. This enables me to give more helpful driving advice in the days ahead.

We are splurging on a big downtown hotel on Robson Avenue. As splurge money goes, it is not in the class of the Château Lake Louise, but it is not exactly a B&B either. All of the ones Nancy phoned were booked solid (as is the Port Hardy ferry, still), another discouraging sign that we are not alone any more. But the Blue Horizon is a thoroughly professional operation, one of those hotels that give you the sense that people know what they are doing. The room has everything, is laid out efficiently, has lots of space, windows that open and air-conditioning that works, functioning coffeemaker, remote control, everything. The view, from the ninth-floor balcony, including the street below, is striking.

Thinking of McCourt's notion about the best way to approach Kenora, I have a theory of my own about Vancouver. The last time I was here was about a year and a half ago when John was in Vancouver studying theatre. I flew in at night, then went for dinner with him and some of his friends. The next morning, I woke up, looked out my hotel room window, and there was a mountain. What a pleasant shock to my Central Canadian system.

This time, after driving out through the Rockies and the Selkirks and the Cascades, we no longer feel the same impact of mountains. Which is not to say we are not impressed, just that we are not stunned.

We will be here a couple of days and decide to spend them on foot. Vancouver is a great walking city, although a bit spread out, but the bus system is okay and I used it the last time.

For some reason, my sense of north and south gets really screwed up out here. It may be because the downtown is tilted a bit. The approaches are north–south and then it goes a bit wonky. So do we. Both Nancy and I have been here just enough to think we know where we're going and not long enough to know. So our first outing on foot, which is to get the ferry over to Granville

Island, takes quite a bit longer than it should. I am completely confident, after we walk ten minutes or so, that we are going the wrong way. So we go the other way for quite a while before I, humbly but perhaps a bit late, admit I was wrong.

The ride, on False Creek Ferries, takes two minutes and costs $1.75. It is a funny little corklike oval ferry, with a bench around the inside, and a capacity of fifteen or twenty. Apparently it was made specifically for this purpose. Once onto Granville Island we stop at the first restaurant we see, sit on the patio, and I order a vegetarian something, just to get in the West Coast spirit of it. It is warm and sunny, but cools quickly when the sun drops behind a cloud, a feature of climates without humidity.

I think we are having a little culture shock here. It comes from driving, getting out of the car and suddenly being thrust among large crowds of people in a place we don't know. Much as I admire Vancouver, love the climate and the setting, there is something about the city that begs to be mocked and I have a difficult time resisting it. What can you do when you walk into a large craft store that has its Mission Statement printed in big letters over the cash? How else can you treat all this coffee stuff?

We walk Granville Island, conscious that this, the Monday of the long weekend, and a nice day too, might not be the ideal day for it. There are so many people. And cars. Why in the world would cars be allowed in this place? They can barely move, for one thing. For another, when they do move they interfere with the freedom of people walking. At the helpful and well-organized information centre, the suggestion on one of the panels is made that it is somehow a virtue to allow cars and pedestrians to coexist. Not today.

The aim of the redevelopment of the island, it is said, is "to recycle an industrial neighbourhood" and this has been done beautifully, aside from letting the cars crawl around. The island is pleasant and interesting, trendy but not phoney, distinctly urban, but softened by the nearness of water. In the markets, a central

Canadian can gawk at all the varieties of fish. There is a good bookstore, many galleries, and a nice park adjoining an area where kids can ride a waterslide and spray each other with water out of hydrants. That's something else that strikes you out here: the attitude to water. There's lots, kids. Spray it around. There is a kids-only market and quite a few rather upmarket businesses, such as International Yacht Brokers. I suspect that on a more ordinary day, this would be a terrific, laid-back place. Right now, laid-back might not be the word for it. I see another child threatened in a store, her father saying "Erin, should I get your little ear again?"

Off the ferry, back at Beach Avenue, we dodge skaters and bicycles and look out to English Bay, picking freighters out of the haze. Around us people lie along the grass. Behind them and across the street are apartment buildings. We walk back to the hotel behind two kids wearing mice (or maybe rats, but I don't want to think about it) on their shoulders; we walk past a park with a sign saying NO PERSON PERMITTED IN THIS PARK 10 PM TO 6 AM. I run into a journalist friend who used to live in Ottawa. Finding out where we're staying, he says we're lucky. Robson Street is his favourite street in Canada.

Nancy makes some unsuccessful calls trying to find us places to stay in Victoria and Tofino, and the Inland Passage ferry is still saying call again tomorrow. Then we go out to dinner. Dinner is at the ballpark, Nat Bailey Stadium, which we get to by taking a bus through some fairly seedy areas of the city. The stadium, however, is in the middle of an agreeable residential area. It's a great old stadium, opened in 1951 with a capacity of 6,500. Average attendance has been 4,751. Old-style pillars hold the roof up. Seats extend only a bit past the bases, to the edge of the outfield grass. The scoreboard is the traditional kind, with the numbers lowered into place, rather than flashed upon a screen. There is also an auxiliary scoreboard that gives batting average, home runs, and RBIs, but no fancy stuff. No imploring the crowd for NOISE / BRUIT, like we are used to seeing at home.

We have a fine seat, just past first base, half a dozen rows up, and the tickets cost $7.50. There is a nice small-town feeling to the stadium, although the concourse area offers an amazing variety of food and, it goes without saying, many kinds of coffee. The outfield wall offers the full range of advertising signs, from Earls to the Forest Alliance of British Columbia.

The Vancouver Canadians, their uniforms reminiscent, and not at all accidentally, of a beer label, are the Triple-A farm team of the California Angels. They are playing the Edmonton Trappers, whose parent team is the Oakland Athletics. As in the games we see in Ottawa, once and future major-leaguers are on the field, as well as some players who are just holding down spots until a real prospect comes along. The home team gets off to an early lead and keeps it. Along with the pleasant temperature, that keeps the fans happy. Adding to their joy is a steady succession of the most truly goofy between-innings promotions I have ever seen. I had never seen the one where the first fan who phones an order to Kentucky Fried Chicken gets it free. In simpler times, that would have meant a rush for the pay phones. Now, it just means people haul phones out of their pockets or purses and call from their seats. Then two tourists from Britain get to throw a ball against a five-foot-wide screen from about ten feet away, the one achieving the greatest velocity winning a full-length mirror from Crystal Glass. Just what a tourist from Britain needs most. Perhaps it is the thought of carrying the full-length mirror back that causes both to miss the screen completely on their second tosses.

The crowd loves all this stuff, loves all the dumb mascots, the blue Smurf and the yellow chicken and the fox that races a young kid around the bases. The kid starts at home plate and the fox is already at second but somehow the cheers of the crowd and the fox's unaccountable combination of hubris and clumsiness allows the kid to win. Surprise.

The best gimmick, even better than the two fans racing the remote-controlled cars from first to third, is the one where the kid races from the first base on-deck circle up the line, picks up a Dust Buster, races back to the on-deck circle, vacuums up some dirt, races back, drops the Dust Buster where he picked it up, and races back to the on-deck circle, all within forty-five seconds. He does it. I hope he won something other than a Dust Buster.

I have a hot dog, an ice cream sandwich, and a cappuccino. The home team wins 11–3 and the fans go home happy. We do too. On Main Street, waiting for the bus, I see a fan filling in his scorebook. Only the truest of fans would bring their own scorebook. Hardly anyone keeps score any more and most of those who do pick up a scorecard at the game. Compulsively imitating my father now, I say something about this to the fan, and he points out that he has scored the game in Japanese. Flipping back a couple of pages, he shows me a previous game, which he scored in Japan, and which featured the Hiroshima Carp. He asks if I know Shane Mack. Sure, I say. San Diego Padres, Minnesota Twins. Shane Mack is a big star in Japan now, he tells me. I tell him about some of the games I saw in Japan forty years ago. I skipped out of school once on the opening day of the Japanese baseball season. I think it was the Mainichi Orions playing, maybe against the Taiyo Whales, or perhaps the Chunichi Dragons.

Did I think, when we started out from Ottawa, two months ago, that I would be on a Vancouver street at eleven at night talking about the Hiroshima Carp with a total stranger? I think of this as a Pacific Rim experience.

## Once Around the Rim

The Pacific Rim experience continues the next day on a walk around the seawall in Stanley Park. At the Port of Vancouver Lookout a plaque says: "For the enjoyment of Canadians and for the other visitors whose homelands are linked to us by the oceans of the world." One of the guidebooks has instructed us to walk the entire seawall to get a perspective on Vancouver, so, performance-oriented once again, we do. The hike, which takes about two and a half hours with time out for lunch, begins with a sign giving instructions: walkers on the right, bicycles and rollerblades on the left. This turns out not to be sissy over-regulation (it is not like Ottawa, in other words). There is much traffic, many people of different speeds sharing this path, and the filtering works.

Looking back at the downtown Vancouver skyline we see cranes, five of them. In the water near the road there are people fishing, using shrimp for bait. There are kids spraying each other in a waterpark. The only graffiti encountered is at least on the political new frontier: CIRCUMCISION REDUCES AND DIMINISHES. We see a log swimming casually by and realize eventually that it is a seal. In such an urbanized setting, you forget about sea creatures.

For the entire walk, during which we pass a rowing club, a sailing club, two cricket pitches, a rugger field, and many tennis courts, we are passed by people running, people bicycling, people roller-blading. This is the fabled B.C. fitness craze. It sticks out less than it used to, since other cities have followed Vancouver's lead and created areas where people can run, bicycle, and roller-blade. Toronto and Vancouver are closer than they used to be. (Some complain that Vancouver has adopted some of the Toronto Type-A style as well, diminishing the differences still further.)

At Siwash Rock there is a plaque erected, as a warning to others, by the friends of a young man who died diving off. Another plaque tells of the rock itself and the legendary guy who, as a reward for unselfishness, was turned to stone. What if he had *not* been unselfish? At Third Beach, signs point out what is allowable – volleyball and windsurfing – and what is not – booze, inflatables, dogs, and fires.

It is an enjoyable and vigorous walk, affording different perspectives on the water and varying aspects of the park. At some points, the trees stretch out beside us. At others, the park rises and sits above the cliffs that hang over us. We stop for lunch and listen to four women at the next table play with their phones. It is at such times you realize that one of the great appeals of nature is the alternative. On the way home, we walk by a grocery store on Robson that, without mentioning bears, advertises pepper spray.

The rest of the day is spent meeting some of John's friends from the time he spent out here, my hope being to get a more youthful take on Vancouver, which is clearly a young person's city. We meet Paul Conder for coffee in the neighbourhood where John used to hang out, around 20th and Cambie. Paul is twenty-eight. He studied industrial design at Carleton, then came out here because of the economy. In Ontario, everybody he talked to about a job was fearful and/or in the process of being laid off. In Vancouver, even those who couldn't offer work could offer the names of other places to try. "Everybody was totally positive," Paul says. Innovative too. He was used to the Ontario culture, in which a young person progresses by joining a large firm and working his way up. In B.C., "it was the two of us working out of our houses with computers and cell phones. I had to relearn everything and there's a lot of that out here."

You are often struck here by people doing business in odd ways, pounding on laptops in coffee bars. "If you take a walk around Stanley Park during the day," Paul says, "you'll see a lot of people out for a run who don't look particularly impoverished. They've got to be doing something."

These notions appeal to him, plus all the other things that make B.C. so attractive, particularly the outdoors – the skiing and hiking and camping. When I saw Paul out here a year and a half ago, I figured him for a lifer. He reminded me of the people I knew twenty years ago in Brandon, who moved to B.C. to escape the Prairie winters and never gave the Prairies a backward glance, except to send postcards in January reminding us all that they were playing golf. Paul could do a ten-minute selling job on B.C. that would make you pack your bags in a hurry. There is no shortage of such Vancouverites, as typified by the remark of one of Paul's more chauvinistic friends: "Everything east of Main Street is screwed up, and that includes the rest of Canada."

Now, Paul seems not so certain. Vancouver's isolation is starting to get him down. In Ottawa he had easy access to Toronto, Montreal, and Quebec City, not to mention Boston and New York. Vancouver is different. "The closest Canadian city of any size is Calgary and that's thirteen hours away."

He carries with him the slightly anachronistic metaphor of Vancouver as the end of the line, the place where everybody gets off the train and there's nowhere to go. "You get a lot of different cultures that don't seem to have a lot to do with each other," he says. The groups are not just national, they are generational too – "a lot of people who got as far as they could get from their parents."

Maybe he's just homesick. No matter how beautiful your new place is, your old one still counts. "There was a Group of Seven show," he says, referring to the touring display at the Vancouver Art Gallery which began at Ottawa's National Gallery, "and I just missed the East so much when I saw it."

We have dinner with Jon Teague, an actor and director and producer. Jon is from Cape Breton and came to Vancouver to attend theatre school. Now his theatre career parallels Paul's design career in an interesting way. Where Paul struck out on his own, rather than join a big Eastern firm, Jon has, of necessity, foregone the traditional big theatre-company apprenticeship. Instead of starting as the second spear carrier on the left and working his way up to second lead, Jon has formed his own company, called Four Prophets, the pun being intentional. Four Prophets just did *Mad Boy Chronicles*, about Viking precursors of Hamlet. He and his partners found a hundred-seat theatre in which to present it, put up the money, and could have broken even by averaging an audience of twenty-five people a night through the run. They averaged more like eight, but learned things in the process. This may be the way our culture works in the time of the much-heralded new realities. At the moment, the old realities don't look so bad, but at least the new generation of cultural warriors is not sitting back and waiting.

We take the bus back down Main Street and walk along Robson a bit. I'm afraid I'm not as sold on it as my journalist friend. It is a lively street, to be sure, with lots of people, mostly young, and much activity. But the activity depresses me, the space art guy, the astrologer, caricaturists working well into the night, the guy who does some kind of art with rice, the juggler, the bagpiper, the jazz alto sax, the crouching electric guitarist, the guy playing one of those multi-stringed things, a dulcimer, maybe even a zither (Sebastian, is that you?). Some people see street artists and musicians and think of a vibrant street scene. I see the same people and think of people being forced to do on the street what they should be getting paid to do in a theatre or a club or a studio. The more talented the artist, the more depressed it makes me.

There is another peculiar thing on downtown Vancouver streets that I have not noticed anywhere else. People don't give way on the sidewalk. Elsewhere, people perform the traditional pedestrian dance. You move a half step to one side, the other person moves a half step to the other and you pass without banging into each other. Here, people don't do that half step. You do the whole step or you collide. A few times I stuck to my course, just to see if I was imagining this. After several bumped shoulders, I knew I wasn't.

I didn't associate this with any particular group, nor did it appear to be in any way hostile. It just seems to be the way things are done. Perhaps it is the way people behave in crowded places, walking more aggressively, asserting their territoriality. I don't know. I just don't like it.

Still, it is difficult to be annoyed at a street where you discover there is a Happy Hour from 7:00-9:00 a.m. and it turns out to be at a coffee bar, the happiness consisting of being able to buy a twelve-ounce coffee for $1.35. We take that thought with us as we drive out the next morning, south to the ferry at Tsawwassen.

# 17

## *Ferries, Flowers, and Eagles*

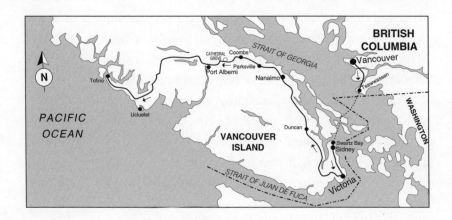

The ferry to Victoria, called the *Queen of Vancouver*, takes one and a half hours. It has comfortable seats, although none outside, several lounges, a snack bar and a buffet. I see eight video games and four telephones. The announcements are in English only and the recorded man making them, I can't help noticing, sounds exactly like the recorded man making the announcements on the ferry to Prince Edward Island. It is a jovial yet authoritative voice, something like the actor Troy McClure on "The Simpsons," welcoming us and making us aware of the existence of lifeboats and asking us to notify the crew "if you notice anything disturbing." Always on the lookout for new occupations in these hard times, I wonder if this is one: ferry boat announcer. Could one guy have all the ferries in Canada, the way that one woman has all the voice mail? If he does, good thing he has Victoria to fall back on, what with the P.E.I. gig falling to the Fixed Link.

It's a sunny day and the route zig-zagging through the islands to Swartz Bay is glorious. We are on the island at 1:30, heading for Victoria, when another driver motions to us that our trunk lid is unlatched. We stop and shut it, remembering now that it had been unlatched the whole ferry trip. Nothing is missing, not luggage and not the laptop which, at this stage, has the entire book in it. Yet another thing has gone right on this trip: people are honest.

As we enter Greater Victoria, we see mountains which, it turns out, are in the United States. We have rooms in a B&B arranged for us by a recently retired journalist friend, Patrick Nagle. The hostess is Swiss-German and comprehensive in her directions as to the proper use of the place. At one point she calls down to ask me to move the car eleven inches. But the place is spacious, away from noise, and a comfortable walk from downtown.

Downtown is unbelievable. We were here once before, twenty years ago for a few hours, but times have changed. Somehow Victoria has become a big-time tourist destination, mostly for Americans, I would guess. We pick up the legislature tour, of course, led by a guide who is clearly a veteran performer. "There is probably enough gold in this building to pay off my student loan," he says at one point. For a change, there are a lot of people on the tour. This may be because there are a lot of people around, it may be because the legislature is right at the harbour, on the beaten tourist track, or it may be because the legislature is in session – although I doubt that, since the tour takes us nowhere near the chamber. Or it may be because the legislature has an interesting appearance. One of the books describes its architecture as "an elegant mix of Victorian, Roman, and Italian Renaissance styles," but it also has a Disneyish look to it, which may draw some passers-by.

After the tour finishes we go back in by ourselves to see the chamber, walk through a metal detector and into the low drama of committee-of-supply debates on budget estimates, in which there is desultory questioning of a desultory education minister. The chamber is narrow and deep, with red carpet, green marble columns, and blue chairs. Not unexpectedly, the building has more of a British feel than its counterparts in either Manitoba or Saskatchewan. But there are many B.C. touches, such as paintings depicting the province's four main activities – agriculture, fishing, lumber, and mining. Now tourism has moved up on the list, although there is no mention of coffee yet. We see also Admiral Quadra and Captain Vancouver, the arrival of Sir James Douglas and the construction of Fort Victoria. And there is a small display of winners of the Order of British Columbia.

The inner harbour stroll reveals a guy with a piano on wheels, several wagons selling iced latte and the like, thousands of tourists, the Empress Hotel, majestically looming, a dock for ferries to the United States, the Undersea Gardens, and a piper, with U.S. money in his open case. There are many singers, four or five people who will draw your picture, three places where you can have your name done in letters that look like birds, a couple of kids playing the flute out of a conservatory book, a solar-powered gondola tour, the tent for the Victoria Shakespeare Festival.

And the Royal London Wax Museum. I try to persuade Nancy to do the wax museum with me, but even "it's for the book" won't work. We saw the real Madame Tussaud's together in London and even that was no roaring hell. I decide to do it later, then the moment is lost and I'll never get the answer to the question that is burning into me – namely, why, exactly, is there a wax museum at Victoria's Inner Harbour? Why, similarly, is there a wax museum at Niagara Falls? What impulse is satisfied by this wax museumization, what need fulfilled?

I picture the first decision-makers, silent upon a hill o'erlooking the Inner Harbour, awestruck by its beauty. Then one of them, breaking the silence, says: "This is so magnificent, so beautiful. Let's put a wax museum on it."

As we walk back to the hotel, the preponderance and the power of the flowers suddenly strike me. Lawns overflow with them, the medians of streets burst forth with them. They cascade from the lampposts, signs are written in them. Near our B&B is a combination grocery and flower store, one that carries, in addition to meat and potatoes and soft drinks, wedding and funeral arrangements. That night we visit former Ottawa friends who have a splendid old house in the Oak Bay area. The trees are insanely tall, the garden verging on out of control, it grows so fast. And as we head out for dinner, an eagle calls to us. Victoria is just like any other place, except for flowers and eagles.

## More Ottawa than London

The next day's walking is mostly in the business district, particularly Government Street. The scene, both around the harbour and on Government Street, reminds me more than anything of Ottawa in the tourist season. The tourists look the same, for one thing. They have the look of not having come from very far. In Victoria's case, they are mostly from Seattle and the northwestern states, I think.

If you assume that what they want is what they get, then what they want is the feeling of being in England without actually having to go to all the Trans-Atlantic trouble of getting there. Government Street, which is reminiscent of Ottawa's Sparks Street, is full of signs with Old Country typefaces, shops with Englishy names – Old Vic this and that, Marks and Spencer, Crabtree and Evelyn, Copithorne and something. Thirty years ago, Edward McCourt was wise to this. "The city of Victoria has perpetrated the most successful hoax in the history of tourism," he observed on what must have been the last day of his cross-country trip. "It has persuaded the rest of the world that it is indeed a little bit of old England. Victoria is not England; she has

simply played on her origins to give the tourist what he wants."
Nothing has changed.

In the middle of it all, we stumble upon Munro's Books and
walk in for a chat. I had met Jim Munro at a booksellers' convention in Toronto a couple of years ago. His store, which is in an old
Royal Bank building, has been here since 1984. It has the big high
ceiling of a bank and that suits a bookstore quite well. As befits a
West Coast establishment, Munro's has a large leisure section, also
a section of metaphysical books. It also has everything else; it is a
most impressive store.

Jim Munro has been in Victoria since the end of the war and in
the bookstore business since 1963. So he knows what he's doing
and he figures literary books by Canadians are good business.
"Tourists buy real books," he says. Americans want books they can't
get in the States.

When he arrived in Victoria he found it a "very quiet place."
Daily ferry service and an expanded University of Victoria are
factors he cites in the new vibrancy of the city, which includes a
symphony, theatre, and jazz, writers', and fringe festivals. This isn't
just for the tourists. "I think it's for us," Jim says.

The store itself has made a contribution, and in more than the
expected ways. Jim says the sidewalk outside his store is the prime
location for street singers. When we get outside, one of those
unavoidable groups with pan flutes is performing and we rush on.
As we cut through the Eaton Centre on the way to a bank, we are
discussing when, or if, we should go to the Butchart Gardens, one
of the big tourist attractions in the area. "Go Saturday," says a voice
behind us. "That's when the fireworks are." The voice belongs to a
Canada Post letter carrier, exhibiting the kind of unsolicited
friendliness we have come to expect by now.

Our walk takes us back to the harbour, which we reach by
short-cutting through the Empress Hotel. I need to check on the
tea scene. Crumpets, fruit, and tea cost $25 and are available at
1:00, 2:30, and 4:00. It is now 12:10 and people are lined up

already for the one o'clock shift. Imagine tea at 1:00 p.m. Imagine paying $25 for it.

We have lunch with Patrick Nagle at a Mexican restaurant – what, no bangers-and-mash? – and talk over old newspaper times, and Brandon, of which he is a native. When I first met Pat I was a kid editor from the little *Brandon Sun* and he was a hotshot feature writer for *Weekend Magazine* in Montreal. He made a point of seeking me out at a reception where I was feeling lost, just because he wanted to talk to someone from Brandon. You remember things like that. When the coffee arrives, the waitress says "You guys need cream?" That happens everywhere. When I order ice tea, as I often do, the question is, "Do you need sugar?" This has something to do with the conservation ethic, not automatically bringing creamers or sugar that will be wasted. I classify it as a B.C. thing, if not exactly Pacific Rim.

After lunch, Nancy goes back to the B&B and I walk along Wharf Street, in the general direction of the Victoria *Times-Colonist*. The feeling of being back in Ottawa comes over me again. Something about Wharf Street's relationship with the harbour reminds me of Sussex Drive's relationship with the Ottawa River.

The *Times-Colonist*, like so many newspapers these days, is some distance from the downtown core. Paul Minvielle works here as an editorial writer. I last saw him thirty years ago when he left the *Brandon Sun* to set up a weekly newspaper in Lanigan, Saskatchewan, which was going to take off with the potash boom. When that didn't happen, Paul, who was a quick and clever reporter, went to the *Hamilton Spectator*, then to the *Reader's Digest* book division. All the while, he kept talking about how the Gulf Islands would be a nice place to live. One day he called his own bluff, by arranging babysitting for his children, buying tickets for himself and his wife, Loretta, and flying out to have a look. Now they live on Saltspring Island, where they have chickens and grow all kinds of things. I always like to hear stories that illustrate how the culture of one place – in this case a newsroom – is different from the culture of

another. At the *Times-Colonist* everybody seems to raise something
and there is a big newsroom trade in fruits and vegetables and
whatnot. At one point, an official from the business office was in
the process of issuing the latest no-conducting-private-business-
in-the-newsroom edict when the publisher arrived in Paul's office
to pick up his eggs.

The night's expedition is to Butchart Gardens, a half-hour drive
north of the city. Just because everybody goes to Butchart Gardens
is no reason we shouldn't, I figure. Plus, the idea of seeing a garden
at night is intriguing.

It is still light when we get there, about 8:30, and it costs us
fourteen dollars each to get in. The route into the parking lot and
from the parking lot into the Gardens is elaborate and well-regu-
lated, taking us, probably not accidentally, past the gift shop, as well
as the restaurant, the first-aid station, and the washrooms.

Hearing music, we go to investigate, finding a stage facing a
large grassy hill populated by hundreds of people on chairs. There
are four musicians, two of them playing synthesizers, in order to
imitate the sound of large numbers of real instruments, and singers
and dancers doing rapid-fire medleys of familiar tunes in a cheery
Up With People kind of way. The stage is covered with flowers.
The audience, which is older, applauds politely.

If the stage show is ordinary, the gardens are quite spectacular,
particularly as the daylight fades and the artificial lights come on.
Some of the lights simply illuminate the flowers, others cast a red
or green glow on the trees and bushes. There are well-marked paths
designed to be taken in a certain order but we – rebels that we are
– seem to have started in the middle and wander about as randomly
as you can in a place full of illuminated trees and gangs of people
headed from the tour bus to the gift shop.

We find a giant redwood. Some visitors, including one small
child, try to see how many people it takes to stretch their arms
around it. Bullied into participating, we now know the answer:
five and a half. Despite the many ponds and fountains, there are no

mosquitoes, so we march on, through the hedges and down the brightly coloured paths, feeling as if we were playing miniature golf without the ball.

Something makes me think of Bill Vander Zalm and something makes me think of Lawrence Welk, but there is no denying that Butchart Gardens is an extremely professional operation, right down to the Plant Information Centre, where you can find out everything about the plants, which is helpful because Jennie Butchart and her husband, the cement tycoon, Robert Pim Butchart, who began serious gardening on their estate here in 1904, didn't believe in actually labelling the flowers in the place where they are. A plant identification guide is available, in seventeen languages, to give you an idea of the draw of the place.

After a bite in a friendly cafeteria filled with plants (or a cafeteria full of friendly plants), we find an illuminated garden sunk into an old quarry, lit up in a strange, spooky-pretty kind of way. Away from the paths all is dark. We walk down a path to the bottom of the quarry. It is quiet down here, with colours you don't expect to see outdoors at 10:00 p.m. The air is soft and the smells are nice.

Further down the path we find a jet of water doing a kind of dancing-waters trick, both the colours and the patterns of the spray changing, in a way that resembles fireworks. It is quite a show. We exit, as we should, by way of the gift store, where we note the following Butchart material: videos, placemats, seeds, CDs, needlecraft kits, tree guides, calendars, and tapestries. The argument for Butchart Gardens, and perhaps for Victoria itself, is that you can never have too many flowers. It is difficult to argue with that.

## Beyond Mile Zero

Mr. J. S. Gowland only got as far west as Vancouver, but Edward McCourt ended his journey here in Victoria. He didn't go to Mile Zero, as far as I can tell. He just stopped at a motel on the outskirts of town and relaxed by the pool. As I have demonstrated in a dozen silly ways by now, I have to see the beginnings and ends of

things, the easternmost this, the westernmost that. That means
finding Mile Zero before we head west of it, to Tofino, which will
be our Mile Zero. We experience, on a nice sunny day, the joys of
getting lost in Beacon Hill Park. These include seeing (a) a cricket
match played where horse races were held a century ago, (b) some
people walking their dogs on Dallas Road, and (c) the world's
tallest totem pole, which is 127 feet and seven inches high. Then
we spot a big Canadian flag and figure that it must mark Mile Zero
so we drive right up to the top of Beacon Hill Park to get to it, I
leap out of the car and race over to the plaque there, and it says:
"Beacon Hill Park."

We finally find Mile Zero, arriving just before a small busload
of Korean tourists. Mile Zero is 4,860 miles from St. John's, which
would be 7,766 kilometres. We have gone 16,116 kilometres, or
10,072½ miles, so far. As for the Mile Zero monument, the
Victoria Auto Club put it up in 1958. There are flowers on it, of
course. Since then, it has achieved significance on several occasions, notably Steve Fonyo's Journey for Lives, March 31, 1984,
to May 29, 1985. Down a steep flight of stairs is the spot where
Fonyo must have put his wooden leg into the water. It is a beautiful spot, with the Olympic Range mountains of Washington in the
distance, and as we look along the shore, there is a person standing
at every point of land, staring out over the water.

We still don't know about the ferry to Prince Rupert. Nancy
keeps phoning and they keep telling her to try again. Now there's
a Plan B. If we don't get on the ferry, we'll try to stay in Tofino for
a few days of no note-taking, no writing. The road to Tofino
begins north on the Trans-Canada, Highway 1, then continues
with Highway 4, west from Parksville, via Port Alberni. It looks
like it should take about three hours, but will wind up taking much
more than that because it is not fast – crowded, through populated
areas, and later mountainous. We stop for coffee at a beach,
Bamberton Provincial Park, which is quite populated and unmem-
orable except for the fact that two little kids get into a fight and the

mother patiently takes the time to find out what happened instead of automatically punishing the one who isn't crying. In the interests of balance, this must be reported.

The road goes through forest, popping out occasionally for a good high vista onto the Strait of Georgia. Other points of interest: Duncan is the City of Totems, the fire danger is high, there is lots of traffic, and the CBC open line show, before we turn it off, is on whether bear hunting should be outlawed. The news, both here and in the Rockies, has been full of stories about bears and cougars attacking people.

I invoke "it's for the book" successfully to have a look at the Bungy Zone, just south of Nanaimo. This is where people jump off high places with cords wrapped around their legs and come bouncing up before they hit bottom. As far as I can figure out, people do it so they can say they did and maybe so that they don't have to do it any more. The Bungy Zone consists of a building, where you pay your money, some vehicles, which advertise the telephone number 753-JUMP, and a bridge. The bridge spans a gorge and at the bottom of the gorge is the Nanaimo River. A few dozen people stand beside the gorge and watch people jump off the bridge, bounce up a few times on the bungy cord, and then be helped onto a boat. An older teen, perhaps wanting to appear brave, says, as if he means it, "I wish I had my shorts." A youngish mother is going to do it, along with a couple of her teenage children. She kisses her husband and says: "I love you no matter what happens."

Oh yeah? What about the cost of the thing? $140 for the jump, the tee-shirt, and a video of the jump.

Considering the risk involved, or at least the courage required to do the jump, the spectators seem curiously uninvolved. As a people, we certainly are becoming quite blasé about almost everything. I talk to the woman who does the videotaping. She says she does about fifty a day, sitting at the top of the gorge in a little shed. I say it must be difficult to catch all that up and down movement. "Just zoom in and zoom out," she says. "I can do it in my sleep."

Filing away this new definition of laid-back, we drive through Nanaimo, which sprawls like crazy. It may beat the previous sprawl record, held by Kelowna. I finally decide to listen to a tape – Diana Krall: this is her home town. Turning west at Parksville we see a bit of cloud and Mt. Arrowsmith to the south. There is a bird and a reptile garden and the store at Coombs with the grass on the roof. Too late I realize that we were supposed to look for the goat on the roof, a big tourist attraction. There is a lot of construction and each irritating delay coincides with a sign a sign saying "Your tax dollars at work." The government public relations people might want to rethink that one.

Highway 4 is heavily wooded with evergreens. We pass campgrounds with signs saying they are full, and lakes with cars parked along the shoulder. Cameron Lake looks like a nice place to swim, with huge trees and a steep cliff. The roadside along it is jammed with cars. At Cathedral Grove, another old growth spot, we encounter the shopping-centre parking lot syndrome again, but the walk is well worth it. The provincial park contains some trees that are as old as eight hundred years, although most date back only(!) three hundred, when there was a fire. The bigger trees must be ten feet across. The name Cathedral Grove feels right. People talk in hushed tones, as if in church, and it jars when we hear some European tourists laughing too loudly.

There are wooden walkways to protect the moss and the ferns and too many warning signs (no smoking, watch out for branches falling on your head) but nothing can detract from the majesty of the trees and the immense calm they produce (even while we watch for branches about to fall on us). You can regret the civilizing presence, the public washrooms and the postcard booth, but if this wasn't a provincial park, tourists might be cutting bark off the trees or logging companies might be cutting the trees down. Who can tell?

Emerging into the light, we drive on and climb, feeling it in the ears, behind a logging truck, across the spine of the island, to the Port Alberni summit. There are long lines of cars, then an 18-per-cent grade, which I think is a record for us. We stop at another provincial park for a late lunch, then a gas station, where Nancy tries B.C. Ferries again and finds out that we're on. Great. Except that we were beginning to get committed to Plan B.

We arrive at Tofino at 6:30. A B&B had been recommended to us by cousins, but was full. Most B&Bs in the area won't take you unless you are staying for at least three days. Tourism is definitely a sellers' market out here. Instead, we have a reservation at a place called Pacific Sands Beach Resort, which is not too expensive, given where it is. We register, carry our stuff into the room, and look out the window. There are pine trees, twisted by the wind in a style I remember from being on the other side of the Pacific. There's the beach, stretching for miles. And there's the Pacific Ocean, nothing between us and Japan. About six weeks ago we were at Cape Spear, looking at Ireland. I take the mileage: we have gone 16,435 kilometres. Then we go stick our feet into the Pacific Ocean, which is cold.

This is a winner. We walk down the beach, hearing a foghorn, deeper than the one we heard in Nova Scotia, but probably no less electronic. There is a bank of fog to the south along the beach and we walk down the beach into it. Nothing can spoil this. Fog is our friend. The fog hangs onto Cox Point as the breakers roar in. There are warnings against swimming because of the rip tides. The temperature of the water is warning enough.

Since there is a kitchen in our place, we drive into the town to pick up something to cook in it. Our number-one aim is to get back in time for sunset. We go to the Co-Op, passing a lot of hotels and B&Bs. Tofino is cute, small, but clearly a place where people live and work. Much of the business caters to people who want to celebrate the sea in some form, whether sailing on it, kayaking, or watching whales. We do our shopping and hurry back.

The sunset probably won't get through the fog bank, which is too bad. But the light is great anyway and people stroll reverently in it along the beach. It is quite chilly now and they are all bundled up. There is a solitary surfer in a wet suit who has his work cut out for him. When dinner is ready so is a genuine Top Ten Belvedere. The sun is down but fog clings to the point, the waves are silver-grey and there is light in the sky and on the water. We put an artificial log in the fireplace and have dinner, looking out the floor-to-ceiling window. We have gone as far as we can go and it is worth it.

# 18

## *Follow the Yellowhead Road*

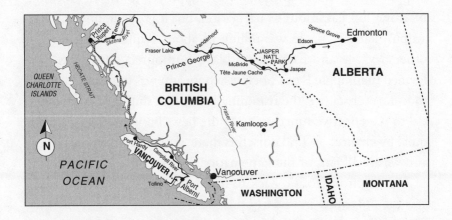

Despite everything, I'd do another fifteen hours on the *Queen of the North* any day. The everything includes indifferent food, bad weather, and passengers who insist on saving at least three seats for themselves by strewing their hand baggage all over them. So what. Bundle yourself up warmly and you can sit out on deck, under a canopy out of the rain, and watch an incredible sight, the Inland Passage to Prince Rupert.

I wonder how the guy we met yesterday would rank this. He was from Hamilton and had been driving all over Canada by himself for two years, going to many of the same places we've been. We bumped into him at the Seymour Narrows Lookout, north of Campbell River, and I asked him, looking out over an excellent vista in itself, what his favourite spot was in all his travels. He said Gros Morne National Park in western Newfoundland. When we were there, we saw just the bottom half of it but it hadn't been foggy for him. This trip through the Inland Passage probably compares to the boat trip through the Newfoundland fjords that was cancelled on us because of fog. Even in the rain the view here is impressive.

That coffee stop at Seymour Narrows was a funny series of coincidences. At this same lookout was a plaque marking the blasting of Ripple Rock in 1958. This was supposed to make Seymour Narrows less hazardous to navigation, but it is apparently still hazardous. Patrick Nagle was telling us about Ripple Rock just the other day. He and some other black-humoured journalists once formed the Ripple Rock Society, whose aim was to restore the rock to its former stature, the reasoning being that shipwrecks are essential to the effective functioning of the news business. Suddenly, and quite by chance, we find ourselves there, with a guy from Hamilton, and we are all fans of the same national park in Newfoundland.

Driving from Tofino back to the east coast of Vancouver Island was the only time in this trip that we have had to retrace our path for any distance. On Highway 19, which goes north along the east coast of the island, then turns inland and west across to Port Hardy, traffic thinned out, until it was more like June, and lumbering activity became quite obvious. The lumber companies note on their signs when the trees were cut and when the land was reforested. The growth is quite dramatic. One stand, planted the year I was born, is as tall as some white pines at Lake of the Woods, planted when my father was born.

Working the phones, Nancy found a good B&B for us in Port Hardy, a modern house called the Eagle's Nest. The one she called first didn't have a room but recommended this one. We learn once again to trust the advice of the B&B people. The Eagle's Nest has an eagle motif and we saw why when we drove downtown for dinner and watched the eagles flying overhead. Although we're still on Vancouver Island, this country has a different, more northerly feel to it. We crossed the fiftieth parallel yesterday. Our hosts, Pat and Lindy Fry, were Newfoundlanders until twenty-five years ago. He was maintenance supervisor at the Island Copper Mine here, which has shut down. Last August the mine where Lindy worked was the deepest point on earth, he says, deeper than the Dead Sea. Now it is filled in with water, a lake. Lindy has a collection of news videos showing the process, called reclamation. I continue to be amazed at the range of experience you pick up in casual conversation in this country. Until you hear them, you would not believe how different people's stories can be.

Pat and Lindy have had guests from the Netherlands, the United States, and Australia, but more of their guests are German than any other nationality. In fact, there are more Germans than Canadians. More Germans come to this part of the province than to Vancouver, Pat said. "They don't like the cities," she said. "That's the reason they come to Canada, to get away from cities."

## Too Bad It's Not Nicer: Part Five

They certainly didn't come here to avoid ferries. I'm sure there is more German than English spoken on this one. It makes me wonder again about my countrymen, where they are. I can only assume that they have better and less expensive things to do. I hope it is not that they are saving up all their travel money for a trip to Disneyland, or Toronto.

We got up at five to catch this ferry, which left at seven. You should see all the campers in the lineup. The ship looks small from the outside but is quite large, more than a football field long but not as wide, holding 157 average-size vehicles, up to 750 passengers in the summer, and a crew of 60 to 65. It makes the 507-kilometre journey every other day in the summer.

Prowling the ship, which I like to do, I find the above information and a good little display about the history of the area. Captain

Cook was around in 1778, on his way to being killed in Hawaii,
Port Hardy was settled in 1912, Prince Rupert in 1906.

Every ship has its own etiquette. This one has written warnings,
plus spoken ones from the PA system that the ship's horn will
sound. This is for people with hearing aids. There also are signs,
reinforced several times over the PA system, saying that you are not
allowed to save seats by placing your belongings on them when
you leave them. This must be a recurring problem and it is clear,
on this day anyway, that the warnings have not worked. The ship
doesn't seem to be that crowded, but there is not an unoccupied
seat that does not have a coat or bag or book or something on it.

We have a little stateroom, mostly to put our stuff in. It has a
Bible but no window. We spend our time on deck, bundled up a
bit, doing some reading and mostly watching the world go by. The
world, once we cross the Queen Charlotte Strait and reach the
Inland Passage, which winds its way through a series of islands all
the way to Prince Rupert, consists of high hills wrapped in fog.
Crossing the strait, we saw several smaller boats in our wake. We
spotted a porpoise. Someone saw a whale.

The rain starts and stops. The passage is quite narrow at times,
like a river. Some young eagles fly along with us. Mist clings to the
top of trees, curls up from the valleys like smoke. It gives different
shades of green and a sharp, layered effect to the hills, a Lawren
Harris quality. It may be a better show than sunlight. On the hills,
there are signs of avalanche activity, with new and greener growth
down the gullies where the rocks went. A guy beside me is reading
J. R. Tolkien's *Der Kleiner Hobbit*. Inside the ship, about seventy-
five people are watching a movie.

The number of smokers is unusually high, I would say. The
number of cameras, particularly videotape cameras, is impressive.
A rainbow appears off the stern, and two dozen video cameras are
turned upon it. Sometimes I wonder whether we should have
thought about bringing one but the camera seems to flatten out
the scenery. And I don't like the idea of a filmed record pushing

my memories into the background. Besides, Nancy is taking lots of stills.

We have a not very good dinner, noticing, first, that the staff is friendly and nice. They run little pools amongst themselves and today's is on the number of moustaches. One waitress, obviously with a high number, is very glad to see me. The other thing we notice is how the passengers keep to themselves. No one, including us, strikes up conversation with anyone but the staff.

Back out on deck, there is no sunset, but a strong silvery light, combining with the haze and water, islands and layers of mountains, turns into a Top Ten Belvedere candidate.

We arrive at Prince Rupert at 11:15 p.m. and find our hotel, which has neither air conditioning nor remote control and is on a noisy street. But nothing could spoil this day. When we saw how beautiful Tofino was, we wanted to stay and were almost sorry we got a spot on the ferry. On this trip, things have a way of working out.

## Highway 16: A River Runs Beside It

One of the reasons we're glad to be here is that it makes sense from the point of the route. Prince Rupert is at the beginning (or the end) of the Yellowhead Highway, No. 16, which will head gradually south, taking us almost as far as Winnipeg on a direct but quite different route. At the moment we're about as north as I've ever been, just south of the fifty-fifth parallel and a bit east of the bottom of the Alaska Panhandle. This, of course, is nothing for true northerners. But I'm impressed anyway.

We have a bit of a sense now, after fifty-seven driving days, that we are on the way home. But there is nothing anti-climactic about what we're seeing. The Yellowhead, from Prince Rupert to Terrace, is a beauty, running beside the Skeena River all the way. It is cloudy, so we don't get a good idea of the river's colour, probably a muddy green. There are mountains all around, but we don't have to drive in them and it's possible to make good time. There

are lots of creeks to cross and even see, although there is the beginning of that alarming Ontario tendency to put up barriers on the
sides of the bridges to shield the view from the drivers.

This part of the Yellowhead features long distances between
towns and not much roadside enterprise in between. That fish-on-
the-wall restaurant in the middle of nowhere won't be found here.
So we stop at the A&W in Terrace.

In the Bulkley River Valley we see cars parked beside the road
at a native crafts place. At first we think it is just the tourists
gawking at the natives, but there is much more to it than that. This
is Moricetown Canyon, a place where the chinook salmon fight
their way upstream and Wet'suwet'en young men try to catch them
with gaff and net. From the hillside, it makes an arresting sight.
The river flowing through the evergreens with mountains in the
background, then plunging sixty metres down the canyon where
the kids skip along the rock at their work. A big truck, full of logs,
goes by in the background. Up on the hill with us are stands where
fresh and smoked/dried salmon are being sold. A guy selling fresh
salmon says the fish may be passing through for only a couple of
weeks, so we were lucky to see this.

After this, the land gentles. We even see sheep – not the bighorn
kind. But the mountains are always there. We are thinking of trying
to get to Vanderhoof, perhaps even Prince George tonight, but
when we reach Fraser Lake, after 584 kilometres of driving, I have
one of my whims, which is that it would be nice to stop early, find
a nice B&B by the lake, and relax. It turns out there is one such
B&B but it is a bit of a distance from the lake, a very long walk
from the nearest restaurant, which isn't very good, and the lake is
used as a place for the flower of the town's youth to practise their
night yelling. So this doesn't work out too well. I think Nancy sus-
pects, after thirty-odd years of it, that my impulses are not very
good. For some reason, I still trust them.

We are also close to the tracks. Just as some people from France
are looking over the adjoining room, the train goes by, rattling

things just a little. The people from France leave and the shared bath reverts to a private one for us. God bless the CNR.

## A Gentler Route Through the Rockies

The next day we can laugh at this, at my determination to walk everywhere once we are stopped for the night, at our setting out on foot in the wrong direction and stopping to ask a bemused man outside his house where the downtown is. Downtown Fraser Lake? The fact that he replies in an Australian accent only adds to the surreal quality of the evening, which deepens when Nancy asks in the restaurant what the house white is. "It doesn't really have a name," the waitress replies. "It comes in a big white box. Everybody likes it." Nancy tastes it and she likes it too. Wait'll the big-shot wine stewards in T.O. hear this.

Over breakfast, Cindy Harms tells us about her two years running a B&B, the White Swan (commemorating the fact that Fraser Lake is known as the White Swan Capital). Her summer customers are mostly French and German tourists, although Cindy shows us a guest book entry from an English woman from Cheshire. "Thanks for showing us your rubbish dump bears – a real treat." The woman had never seen a bear before and Cindy showed her how to get to the garbage dump.

Fifteen thousand white swans turn up in Fraser Lake in October, staying until the lake freezes. Vanderhoof, just down the road, gets geese. It is better known as the Geographical Centre of British Columbia. Every town is known for something. We drive through Prince George, a nice, open, big-sky kind of city known, among other things, for a giant tree person, known as Mr. P.G., who seems, in his pictures, to be waving a flag. We don't see Mr. P.G. beside the road, so drive on, perhaps showing insufficient dedication. Coffee is at Willow River, where eight kids, aged sixteen to eighteen, lost their lives in 1947 canoeing an impassable canyon. I want to see the impassable canyon but the path to it becomes impassable as well. This doesn't seem like a great day for perseverance. We stop at McBride for lunch, then, in a narrow valley between two mountains, see a sign: GUSTY WIND AREA. Then we see HIGH MOUNTAIN ROAD. SUDDEN WEATHER CHANGES. BE CAUTIOUS. We're in the mountains again.

Just on this side of the British Columbia/Alberta border, the Yellowhead splits, at Tête Jaune Cache, the southern route going down to Kamloops and eventually meeting 3 at Hope. We continue east towards Jasper and stop at the Mount Terry Fox Lookout, taking a bit of a stroll to get a good view of it and the valley in front. The various proclamations about it, all signed by Bill Bennett, when he was premier, don't suggest any connection between the mountain and Terry Fox, just that they named it after him, a British Columbia boy. Another sign points to Mount Robson, at 3,954 metres the highest in the Rockies.

This is a gentler route through the Rockies, at lower elevation, and a nicer way to approach them. From Calgary to Banff it was like a race. This is more relaxed. The mountains quietly surround you. From the east, the mountains are more of a surprise. Nancy says that from this direction, there is a greater sense of the Rockies as a barrier, dividing B.C. from the rest of the country. Reminders that we are in a different world now crop up at regular intervals, in the form of gates for closing the highway in case of snow or avalanches. You don't see those around Ottawa. The lakes and rivers, Moose Lake, Moose River, are roughly the colour of Lake Louise, that same bright chalky green. In rapid succession now we see a time zone change, the entrance to Jasper Park, Alberta's slogan, Wild Rose Country, a sign saying the fire hazard is high, a bear warning, and a haze that turns out to be a fire. Here we are.

Our B&B in Jasper seems to have no name. The town has another wrinkle on the B&B rules. Here there is a simple black-on-white sign outside each of them that says APPROVED ACCOMMODATION (and usually NO VACANCY). Our hosts, Frank and Jean Krauss, don't mind. With only two rooms to rent, they would spend most of their time turning people away if they hung more of an advertising sign out.

When Jean says that it would fine for Nancy to do some laundry, we discover that we have left our dirty clothes (tastefully enclosed in a green garbage bag) at Fraser Lake. Nancy phones Cindy Harms, who says she will put it on a bus and we can pick it up in Saskatoon. I am reminded that people are nice. I am also reminded, uncomfortably, of Mr. J. S. Gowland, who left his laundry in Cochrane, with instructions that it be sent ahead to Calgary. How would he have handled this one? (The last time I checked his book, he had reached Vancouver and had so far spent only a hundred dollars. But he seemed to get a lot of free meals at restaurants.)

Our perspective on Jasper may be affected a bit by the fact that we are staying in a residential area, a few blocks away from the main business area. So we find it quieter than Banff, also smaller, with many tourists but fewer tours and a large number of actual Canadians. The commercial emphasis seems to be more outdoorsy than Banff's. Dinner is at a good fish restaurant, the Fiddle River Seafood Store, which is woody in that nice northwest way rather than the phoney pseudo-Alpine way. The fish, salmon and trout, is fine and not expensive. While we eat it we get to watch the mountains, and three elk walking along the railroad tracks just across the street. Afterwards, we walk a bit more, the smoke having disappeared, and I find an ice cream place. Life is good again.

## The Jasper Bulletin Board

The next day we see more elk and still more elk. It begins as we leave Jasper on Highway 16, with what I think of as a "bulletin board" experience. If two people stand and look at the office bulletin board, they will soon be joined by others, wanting to know what the excitement is. Here, we see a bunch of cars and campers parked beside the road. Taking this as a sign that there is an animal to look at, I pull over too. We never see it, although we do see two guys go walking into the woods. I'm assuming, because of that, that it isn't a bear. But you never know with people. A bit later we see a bull elk beside the road and a man standing right beside it, setting up a tripod. Let's see, is it the rutting season or the calving season?

Maligne Lake, not to malign it, doesn't seem all that special to us, although it certainly seemed special to Lawren Harris and it does draw a crowd – the parking lot is full of rented campers. We see an object lesson in what happens when animals get used to being fed by humans. In a grassy picnic space beside the lake, woodchucks (or are they whistling marmots, or hoary marmots, or just gophers?) pop up and approach tourists for food, as grey jays fly low and land on our table. On the way back to the highway, we stop at Maligne Canyon, which is exciting, deeper and narrower than Johnston Canyon, the water falling into deep caves. Many people are with us, as we walk along the edge of the canyon and peer over the fence, but we're used to that by now.

The roadside wildlife population seems greater here than in Banff, although tame life might be more like it. The mule deer and elk show not the slightest interest in getting away from people.

Heading northeast out of the park, we stop for a picnic beside what we think is Rocky River. The sun is out and the water is green. The mountains above us are more rocky than treed. Although no picnic could compare with our lobster sandwiches along the Cabot Trail, this one could come a close second.

The end of the park is reached at 2:45 and we say goodbye to the mountains. There are hills ahead but it is not the same. Signs of a different culture appear. YOU'RE IN BULLTROUT COUNTRY. KEEP ALBERTA KNAPWEED FREE. We will probably be out of Alberta and free of knapweed ourselves before we find out what it is. We pass through the Obed Summit, highest point on the Yellowhead, hard to believe since it does not feel like we've been climbing.

Now the road, four lanes of it, becomes more dominant. Clouds appear overhead as we go through Edson, whose slogan is SLO-PITCH CAPITAL OF CANADA. I picture an entire community of people with uppercut swings. Among the highlights is the Derrick, billed as the largest liquor store west of Edmonton. Again, this is the kind of promotion we are not used to in Ontario – so far. We see another unfamiliar sign: SMOKE AREA LIMITED VISIBILITY USE EXTREME CAUTION. We are cautious but see no smoke. It is not a very interesting highway now, except for Evansburg: Home of the Grouch. From Spruce Grove into Edmonton the highway is six lanes, crowded, but it would be rush hour now. It is always a bit unsettling for us to arrive in a place and find that people are actually going to work and coming home from it. Who do they think they are?

Edmonton is called the City of Champions. My parents lived here for about five years in the sixties and enjoyed it very much. This has given me a slight sense of knowing where I'm going, which is always dangerous. We follow signs pointing to the city centre and wind up considerably south of the city centre and on the wrong side of the North Saskatchewan River and its wide valley.

Our hotel, the Château Lacombe – now called, in the dumb corporate fashion of the day, the Crowne-Plaza Château Lacombe, and who knows what it will be called next year – is modern, well laid-out, and comfortable, reminiscent of the Blue Horizon in Vancouver. Except that someone has cranked the heat up to 40°C in our room and left it on. We get moved without incident and wind up on the sixteenth floor, feeling higher than that because the hotel sits on the edge of the valley and our room faces across it. We make some calls to set up stuff for tomorrow, then decide to take the night off. Room service brings a steak sandwich which we have with the view and the baseball game, which the Expos lose.

### Ralph Klein's Magic Spot

When we get to the Alberta Legislature after a nice ride on Edmonton's LRT subway, we're late for the tour, but the woman at the desk says we can catch up. "I'll call security and let them know you're coming." We then hustle down the impressive promenade, with its fountains and pool, and find security at the legislature door. "Security" turns out to be another university-age woman.

Our tour guide, Virginie, is from Quebec City, and was a tour guide there. She has a French accent and knows everything about the Alberta legislature, where the sandstone and granite are, the different kinds of marble, the statues of Crowfoot and Princess Louise Caroline Alberta, who, as you might have suspected, has the odd thing named after her out here, the symbols and imagery in the carvings and paintings, all the things that people seem to want to know. I am always struck by the ability of guides to learn all this stuff and somehow stay interested in it.

Here, as in Saskatchewan, are portraits of the premiers, which I somehow find more interesting than even the mace. What I particularly like is context, how each premier wanted to be remembered. Bible Bill Aberhart is here, from the thirties, posing with a microphone and a Bible. Harry Strom, who succeeded E. C. Manning as a Social Credit premier, is shown in a modern context, in front of fields. Until Ralph Steinhauer, who posed in native dress in 1974, all lieutenant governors of Alberta apparently had to wear a heavy uniform with a lot of gold in it. One of my favourite politicians is here: Gordon Towers, a man who used to compose and recite political doggerel from the Tory back benches in the House of Commons, until the Speaker, Jeanne Sauvé, told him not to. Here he's shown as lieutenant governor, putting on the doggerel, as it were, in top hat and tails.

Actually, the mace *is* interesting here. There are two maces under glass. The first one was a rush job done right at the beginning by a local guy when somebody realized at the last moment that the assembly couldn't meet without a mace around. So he put one together out of used plumber's pipe, a bedstead, and handles of shaving mugs. It was used for fifty years and looks pretty good too, quite macelike, and we wouldn't have known the difference if Virginie hadn't told us.

The legislature's great attribute, the one that sets it apart from all the others, is the Magic Spot. It is on the top floor, high above the fountain, and is marked by a metal circle in the floor. If the fountain is on and you stand here, it sounds like the fountain is coming from directly over your head. It really does. Thinking of this and the goofy mace, and the buffalo being slid over the ice in the Manitoba legislature and Dief's shiny nose in Saskatchewan, I conclude that there is a force in the West that conspires against solemnity, even in the most solemn of settings. This is reinforced when we go outside and see kids in bathing suits splashing about in the ornamental pools and fountains. No one is telling them not to.

At the end of the tour we chat with the Carter family from Toronto, who are travelling and seeing a lot of legislatures too. When Tricia hears that I'm working on a book on travelling she says I have to include a chapter on washrooms. We are near the washrooms, which, as in every legislature but Ontario's, are accessible and well marked. I tell her about that. Then we have one of those no-degrees-of-separation chats that may happen more in this country than anywhere else. Tricia says she only knows one writer and I probably wouldn't know him: Greg Cable. I tell her that I play poker at a friend's cottage with Greg Cable every year. He may, in fact, be unwittingly helping to finance this trip.

### West Edmonton Mall: One More for the Book

I spend the early part of the afternoon with friends from the *Edmonton Journal*, one of the few modern newspapers that has had the good sense to remain downtown. The refurbished building is modern and airy and couldn't be better located. Nancy walks on Jasper Avenue, which used to be thought of as the main drag. I report to her that my former Ottawa friends in Edmonton think

Albertans are really friendly, except in their cars. I am glad to have my impression reinforced. Nancy reports that Edmonton's downtown is full of malls.

Then we head out for the West Edmonton Mall. Nancy may be making her greatest sacrifice yet "for the book." As we drive out there, I'm beginning to feel like I have the hang of the directions, which way you turn to go east–west or north–south. Still, we almost miss the entrance for the West Edmonton Mall parking. How could we miss the biggest mall in North America, or is it the world?

It's because, I maintain, everything leading up to the West Edmonton Mall is a mall. So it all blurs together. I have a hard time believing this, that people would put up malls around the biggest mall in the world, or is it the solar system? But maybe that's the dynamic, that malls attract malls, just as one coffee house attracts another. This is not a world I understand very well, or want to.

But it would be irresponsible to pass this one up. So here we come, driving along a six-lane highway past one mall after another, and right in the middle of it is a new housing development. What would you call a new housing development in the middle of a city, surrounded by malls, with a six-lane highway running past it, and the world's biggest mall next door? Right. Whispering Willows.

Our entrance is effected at parking lot 2J, Entrance 1. Once inside, we find ourselves on European Boulevard. There are European-style sidewalk cafés in it, part of a strange attempt to make aisles in a mall look like streets outside it. We encounter another one later on called Bourbon Street, where twenty restaurants and clubs are stuck in a row under a dark-coloured ceiling and twinkling lights. Why can't a mall just be proud to be a mall? Clearly, they are a big part of our culture now, whether old grouches like it or not. They are in many ways the new Main Street. While it is fun to watch the traditional Main Streets – the Rosser Avenues and Stephen Avenues and Government Streets and Water Streets – fight back, it is also instructive to look at the other side, to watch the malls recognizing that they have to become more, for lack of a better word, human.

West Edmonton Mall tries hard to become more human. But it can't, at the same time, abandon its previous goal, which is to become more More. It is in this context that I assess the fact that a replica of Christopher Columbus's ship the *Santa Maria* is in a big pool, along with some dolphins and a submarine. People are standing watching this, and why not?

There is More here, to be sure. We walk by the wave pool and look in through a window. It is apparently the World's Largest Indoor Wave Pool (the world's largest outdoor wave pool being the ocean). There is a change room downstairs and a complete list of things you can rent, in order to make the wave pool experience in the shopping centre more meaningful, such as a family cabana for $19.95, a towel for $3, a yellow inner tube for $5. You can also go on a waterslide here or bungy-jump. What I find bizarre about it is not the fact that there is a wave pool in a shopping centre but that people are sitting around beside it, in bathing suits on lounge chairs, reading, as if on a day at the beach. Do they know that those are electric lights overhead, that they are indoors?

We walk by the ice rink, which is full size, and over which a radio station blares unintelligibly. Right beside it is a fancy coffee place and right beside that is a tank of tropical fish, for some reason. What reason? *Context* is what's missing in this mall, "often called the Eighth Wonder of the World," according to its own literature. Context. Why are those tropical fish there? It doesn't say. There they are, that's all, and if you happen to like tropical fish beside your ice-skating rink, well, this is your place. Later on, in the same context, or lack of it, we see peacocks in one place and a display of minerals in another.

What else is there? Well, eight hundred stores and one hundred places to eat, we are told. Plus a miniature golf course and an amusement park, which we go by several times without noticing. How can you not notice an amusement park? I don't know.

Perhaps we were distracted by the minerals. The amusement park is impressive, like the wave pool and the ice rink, but, walking around, mulling it over, I am forced to the conclusion that this is just another shopping centre, really, if you take away the wave pool, the ice rink, the miniature golf course, the submarine and the amusement park. Oh – and the hotel, the Fantasyland Hotel, with the rooms made up to look like igloos and trucks and horse-drawn Victorian coaches and whatnot. Aside from all that, it's the same old bunch of stores and fast-food places.

We keep wandering, looking for something special, something different, something bizarre. I do see an inflatable mascot for the restaurant chain Hooters dancing to the music of the inevitable Peruvian pan flute band, but I suspect that's almost a commonplace sight now in urban Canada. And I do admire the fact that the Orange Julius at the amusement park doesn't have orange juice and refers us back to the *main* Orange Julius, which is at the skating rink. Still, we are very much in the real world, as it is defined in the nineties in North America.

There is only one way to have a unique West Edmonton Mall experience. I must ride the submarine. Nancy, somehow declining to join me, walks off to buy a newspaper and is unable to find one store, amongst the eight hundred, that sells them.

Meanwhile, I pay my $13 and, after a nervous trip to the washroom, stand in line for the next trip, which I'm told will be in ten minutes and I'm supposed to be there ten minutes early. Heaven knows why. Anyway, there I stand, realizing that I am setting myself up for the ultimate humiliation – namely, to be seen by someone I know, standing in line to ride a submarine in a shopping centre. There is no way that I can pretend I'm doing something else. I'm lined up on a gangplank kind of thing and the submarine is coming in for a landing. I can see it, its top at least an inch below the surface of the water. What would I say if I were to be spotted? "Oh, hi. Did you know that this is the absolutely best place, acoustically, to hear the Peruvian pan flute band?"

The hatch opens and about twenty of us get in. I have not been spotted. I sit by a window and it occurs to me, rather too late, that I sometimes get claustrophobic. I always take aisle seats in planes and theatres because of this. I wish this hadn't occurred to me. Or, alternatively, I wish that it had occurred to me $13 ago. Now I'm really stuck. I try to imagine the scene: Me, in a cold sweat, pleading to be let off a submarine that is one inch below the surface of the water, on a track, in a shopping centre. No. I will have to tough it out.

Before we depart, our captain, Susan, describes the submarine's safety features. "Although we are in a mall, we are governed under the laws of the Canadian coast guard," she says. There are life jackets, fire extinguishers, a two-way radio ("Can you describe your exact position?" "West Edmonton Mall.") and flares. Then we are off, on a twenty-minute odyssey, or whatever you call it in a mall. The submarine takes us past tanks of Hawaiian, then Australian, then Atlantic fish, then a tank with some baby sharks in it, then Alberta trout. It is a kind of aquatic version of multiculturalism we are being exposed to here. We see a giant turtle and then, as we continue slowly around the track, a replica of a sixteen-foot white shark, then the side of the *Santa Maria*, then a mock-up of a submarine like ours being attacked by a giant squid. I completely forget my claustrophobia. Then we see a representation of the Lost Civilization of Atlantis, the representation consisting of some broken statues. This gives me a sudden flash of insight into decision-making at the mall: if they don't know what to do with something but don't want to throw it out, they can dump it into the pool and let the people look at it from the submarine. Next year at this time, I bet we could look out the submarine's windows and see a display of minerals. I hope not peacocks.

Over the loudspeaker, the captain calls our attention to all the sights, telling us whether they are on port or starboard sides and making sure that we know which is left and which is right. There may be some landlubbers in our group. We pass, on the port side, a model of a giant clam, then some coral. "The coral is real, though no longer living, due to the chlorination of the water," she says. Then we see the dolphins, which are real.

As we land, someone asks her about the blank TV screen at the front of the submarine. The captain says that promotional material about the mall used to play on it, but they found that people were watching the TV instead of looking out the submarine windows. "Now we just use it for the weight," she says, demonstrating that sanity can still be found, even in a submarine in a shopping centre.

As we drive around Edmonton in the early evening, I remember how much I liked it back in the Sixties. By that time, I had left home but often came out for visits at Christmas and other holidays. We locate the house where my parents lived, on 117th Street, near the university. It looks great, nicely painted, and with the trees grown tall. Nancy says she wants to tell my mother we saw it, and I remember her as being happy here, living in Canada for the first time after a life in the States and overseas, finding things to do and friendly, open people to do them with.

We drive to Whyte Avenue, in the southeast part of the city, not far away, one of the streets that has defied Edmonton's numerical naming system, even though it is, on most maps, called 82nd Avenue. Whyte Avenue, in a three- or four-block avenue around 104th Street, has become trendy, full of interesting restaurants, coffee places, galleries, and the young people they attract. We park but I need loonies to feed into the machine so I go into a bar and ask for two loonies for a toonie. "We call that a Lucien," says a guy in uniform. "A Lucien?" I ask, excellent straight man that I am. "That's what I call it," he says, "because it likes to split." I remember that in the early days of the two-dollar coin people were hitting it with hammers, causing the middle part to come out. Then I remember that this may be the first unity-related remark I have heard in two and a half months.

Whyte Avenue reminds me of hip-looking streets you see in other Canadian cities, with one very western exception: it is as wide as the sky. So you don't go casually bopping across the street and back the way you might in, say, Ottawa's Byward Market. Still, it is a progressive place, so progressive that the best bookstore on it has separately labelled sections for each of the following categories:

Men's Studies
Relationships
Abuse/Loss
Recovery.

We eat at an attractive, upmarket yet casual ribs-and-chicken place called Pack Rat Louie's, then wander down to 83rd where Edmonton's fringe festival is about to begin. It is a bustling scene, with booths and tents, and lots of people. Because Edmonton is smaller and more community conscious, something like the fringe festival will make a bigger impression here and get more coverage than in a larger city, like Toronto, where at any given time it is just one of dozens of big events. Edmonton, my kids tell me, is one of the best theatre cities in Canada, and I'm not surprised.

# 19

# Across the Top of the Prairie

Our drive to Saskatoon is uneventful, still on 16, the Yellowhead. Aside from the drive through the Rockies, the two branches of the Trans-Canada don't show Alberta at its best. It's not until we get back into Saskatchewan, after Lloydminster, that the land really begins to green up with farms and roll a bit with the North Saskatchewan River Valley. We lose the 110 km/h speed limit, the divided highway, and the cheap gasoline, but regain the multi-coloured fields.

Our first full day in Saskatoon covers the range of spiritual experiences. It begins with a visit to the bus terminal, to pick up our laundry from Fraser Lake. The whole downtown has a kind of empty look and nowhere more so than around the bus terminal, from which there is nothing in sight but parking lots.

From there we drive north to Wanuskewin Heritage Park, a National Historic Site, a centre of native spirituality and an awfully good advertisement for native culture. When I talked on the phone to the novelist Guy Vanderhaeghe last night and asked for advice on what to see, he recommended this. It is about a fifteen-minute drive, north on Highway 11, seemingly in the middle of nowhere. When you walk through the middle of that nowhere, you find out how much nowhere can contain.

Wanuskewin has been open since 1992, financed by the city, the province, and good old Saskatchewan Lotteries. At the centre of it is a modern building, built in a style that evokes tepees (tipis, they are spelled here). The interpretive centre has a gift shop, a restaurant, a museum, and an auditorium. There is a seventeen-minute slide show, we are told, and there is a network of trails around the site. Against our better judgement, we go and sit through the slide show. It turns out to be a slick multimedia performance in which the words "before the white man" are never uttered. Conveying more mood than information, it talks about the importance of the land, the symbolism of circles, the interdependence of people and animals, and somehow does it in a way that avoids the New Age goo we have become accustomed to. At the same time, it also avoids the kinds of facts we have been raised on. It doesn't answer any of the Inner Journalist's questions – How many buffalo? What year was that? How strong a wind? "Maybe we don't need to know everything," says the narrator, a native woman looking for the meaning of Wanuskewin. "Maybe mysteries have a right to exist."

Okay, granted. The Inner Journalist goes back wherever he was hiding and we continue, now well primed for the rest of the North Plains Indian experience. The main exhibit hall has skins, stuffed animals, tipis, sounds of drums, birds, and water. Touch-sensitive screens guide us through various topics. I learn about three ways to catch buffalo, the buffalo jump being my favourite. There are words

that I like: "The life of a man is a circle from childhood to childhood, and so it is in everything where power moves."

Outside it is a cloudy but warmish day, shorts and sweatshirt.
The interpretive centre sits at the top of a valley, and trails wind
down through it. Prairie is at the top. Creek is at the bottom. We
pick the Trail of the People, which is supposed to take about an
hour. It winds behind the interpretive centre, down to the
Ophamihaw Creek and then back up. We find a buffalo jump and
a buffalo pound – the former being a cliff the buffalo are driven
over, the latter an enclosure in which they are trapped. We stop at
a medicine circle, gaze down on the South Saskatchewan River.
Along the way are a few interpretive sites (sponsored, in the
unavoidable modern way, by such institutions as the Saskatoon
*Star-Phoenix* and the Bank of Montreal). At each, a board tells us
what would have been happening at this spot two hundred years
ago, or two thousand. Looking up the hill we can see where the
buffalo were lured over the edge.

What is moving about this – and it is far more moving than a
museum could be – is to walk an unchanged countryside, the little
humps and twists of a prairie trail, and to experience the landscape
the way others must have, the breeze and unbroken vistas at the
top, the stillness and sweet smells and infinite variety of the narrow
valley. Walking the land and seeing how it was used, it is possible to
understand why people loved it and needed to live in it. The prairie
is capable of so much more than it is given credit for. Here are the
wild flowers and grasses, the animals. Standing quietly on a
wooden bridge over the creek, we hear owls and the wind, see
prairie chickens, a thrush, cat-tails, butterflies, ducks and yellow
flowers. It is not the most vigorous walk we've had, but perhaps
the nicest.

In its way, Wanuskewin is akin to Upper Canada Village. It is
less detailed, less commercialized, less on-the-nose in its representation of a people's history. But it gives the same opportunity, to
walk where an earlier people walked, and it has the same effect.

In Saskatoon, on the way back to the hotel, we stop at the Mendel Gallery, one of the best small art galleries in the country. It is an unprepossessing building on the bank of the river. Two large landscapes by Dorothy Knowles greet us. Margaret Vanderhaeghe, who is also represented in the Mendel, says Knowles is the best landscape artist in the country these days, has been for ten years. For some reason, landscapes are what people buy. Perhaps it's because we crave scenery.

The permanent collection is varied and colourful. I like Paul Sisetski's *Death of a Small Town Bar*. Ottawa artist Alex Wyse is here, along with William Kurelek, Jack Shadbolt, Ivan Eyre, and Lawren Harris. Other Saskatchewan artists, in addition to Margaret Vanderhaeghe, include Ronald Bloore and Allen Sapp. Two artists, Darrell Bell and Darryl Hughto, an American, have painted Wanuskewin. The Mackenzie Art Gallery in Regina displays its collection more dramatically, but this is an impressive collection.

Later in the afternoon, we split up, expanding our range of cultural experiences. I wander by myself down Spadina Crescent to the Ukrainian Museum of Canada, which is small but interesting, another culture both displaying and preserving itself. Unlike Wanuskewin, the Ukrainian Museum emphasizes facts and artifacts: dates of settlement, populations, costumes, implements. Ukraine is the second-largest country in Europe, I learn, with a land mass the size of Ontario. The period of the greatest settlement in Canada was between 1891 and 1914. The major destinations were Winnipeg and Edmonton. I learn how *pysanky*, the inscribed Easter eggs, are made, with a beeswax pen and layers of dye.

Nancy takes our newly rescued dirty clothes to a basement establishment on Broadway that combines laundry and bar facilities. It is called the Wash 'n' Slosh. Apparently that sums it up.

After the museum, I walk back to the hotel through Kiwanis Park, which runs alongside the South Saskatchewan. Somehow I miss the flock of white pelicans for which the river is known, or they miss me. Saskatoon makes good use of its river and the river

distinguishes the city. There is a trail and a bike path, a statue of
Ray Hnatyshyn. Behind the Bessborough (now called, in that
stupid corporate way, Delta Bessborough; these capitalists insist on
sticking their ugly corporate names in front of the names that actually mean something to people), there is a garden, a railway-hotel
kind of garden. Wedding photos are being taken at the Vimy
Memorial Bandstand.

We cross the river and drive south for dinner with Guy and
Margaret Vanderhaeghe. My sister, Alison, as it turns out, was
through only two days ago. She is in Saskatchewan to speak at the
Saskatchewan Baseball Hall of Fame dinner in North Battleford,
which we passed without stopping on the way here. I wonder what
she would have said, when she was thirteen and living in Tokyo,
if someone had told her she would one day speak at the
Saskatchewan Baseball Hall of Fame.

While we have dinner at the Vanderhaeghes' – outside and bug-
free – we talk about such things as the alleged superiority of
Saskatoon to Regina. Saskatoon, not being a capital, has had to
achieve its level of culture without government support. Guy and
Margaret lived in Ottawa about ten years ago when Guy was
writer-in-residence at the University of Ottawa. Now they think
Saskatoon's theatre scene may be livelier than Ottawa's. There is a
good jazz festival as well as a vigorous local scene, a good fringe
festival and Shakespeare on the Saskatchewan. It may be that
Saskatoon's feeling of isolation has something to do with this, creating a sense of identity and common spirit that bring people
together to work for the arts. Whatever they have, they should
bottle it.

## An Unexpected Road to Brandon

Our destination today is Greenwater Provincial Park, about three
and a half hours east, where our Brandon friends Terry and
Colleen Mitchell have a cottage. We think it might be nice just to

flop for a couple of days. Not that we've been breaking our backs with a lot of long drives lately. Just that it's nice every once in a while to sit quietly in a comfortable place with people we know. First, we want to go to Batoche, which will entail a small detour to the north.

Mindful of Guy Vanderhaeghe's recommendation and thinking of our experience yesterday at Wanuskewin, it seems like a good idea to walk around in Louis Riel's footsteps too. We turn east from Rosthern onto Highway 312 and go down into a valley, across the South Saskatchewan (you never cross a Prairie river just once), arriving at the National Historic Site, which is one of the few Canadian battlefields you can visit. This time we don't need persuading to sit for the slide show, even though it is forty minutes long. This one is quite elaborate, using eighteen projectors, a scrim, some sets and mannequins. The comfortable theatre holds about 120 and is half full.

What we get is a simplified version of history that doesn't really tell us why the Métis were so mad at the federal government in 1885 or why the federal government was so worried about the Métis. You could, of course, put it down to distrust and paranoia and anyone familiar with modern politics would accept it without argument. If the show is weak on context, however, it is powerful in depicting the emotions and the struggle involved. It certainly sets up our walk.

The walk takes us to the church, which is busy and overdecorated, but it is possible to imagine it busy and full of anxious people alarmed by the gunfire. Then we walk to the cemetery, which has some new graves in it, but also many old ones, and old names – Boyer, Caron, Pilon, Gervais. A plaque summarizes Gabriel Dumont's life. He was born in 1838 and died in 1906. In 1884 he led a party to Montana to bring Riel back to help at Batoche. When Batoche fell, Dumont escaped and wound up in Buffalo Bill's wild west show. (A harbinger of a depressingly familiar

Canadian pattern: even then, there was a brain drain.) Pardoned, he returned to Batoche and became a hunter again. As for Batoche, it actually recovered after the battle in 1885, even prospered, but eventually succumbed to other economic forces.

From the graveyard we walk down a narrow path to a spot over-looking the river where it bends. Poplars are all around. Across the river there are fields. It is very beautiful now and difficult to imagine fighting here, but not difficult to see why people would fight for it.

The visitor centre has, in addition to the theatre, a gift store, snack bar, and art exhibit. It is well done, with taste and intelli-gence. A staffer says that most visitors are Canadians, the greatest number from Saskatchewan, then Alberta and Manitoba. So we have left the beaten tourist track. I look at the guest book and see only one American out of the last fifty visitors. Interestingly, the comments are all favourable. I would have thought that Riel and Dumont might still inspire unfriendly comments. It is certainly a misunderstood, often trivialized period. I think of Riel's Manitoba associate, Cuthbert Grant, called Warden of the Plains, who was adopted for a time as a kind of historical mascot for Brandon's Winter Carnival, sort of a Métis Bonhomme Carnivale.

The Yellowhead is quite a bit south of us now. We take 41 to Melfort, 3 to Tisdale, putting faces on places that were just names on a map. Tisdale is still called, against all odds, the Land of Rape and Honey. When we arrive at Greenwater, in time for supper, we hear that Lew Whitehead has died. The funeral is in Brandon, five hours away, the day after tomorrow.

I decide that I want to go, but I also want to continue with the route we had planned, which would take us still farther north, to Flin Flon. Eventually we decide that Nancy will stay here with Colleen. Terry and I will drive to Brandon for the funeral, stay overnight if a good wake develops, otherwise come back the same night.

## The Power of Distant Light

Terry and I set out after an early supper the next day and spend a lot of time during our drive talking about Lew, who was a neighbour of Terry's, and about my early days at the *Brandon Sun*. A week after I started at the *Sun* late in 1964, we moved down Rosser Avenue to the new building Lew Whitehead had put up for us. It was an impressive thing, fancier than it needed to be, an ornament to the street, a demonstration of the faith he had in the community and the place of the newspaper in it. A couple of years later, he sold a minority share in it to Southam. This was to make sure that it didn't fall into the wrong hands should he die. Lew was a bachelor and there was no obvious person in the extended family to take it over.

By virtue of sticking around, I rose in the paper, eventually becoming managing editor for my last five years there. Lew, who carried the title of editor and publisher, backed me up when I got the paper into trouble, which I did from time to time, and sent me off to seminars in the States and conferences all across Canada. Of course, it all seemed rather natural at the time, but when I look back on it I realize what an amazing thing it was for Lew to put so much trust in me and the other young and quite inexperienced people who were looking after the news side of his investment. He continued to pour resources into the plant – the *Sun* was one of the first Canadian converts to offset printing – and into the training of the staff. In the meantime, he travelled widely, looking after his many business interests in the United States. When he returned, often to some fresh horror, he listened to the nervous complaints of the folks on the advertising and circulation side, then listened to my side and then told the nervous folks to back off. Because I was young and had never worked anywhere else, I didn't realize how rare that was.

Terry and I drive south, then east and into Manitoba around Benito, then south on Highway 83 to Highway 1 at Virden. It is a clear evening and we see a Top Ten sunset as we drive south. In

Saskatchewan, we pass through Nut Mountain and Kelvington, whose slogan is THE HOCKEY FACTORY, at the top of a sign that lists many hockey players, most notably Wendel Clark, who have had careers in the National Hockey League. We will see other Saskatchewan towns that celebrate their hockey players, not to mention Foxwarren, Manitoba, HOME OF THE NHLERS. In Manitoba, we go through Roblin, JEWEL OF THE PARKLAND, and see a coyote beside the road.

Approaching one town I remember how disorienting it can be driving on the prairies at night. When it is flat and clear, a light five miles away can look like it's fifty yards down the road, and something flashing in the distance, a radio tower, a tow truck, a railway crossing, can fool you into slowing down far in advance. Terry and I must have spent ten minutes trying to figure out what one particular distant light was. It is easy to understand, on such a night, the sincerity of those who see UFOs.

To make matters more complicated, the eyes become so accustomed to the emptiness and darkness that the arrival at civilization – in this case Virden – produces a confusing riot of light and colour. Still, we make it to Brandon, around eleven, back on Manitoba time.

## Setting of the Sun

I never regretted leaving in 1974 but always missed the *Sun*. And Nancy and I both missed Brandon, where we had been active and had great friends and where our two children were born. We visited a few times and I kept up with various former colleagues. Once Lew came to Ottawa and we had lunch, but I was never able to get together with him on any of my trips to Brandon. In 1986, he was walking his basset hound when he was attacked by two men. I think what they had against him was the fact that he was there and they were viciously drunk. They had no idea who he was, but they beat him and stabbed him many times. He almost died, and his spirit may have. He became fearful and reclusive, lost interest in the paper. When he sold it, a year later, it was, most ironically, to the Thomson chain. His health went, and he dropped out of public sight. Few of his old friends saw much of him in recent years.

The funeral is at 1:00 p.m. It is not in the Anglican Cathedral, where a person of Lew's importance should be, but in the funeral home. It would hold about two hundred people, the Inner Journalist figures, and is about half full. There are *Sun* people there, but not too many of the current ones and no one of my generation – at least not from the newsroom, although I am heartened to see a few former colleagues who are even older than I. The composing room, probably the group with the least turnover in the building, has turned out in force and I see some old friends there. There are some of Lew's contemporaries from the town and from the university, in which he was active and to which he was generous.

The service is terribly disappointing. There is no eulogy, no old friend to talk about Lew's life and work. The minister tries, but his words could be about anyone. Lew knew triumph and tragedy, joy and sorrow, success and failure, etcetera and etcetera. The solo is slow. The fact that it is an Anglican service deepens the impersonality of it all. You start at this page in the book and continue on to this page, inserting the name of the deceased where appropriate. At the end, the family leaves quickly without staying to greet anyone. No provision has been made for people to get together. We all feel unsatisfied. While it is true that no man should be known by the quality of his funeral, a funeral should at least reflect the quality of the man. And it should give the friends a chance to gather and remember. I think of my mother's funeral, only six weeks ago, about the warmth that was there, despite the sadness, the feeling that she was being well remembered.

There is no point in sticking around. Terry and I pick up some sandwiches at a good delicatessen and head back to Saskatchewan. This time we take the Trans-Canada into Saskatchewan and turn up at Whitewood, crossing the Qu'Appelle Valley, which is quite a

sight. Driving along a flat road, you see a sign indicating a downward grade and then all of a sudden you're driving straight down
into the valley, with its gnarled walls, the crops bright in the twilight, the river small and slow, always less majestic than the size of
the valley would suggest. Then it's up the other side, the car down-
shifting to make the hill and saying (I have begun to hear the car
talk now), "Hey, I thought this was the *prairie*, dammit!"

We drive past Stockholm and Dubuc, a peaceful drive, ducks
and birds in the sloughs beside the road, the slower cars pulling
onto the paved shoulder to let the faster cars go by, perhaps to
Alberta. Around Yorkton we see a storm which we manage to skirt,
first to the south, then to the west. We go through Canora, where
there was a big settlement of Ukrainians, then onto Highway 5,
Buchanan, Invermay, Margo, Kuroki, then back to Highway 38
and home at 8:30, Saskatchewan time. I'm glad we went and sorry
the day didn't mean more to more people.

## Just in Time for Flinty's Birthday

I know two people, and only two people, from Flin Flon. They are
both poets. This is all the more reason to see Flin Flon. Enid
Delgatty Rutland is a poet in Ottawa. Jerry Heath is a poet, a trom-
bone player, and an environmentalist on a farm near Delta,
Ontario. When I asked Enid if she knew Jerry in Flin Flon, she
said of course. Neither has lived there since the fifties.

Off we go for Flin Flon, setting out from Greenwater on a
cloudy but warm enough morning. It would have been easier for
both of us to go to Brandon and then keep going east – we are
both starting to have thoughts of home after having been away for
more than two and a half months – but this seems important
somehow. For one thing, it is a route no one takes. No one can
advise us on places to stay, things to see. We hear that the three
hundred kilometres of the Hanson Lake Road, as it is known, may
not be so good. And we have to go a couple hundred kilometres
to get to it.

So this will be an adventure, an ordeal perhaps. But first we have to detour to Porcupine Plain to see the world's largest porcupine, Quilly Willy. We do that, and indeed there he is, a big statue wearing what looks like a lumberjack outfit. I picture that council meeting of a long time ago, when the question of whether to put up a statue of a giant porcupine (or giant goose or giant lobster or giant muskie) was being debated, the pros and cons bouncing back across the table, the final decision an act of faith in the ability of this giant thing to bring in tourists and spark economic growth. Now maybe they only stop if they have to use the washroom or are writing a book. Meanwhile, Porcupine Plain has another sign, proclaiming itself the HOME OF KELLY CHASE, THE PRIDE OF PORCUPINE PLAIN. He is a hockey player with the St. Louis Blues.

Nancy humours me on all this. Sometimes these things work out and sometimes they don't. Sometimes there is material, and sometimes there is just a sign. We turn west now to Melfort, CITY OF NORTHERN LIGHTS. We pass through Gronlid, BRIDGEWAY TO THE NORTH. From coast to coast, so many towns we've seen boast only about being the gateway to somewhere else. Of course, if they had a hockey player, things would be different. We cross the Saskatchewan River on a causeway – it is now wide, since the North and South Saskatchewan rivers have joined and are heading northeast towards Hudson's Bay. We stop at a roadside park for coffee. We are the only people. There are the sounds we make and the sounds of the wind and the sound of one squirrel. It would still be possible, if you wanted to do it, to find a route across Canada, even in August, where you wouldn't see tourists.

The Hanson Lake Highway, 106, turns out to be far better than advertised. It is not particularly scenic, but the thought of driving north gives it a certain allure. The lake where we stop for a picnic lunch, Little Sealy Lake, looks a bit like some of the smaller ones around Kenora. A forest fire was here not too long ago. There is intermittent rain.

As we get farther north we see more turnoffs for fishing lodges. The landscape begins to get rockier and the trees bigger about eighty kilometres this side of Flin Flon. The trees look like red pines. When we finally get a Flin Flon radio station, it is doing the Arctic Radio News (we *are* in the North), pre-eminent among which is that Flinty's birthday is coming up and there will be cake for everybody, plus rock-painting and other things. Flinty is a statue of Josiah Flintabbatey Flonatin, a character in a novel that was, so the story goes, found on this site, which was then the wilderness, by prospectors. When, years later, they found gold, they decided to name the place after him. Fortunately, someone shortened the name, otherwise what would poets do? What rhymes with Flintabbatey Flonatin?

It really is one of the unlikeliest ways anything ever got named. And what if they'd found another book? Flin Flon could be named Moby Dick or Uriah Heep or, for that matter, Glengarry School Days.

Entering Creighton, Saskatchewan, a kind of twin city of Flin Flon, we see a big smokestack and that combination of bare rock and scrubby trees you see around Sudbury. These are mining towns, as indicated by the Copperbelt Hotel in Creighton. Flin Flon has that same very rugged, rocky look to it. It is early, because the drive took far less time than we thought, and we don't see anything that knocks us out in the way of hotels, so we drive over to the tourist bureau to see if we can find out anything there. And there's old Flinty, in the flesh, or at least the wood, the statue designed, in another bizarre twist, by Al Capp, the American cartoonist and looking, if the truth be told, a bit like Quilly Willy, only more dressed up and wearing red spectacles. No one's complaining, mind you. Better to have Flinty than Fred Flintstone or some Disneyfied creature.

The tourist bureau lists a new resort by the water at Denare Beach, back in Saskatchewan. Denare Beach has an interesting story to its name too. It comes from the first two letters of

DEpartment of NAtural REsources. And you thought it was some exotic native moniker. Anyway, we drive back through Flin Flon, back through Creighton, to get to it, and find the resort, which is exactly what we want and more. It sits on the edge of a steep hill high over Amisk Lake (Amisk is, in fact, a Cree word, meaning beaver). The exterior is solid log. The room is inexpensive and has a treated wood balcony, facing west. The dining room, which is informal and outdoorsy, serves pickerel, albeit frozen, and we finish it in time to get back to our balcony for the sunset, which may be the best we've seen. The lake resembles Lake of the Woods. Our height is like the height from the highest point on Birkencraig and from there the wind gives the water the same sense of rivers flowing between the islands. The spruces are taller and skinnier, perhaps a sign of our northerliness (we are up near the fifty-fifth parallel again). It cools off and a rising half moon accompanies our sunset. We went 598 kilometres today and it was worth it just for this.

## Out of the North

The next morning we delay our departure in order to watch a beaver swim across the bay. His wake is visible all the way across, the water is so still. On Main Street, we park in front of the Flin Flon Bakery, get cinnamon buns and coffee for the morning's first stop, sandwiches for our lunch. Heading back to the car, I walk by a youngish guy and he nods hello and smiles. Usually you only see that from older folks.

We drive around town a bit. I'm thinking of Jerry and Enid and what it must have been like growing up here. Enid has a poem called "The Cranberry Tree" that is about coming back to Flin Flon and her descriptions are just right.

> Rock peers out through the roadbed,
> in gardens, in basements.
> No escaping it, not even in winter

when the wind blows the jutting boulders clean.
Living in the foundations of an unfinished house
all year round.

Flin Flon doesn't resemble any place else. That's probably why people leave and why others stay.

We are headed south now on Highway 10 and the first part of it, through Cranberry Portage to The Pas, is beautiful, full of lakes. At Wanless we stop to make a telephone call at a place that is a combined general store, liquor store, and post office. Outside, two young women are talking about the cold. It was three degrees last night. An older guy talks about the summer of '84, "the year Dave died," when it froze in mid-August. Today it is warm and sunny. A few miles later, the highway becomes flat and straight, more like Manitoba. We see a grain elevator at The Pas, then cross the Saskatchewan River again.

After crossing the fifty-third parallel, we see our first farm, which features pigs and cattle, then a range of hills, probably the Duck Mountains. Off to the left we see a vista of fields. We are out of the north.

I think it's when we decide to bypass Dauphin (HOSPITALITY PLUS HERITAGE) that I realize I am starting to think about home. There are more signs of that. We stop at Wasagaming, in Riding Mountain National Park, and check in at the Elkhorn Lodge and Conference Centre. Our room is terrific. It has a little living area, a fridge, a fireplace, and a balcony opening out onto a nice view. I barely notice, just throw my bags on the bed. This must be the way people who travel all the time get – ballplayers, rock musicians, foreign correspondents. Where's the bed, where's the phone, when do we eat, fine. A month ago, even a week ago, I would have been ecstatic about the room. Hell, even yesterday I was excited about the room. After dinner we go out for a walk in the town and I decline to go into the bookstore, fearing, I think, that I might find something to take notes about. Suddenly, a feeling of let's-get-it-over-with is upon me. I guess it's good it didn't come sooner. We have about a week's worth of driving left.

Wasagaming, usually referred to as Clear Lake, after the lake, is cottage country for Brandon. I always thought it was a peculiar setup (never thinking there was anything peculiar about an island in Lake of the Woods with twenty relatives around the table). The cottages are laid out along streets parallel to the lakeshore. Most people are away from the lake. And they are as close to their next-door neighbours as they would be in town. In fact, some of them have *the same* next-door neighbours as they have in town. I always figured that you went to the cottage to get away from all that.

But people enjoy it. Clear Lake has a great golf course, and the park, while nowhere near as spectacular as Banff or Jasper, has a lot to offer. Tonight, for instance, the lake produces for us yet another spectacular sunset. The townsite has nothing of the up-market internationalism of Banff. It is more like a resort community of the forties or fifties. It has that rustic, small-town flavour, with a lot of people out for a stroll, saying good evening to each other. The shops sell souvenirs, basic groceries, and ice cream. Most of the people look like they live here.

## Divining Neepawa

The sense of heading home intensifies. We have travelled more than 1,200 kilometres in the last two days and by the end of today we'll either be in Winnipeg or on the island at Lake of the Woods, back in places we know.

Surprisingly (to us, now that we think about it), there's still some discovering to be done in Western Manitoba. Driving yesterday and today I'm startled at how much we didn't see when we lived out here. A lot of that has to do with spending so much of our vacation time at Lake of the Woods instead of roaming around in the car. Much of that roaming around in the car would have been with tiny children in it, too. Maybe that explains it, at least some of it.

At any rate, we have not seen Neepawa, so that's where we're headed, leaving the park, driving through Onanole, Erickson, and crossing one of the most beautiful valleys in the country, just west of Minnedosa on Highway 10. The river is the Little Saskatchewan, such a small river for such a big valley. Being a prairie river, it appears again, with another big valley, after Highway 10 meets Highway 16. We're back on the Yellowhead. The country becomes flatter, more open. There are fewer trees. The fields look more ordinary now, with the bloom off.

Neepawa's slogan is MANITOBA'S MOST BEAUTIFUL TOWN, and it could be. The residential streets are lined with large elms and have substantial old houses and churches. Mountain Street, the main drag, is typically wide, with diagonal parking. Away from Manitoba, Neepawa is known not for being Manitoba's Most Beautiful Town but for being the home of Margaret Laurence, and for being the real name of Manawaka, the setting for five of her novels, including some of the best known.

We drive to the Laurence house, at 312 First Avenue, where she lived from 1935 until 1944, when she was eighteen. It was her grandfather John Simpson's house, a solid two-storey yellow brick structure on a corner lot, built in 1894. A verandah goes around the house's left front corner. Walking through the house I'm struck, as I was struck at Green Gables, with how much of our Canadian history resembles what we still live in. This may be what a friend meant when he warned us that the Laurence house is dull. It's not dull, just familiar. We may have relatives who live in a house just like this one. We may live in one ourselves. It is strange to see it put on display, walk in to what feels like our house and see signs that say DO NOT TOUCH. That's how young the country is. That's how close to our history we are.

The living room is in that familiar twenties style, with a piano. Artifacts – a Remington typewriter, a teapot – have an everyday look to them. There is an intriguing collection of memorabilia, lovingly assembled and well marked – high school newspapers and yearbooks, photos taken when she was Peggy Wemyss, old magazine articles about her. There is the room where she did her homework and another room that has been set aside to record the honours bestowed upon her – the Order of Canada, ten honorary degrees. Her earliest honorary degree was from Carleton in 1974. Then they came fast and furious. During one heady period in 1975 she received three of them in three weeks, from Brandon, Queen's, and Western – a mixed blessing for one who dreaded public speaking.

The house, in danger of demolition, was purchased in 1986 by the Margaret Laurence Home Committee a year before her death. The mandate was to pay off the mortgage, restore and renovate the house. Money came from the Neepawa Area Development Corporation and later from provincial grants and foundations, gifts from individuals, local and national corporations. The results are impressive, in some ways more impressive than for a more massive undertaking. This one gets no publicity, has no high-powered board of directors to lobby on its behalf or carry on lavish publicity campaigns. It survives only through hard and largely unnoticed work by people who truly love what they are doing. We have seen many such places on our trip. They are as important as the Glenbow or the National Gallery.

At the gift shop – for of course there is a gift shop – Lesia Gawaziuk, a fourth-year Brandon University student who is running the place, gives us a map showing us other points of interest in Neepawa, including Laurence's first home, where she lived until she was nine and her parents died, the cemetery, where both Laurence's grave and the Stone Angel are located, the Neepawa United Church and the *Neepawa Press*, where she did her first professional writing, as a reporter in 1943. Lesia says there have been almost 3,000 visitors this year to the home. Many of the visitors are high school students with *The Stone Angel* on their curriculum.

Among the older visitors, many admire Laurence, others are critical of what she had to say about the town, particularly in *The
Diviners*.

With Lesia's map we drive to the cemetery and find the Stone
Angel, which decorates the grave of the Honourable John A.
Davidson, who was born in Thamesford, Ontario, on August 19,
1852, and died in Neepawa on November 14, 1903. Then we drive
to the *Neepawa Press*, where Laurence once worked. This is news
to Jack Gibson, the editor, who has been here less than ten years.
He was a sports writer at the *Brandon Sun* when I was there.
Eventually, he became managing editor and quit after Thomson
bought the paper. With Ewan Pow, who was advertising manager
at the *Sun*, he bought the *Neepawa Press*. Ewan is general manager.

It looks like they made a good choice. Neepawa, with a population of 3,500, is thriving and appears headed to be one of the
towns that will flourish as supply centres for the surrounding agricultural population – one of the towns where the car and implement dealers go. We leave our car parked on Mountain Street,
where there are no meters, and go in Ewan's to the Neepawa Golf
Club for lunch. As we walk through to the dining room Ewan and
Jack book a tee-off time for later in the day. Nice life: Take off early
on Friday afternoon and shoot a round of golf. The club is busier
other days, Thursday, for example. "If you try to do business on a
Thursday in the summer it's an absolute waste," Ewan says.

Part of Neepawa's prosperity has to do with demographics. An
inordinately large percentage of the population is over sixty-five,
retired farmers with a good income. There may be a good future
in selling the town as a retirement centre and building the facilities
for it.

As for the paper, it looks good. There are eight full-time
employees, two in the newsroom, including Jack, who takes photos
as well as writes and edits. The paper is printed in Dauphin, with
the printers coming to Neepawa to pick up the flats. The business
connection to Brandon is severed, but it is good to think of Lew

Whitehead's influence continuing, to the east in Neepawa, as well as to the west in Moosomin.

On the way to Winnipeg, we cross the Whitemud River four times. Just west of Portage la Prairie, the Yellowhead meets the Trans-Canada, the northern part of our journey meeting the southern part. This is where we came in. For three hundred kilometres or so, we are going to be on a route we have already travelled – travelled many times, in fact.

We stop in Winnipeg for a couple of hours and see assorted aunts and cousins. A bit of history is being played out here too. My aunt Lois, ninety years old, twenty years older than Margaret Laurence would have been, has just moved back to Winnipeg after sixty-three years away (she left in September of 1933, she tells me) in Montreal, Toronto, and most recently Kingston. The city has that strong a hold on her, much of the family is a few streets away, and the island is just two hours down the road. We drive over with her to look at the new apartment, which it seems she will like. It will get great sunsets and is just across the Assiniboine, really, from the old family home.

It is after six when we leave for Kenora, where it is our plan to spend a few days on the island. There is no one there, so we will have to stop in Kenora and pick up supplies. I am fretting a bit about the light. Will we have any when we get to the boat? A lot of other cars are with us. This is the weekly Friday night rush down to the lake. We reach the official end of the Prairies at 6:57, by the clock on the dashboard. With the light behind us, the Prairies look terrific. Now we are approaching from the proper direction. First we see scruffy bush, then a few boulders and some larger rocks, at 7:17. Soon we will see rockfaces, then lakes.

# 20

*Back to Reality (Or, at Least, Ontario)*

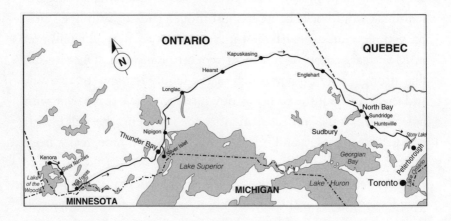

Is everybody on a history kick, or am I just noticing? Saturday we go into Kenora to pick up some more supplies. I drop in on Elizabeth Campbell Books and ask about a heritage tee-shirt on the wall. Elizabeth Campbell tells me it concerns the painting of murals on the walls of town buildings. While I am doing some errands, I pass a guy painting a mural on the side of a building on First Street. He is up on a scaffold working on the detail of the old Kenricia Hotel. When he gets down and walks across the street to look it over from a distance, I walk over there too and we talk.

Frank Lewis is from Victoria, and he did some of the work in Chemainus, a Vancouver Island town many think was saved from extinction in the early eighties by the idea of painting murals on twenty local buildings, depicting its history. Now 370,000 visitors come every year to look at the murals, and other towns are thinking along the same lines, including Kenora. Across the street, on the side of the Scotia Bank, a woman is working on a mural of the waterfront, showing the old Stone's Boathouse that I remember from my youth. Further down Main Street, at the corner of Second, a man is painting miners and loggers. There is already a mural east on Second Street with a sports theme.

A similar theme is what Frank Lewis had in mind when he won a commission to do the work, but he was asked to narrow it down to bicycling. So he got the Lake of the Woods museum to send him photos of the Rat Portage Bicycle Club. (What is now Kenora used to be Keewatin, Norman, and Rat Portage, and it got its name just as Denare did, by the unromantic method of combining first letters.) The time of the bicycle club photo happened to coincide with the Golden Jubilee of Queen Victoria, 1897, so he worked that in as well, a parade in front of the Kenricia Hotel, which happens to be his finishing detail. I ask him when he has to be finished. "Tomorrow night at sunset," he says. After that, he goes to Kuala Lumpur to work, under the Canadian Executive Service Overseas, at the school of design and architecture.

Frank's main work is as a graphics designer. But he has done fifteen murals in the last twenty-five years. It is fascinating to look at the mural and follow his thinking. Talking of the ten faces of the bicycle club members, he says, "Fifteen hundred miles ago when I designed it I didn't have these faces in mind." But he saw the faces around him in Kenora. Among other details are some poppies, done in the William Morris art nouveau style, which serve to locate the period. And there are two chickens in the lower left-hand corner. Chickens, apparently, were one of the hazards of bicycling, always bothering cyclists in those days. "Fifty years ago I remember chickens along the road," Frank says. "It's a reminder for the young people of how close to the pioneer days we are."

Owners of a local chicken place tease him about the chickens, which have a purplish tinge, asking him if they've laid any eggs yet. Frank's last act, just before he leaves, will be to deliver an egg, which he has with him and has painted purple, to the chicken place.

Frank says he began his career wanting to be one of the Group of Seven, but he became more interested in putting art to social purposes. He began street painting. "I was trying to find the faces of who we are," he says. When, as a long-haired muralist, he began doing the Chemainus paintings in 1982, it was to a mixed reception. "Loggers would drive by and throw beer cans and yell 'go home, you faggot!'"

He persisted in muraling, as he calls his work, and his work persists. This may be his last, however. "I'm sixty-three and the scaffolding is getting to be too much," he says.

History drags me down the street now to the Lake of the Woods Museum, another place I've never been. It sits on Main Street, just up from where Stone's Boathouse would be. I don't know why I'm surprised, but it is a thoroughly professional operation, with a good display of native clothing and artifacts, fascinating old photographs, representations of drawing rooms of the rich, pictures of cottages and collections of vintage cottage paraphernalia (which don't look so vintage to me) and outboard motors. There is a photo of Dominion Day on Main Street in 1915, a photo of the Rat Portage Bicycle Club in 1899, a photo of the CPR station in 1899. Another photograph shows the ceremonial opening of the Kenora–Manitoba stretch of the Trans-Canada Highway in 1932, with ten guys standing under a banner saying Ontario Welcomes You – this in unflattering contrast to today's Ontario–Manitoba border sign, which says "Ontario: We'll make you feel incredible!", a no-contest winner for the dumbest slogan of the trip.

There is also a rather modest (in my slightly biased opinion) Ralph Connor display, which consists of three books and a paragraph in the guide book. As luck would have it – and luck seems

to be having it quite frequently in recent days – I am standing at
the reception desk when I overhear a man asking if Ralph Connor
wrote *Glengarry School Days*. I jump in, as my father surely would
in this town, and say yes. A conversation ensues. He wants to know
about Ralph's connections to the lake, whether any of his books
have been made into musicals. I tell him that the Blyth Festival did
a version of *Glengarry School Days* that was frowned upon by the
purists in Glengarry. He turns out to be Gordon Day-Janz, who
has been active in recent summer theatre productions and is thinking a musical would be a good summer attraction. I tell him I know
where he can find some good young actors.

Who knows where all this leads, these plays and museums and
murals we see all across the country. At the very least, it appears that
more places are seeking their identity, even their economic well-
being, in their history rather than in the big mall on the outskirts of
town. On Main Street, I hear bagpipes, and track them down to the
laneway beside Pur-Plus Cleaners, formerly the bus terminal. Two
kids in full highland attire are playing. I don't know why.

## All Alone, and Just as Well

When we return to the island, with the groceries and the laundry,
I notice how green and lush it looks. It's been wet this summer.
This is good for the berry crop and is probably why we haven't
seen any bears on the island this year. We were a bit nervous about
that coming out last night. Last year around this time, when there
were only four or five people here, a bear figured he had the place
to himself and showed up at the house a couple of times. I didn't
like that at all. That was happening everywhere in the area. Just as
in the Rockies, people are moving into previously wild areas and
driving the bears out, and the bears are having to find new places
to go. Some of them wind up in restaurant parking lots. Some of
them go to cottages. Last night, Nancy wasn't keen on walking
down the path to the outhouse by herself, which is unusual for her.
But it looks as if we won't be having company this year.

Everything worked out fine. The boat started, it was dark but there was a moon and we could see to get out to the island all right. We had a late dinner on a warm night with tons of stars and even a hint of northern lights. Today is warm too, a good day to read quietly and listen to the water, which can do amazing tricks if the world is quiet enough. It can disguise itself, sound like footsteps, animals in the bush, humans talking.

## The Long Way to Thunder Bay

There is something to be said for an uneventful day, which we have just enjoyed. We went fishing in the canoe in the morning, the best way to fish, although not necessarily to catch anything. Nancy paddled, I trolled and caught a bass that was too small to keep. In the afternoon it was chilly enough to read under the covers.

It was a day for slow and quiet stuff. I paddled around the island by myself. There was a bit of a breeze so I had to sit in the bow seat and face backwards. I saw an eagle and a few cormorants but there were no turtles in their usual place on the log in the lagoon. They need sun to bring them out. At night, we barbecued a steak, then sat in the living room, for the first time in the summer, and put on a fire.

Now we're headed for Thunder Bay again, after a stop in town to drop off the garbage. We are taking a different and longer route, beginning with Highway 71 south to Fort Frances.

This is certainly more scenic, keeping Lake of the Woods on our right for the first hour. At Sioux Narrows we cross the world's longest single-span bridge (or did we do that somewhere before? Bridge nomenclature is so specialized). We have coffee at Nestor Falls, which is still on Lake of the Woods and still part of the lake economy. There are many lodges and fishing camps along this part of the road.

After we leave the lake, we move inland through poplar trees and some rather unproductive-looking fields. The road, while still more scenic than the related section of 17, needs passing lanes. We turn east on 11, a highway that we will be on for several days. It will take us north, away from Lake Superior, before depositing us at North Bay. Emo, which precedes Fort Frances, has the slogan A FULL SERVICE COMMUNITY. I don't know who thought that one up, but you see it all over the place. What does it mean? That there's a hospital there? A church? A McDonald's? A gas station that's not a self-serve?

Fort Frances is on the border with Minnesota (Slogan: A GOOD NEIGHBOUR COMMUNITY) and big enough, at 9,000 people, to get lost in, which we do. Once back on the highway we see signs directed at Americans, telling them what a kilometre is and that seatbelts are compulsory. Rainy Lake is on our right. There is a long stretch of sixty kilometres per hour through a rather unpopulated reservation, something you see often in Northern Ontario. I have mixed feelings about this: glad the people have enough political clout to get the speed limit lowered; sorry I have to slow down.

We cross a causeway, five kilometres long. It becomes rockier and we see more logging trucks. This is called the Voyageur Route, and somebody would point out that this is for good historical reasons. Near Shebandowan, the time changes, then we get briefly onto 17, before swinging north on 102 to bypass the city. Back on 17, which is also 11 for a while, we are driving through a more rugged landscape, as soon as we get past Thunder Bay, and we get our first glimpse of Lake Superior. The Fort Frances route was about eighty kilometres longer, it turned out, but worth doing at least once, if you have the time, which, as we keep reminding ourselves, we do.

The Terry Fox Scenic Lookout, just east of Thunder Bay, has been moved across the road and higher, to give it a better spot. The view, out onto the lake and back to the city and the Sleeping Giant, is magnificent. There is a government travel information centre, washrooms and all that, which is probably a good thing, to bring people within sight of the monument, which tells of Fox's trip in 1980, his attempt to run across the country on one leg to raise money for cancer research. He started on April 28 in St. John's and gave up near here on September 1, having travelled 3,339 miles, or 5,373 kilometres. He died the next year, in June. A year after that the monument was dedicated here. The governor-general, Ed Schreyer, was there, as was the premier, Bill Davis. It is a lovely spot and a moving memorial. Many of the people who stop there can probably remember what it felt like to be driving and to pass the slow-moving caravan moving along the shoulder, police car lights flashing ahead of and behind a curly-haired young man kind of hopping along, clearly with great difficulty. An attractive little park surrounds the monument and a woman with no sense of irony and little sense of occasion sits there enjoying a smoke.

Our destination is Silver Islet, where Nancy spent her summers when she was growing up here. To get there we turn off at Pass Lake and drive through Sleeping Giant Provincial Park. It takes a while, moving from a gravel road to a bumpy, narrow, and curvy paved road. Nancy thinks the road has changed, that it doesn't pass as many lakes as it used to. I think people's memories put lakes in unlikely places. We pass Surprise Lake, where Islet people swim, then landmarks with the kinds of names you get in a cottage community – The Big House, The Jail, The Store. We have covered a lot of ground, for us, in the last three driving days – 641 kilometres today.

## Walking The Avenue in Silver Islet

Silver was discovered on a little rock a bit out in the water from here in 1868. The vein was vertical and by 1884, when the shaft was 450 metres deep, the water couldn't be kept out of it and the mine closed. In the meantime, a mining community had developed, with houses, a store, a church, a graveyard, and a hotel, all lined up along the shore with a street – residents call it The Avenue – running between them and Lake Superior. The hotel is where we're staying now. Susan Greer, who owns half the building and uses it for a cottage, grew up with Nancy in Fort William and at

Silver Islet. She is now a judge in Toronto. The hotel, as far as she knows, never had a name. It was just The Hotel. As we stroll along the avenue, Nancy and Susan point out the sights, talk about who lives here and used to live there.

The houses owned by the miners are now all cottages – or, in the local vernacular, camps. Some of them have signs indicating what they used to be and how old they are. Near The Store is the mine captain's house, which was built in 1867. The former Methodist church goes back to 1868, the blacksmith's house to 1870. The spaces between the camps are not lawns but outcroppings of rock. Missing are any signs of gentrification. The houses are as they were, the improvements either structural or just simply functional. Decks made of treated wood have been tacked on, solar panels put on the roof, generators and propane tanks stuck outside. The camps have only the electricity their owners can hustle up on their own with generators and solar panels.

At the former hotel, Susan gets by with none. She has a wood stove, a propane fridge, an oil heater, propane lights, and a lot of kerosene lamps. Dinner in the darkened hotel dining room accompanied by twilight on the lake or, better yet, an intense thunderstorm, which we had here a couple of years ago, is an experience you remember.

We walk to the old graveyard, which is in the middle of what was once a native campground. Worn-out wooden tombstones are surrounded by leaning picket fences. Here is a forty-two-year-old who died in 1882, a ten-day-old who died in 1872. Large pine trees, younger than the graves, rise up from within the pickets.

Our walk back – it is called The Loop – takes us over Sibley Creek on a bridge with the childhood smells of wood and hot tar. We pass a house called Green Gables. Everybody we pass Susan knows. If they don't know her, they say hello anyway. I often tease Nancy about this place – the fact that all these people come to camps that have an avenue between them and the lake, and the lake so cold that no one has swum in it since 1953 and they have to walk to another one. But there is a community feeling that is inviting and it is gratifying to see a place where the bicycles sit beside the houses, unlocked. A friend who didn't grow up here says it is because it is the end of the road: no one is passing through on the way to somewhere else; everyone belongs here and acts like it.

Everyone swims at Surprise Lake, which is a ten-minute walk away from Superior. On the way back we stop at The Store, which has been restored and refurbished. You can tell that people won't let Silver Islet decay. After a dinner by oil lamp, we watch the path of the moon on the lake and I understand the appeal of this unlikely place.

## Highway 11: The Ultimate Sacrifice

This is the day Nancy thought would never happen, the day we leave her beloved Lake Superior route and turn north to Highway 11 – Longlac, Hearst, Kapuskasing, and points east. It is the route favoured by many of those whose main aim is to make time, but it is a route not even covered in some of the guide books. Still, it would be wrong not to see it. This is the ultimate sacrifice Nancy makes "for the book."

We turn north at Nipigon (HOME OF AL HACKNER, WORLD CURLING CHAMPION), remembering what a Thunder Bay friend once said: all east–west highway traffic in Canada has to cross the bridge over the Nipigon River. The road goes initially along beside the river and is pretty. There is a provincial park at Lake Nipigon where we stop for coffee. It seems badly maintained and understaffed – we find no garbage cans, no one at the gate – and I begin having political thoughts, my first in quite a few days, showing that we are not only back in Ontario but back in an Ontario state of mind. These continue while we drive on fifty kilometres of highway that have had the old surface skimmed off with no sign of anyone putting a new surface on. Welcome to the Cutback Route.

Beardmore has a giant snowman (apparently the world's largest) on the outskirts but nothing to indicate what he represents. The ballpark is weeded over, always a bad sign. Then the road improves and the scenery becomes distinctly Northern Ontario – muskeg and large stands of spruce. There is almost nothing on the road but big trucks, but they move at a good clip. We stop for lunch at Longlac, which looks more prosperous, and have a good western sandwich. On the menu it is called both a western and a Denver, so I ask the waitress which it is and she says western. So it's a western at Longlac, a Denver at English River. There is a stretch of about five hundred kilometres in the middle that needs further investigation.

There are no Persians.

There are farms for awhile, then the spruce resumes. Seeing some nasty-looking storm clouds to the north and having travelled more than six hundred kilometres, we decide on Kapuskasing (MODEL TOWN OF THE NORTH) for the night and begin looking around. It is the halfway point between Thunder Bay and North Bay. The downtown has been, pardon the expression, spruced up and looks good. Not far away, we find the Kapuskasing Inn, a grand-looking brick structure that goes back to the days when hotels were hotels, even in towns of 12,000. I think of the Kenricia in Kenora and the Prince Eddie in Brandon. This one must have been really something. In the lobby we see a signed photograph of Princess Elizabeth and Prince Philip, who stayed here during a royal visit in 1951. Things have changed, for the worse, and the room we are shown is in a motel unit out behind the main building. We try a couple of other motels. At one, the proprietor says: "We've got one room but you wouldn't want it." We decide to take his word for it. He recommends another place down the road. We ask about another. He glowers at us. "I'm recommending to you the one that I know is clean," he says. Hmmm. We take his advice, and it is clean, although sitting right on the highway with a tiny room, parking in front of it. Still, it could be worse. We could be driving in the storm that suddenly lands on us.

After the rain stops, we walk to the truckstop down the road where I lose my head and disobey the western sandwich rule. The thing is, I've had one already today, and the hot hamburger is on special, along with the bean soup, and I am pleased to be in a place with no pretensions. It turns out there is a reason for that. The bean soup is okay and the chocolate cake is fine. But I learn that it *is* possible to mess up a hot hamburger sandwich. Still, the bill for the two of us is $16. That, combined with $44 for the hotel, including tax, makes it one of the cheaper nights we've had. Not one of the best, though – something about the trucks roaring by so close, the bed so close to the window, the window so close to the car.

My Northern Ontario book is *Bastion Falls*, by Susie Moloney. It's about a town in Northern Ontario where it begins snowing in September and never stops, and scary things come out of the snow. It is a ghost story, but it reminds me of the gleeful way northerners talk about winter, such as Ted Lake's story about the truck not quite being able to jump the river when the rain washed out the bridge.

## A Turn to the South and Other Symbolic Stuff

We beat all our records in our haste to get going, up and checked out, picking up breakfast and hitting the road by 8:17. The proprietor says, as we leave, that this has been a busy summer.

As we begin to see the barn door, every turn in the road becomes symbolic. Past Cochrane, we will take a turn to the south. On our way to Cochrane, the landscape, quite flat, begins to resemble what we remember of the stretch between Sudbury and North Bay to the south of us. We start to see a few purple houses. After Moonbeam (which could have been named by Leacock) we go through Smooth Rock Falls, where one of my newspaper colleagues grew up. I try to make significant notes for him. There's

2,300 people, a smelly paper mill, the Mattagami River – a typical northern paper town. I've always liked them for some reason, maybe just to be contrary. I remember the slogan in Dryden, one of the smelliest of all paper towns: "It's the smell of prosperity." If you live there, you've got to believe that.

It takes an hour to get to Cochrane, HOME OF THE POLAR BEAR EXPRESS, which runs all the way north to James Bay and with a giant polar bear statue to prove it. The chip stand is closed for the season, which seems to go along with our turn to the south. Things are coming to an end, although we see no sign yet of leaves turning. We cross the forty-ninth parallel. It is the twenty-ninth of August.

The north does not have the only highways where you see shuttered motels and restaurants with CLOSED signs. I remember there were many on Highway 7 close to home. Still, you see a lot of them on Highway 11 and Highway 17. Every time I see one I think of the dreams people must have had when they opened them. And what killed them? In most cases, a bad economy, but also bad luck and bad location, the bad luck being that the owners did not recognize a bad location until they had been in it for a while.

We pass the turnoff to Iroquois Falls. The land becomes scrubbier, with some roll to it and some farms. We stop at a roadside picnic spot near Matheson. It is chilly. A woman in a hardhat gets out of a truck and goes into the washroom. "What a relief!" she shouts to no one in particular when she comes out. Just down the road we see her taking over flagperson duties on a highway construction project.

To the list of small towns it is impossible to get lost in for anyone but me, add Englehart, population 1,700. Grant Thain, Nancy's father, had his first teaching job here, so we get off the highway to have a look around, not paying much attention to street names. There's a gas station we want to get to and we can see it every once in a while, but it seems to be an elusive sort of

gas station. Eventually we nail it down. We pick up our lunch at a
Subway in New Liskeard and drive to a picnic spot at Latchford
beside the Montreal River, which seems to be a different river
than the one that empties into Lake Superior. This is a nice spot,
with a choice of iron bridges to look at. One is the Aubrey Cosens
Memorial Bridge, named after a local lad who died heroically in
Germany in 1945. There are two flagpoles at the cairn, one of
which is bare. A woman at the tourist bureau says the missing flag
is an Ontario one that has been on order for some time. I have
another political thought.

Although the towns have hard-rock mining names like Cobalt,
indications that we are leaving the north continue to appear. The
garbage containers at Latchford were not bear-proof, we noticed.
We begin to see certain words on signs that hint at the growing
influence of the big city. Some of these words are: family restaurant, collectibles, sea doo, ice cream parlour, tea room, mews, bed
and breakfast. On the other hand, we see other words – moccasins,
live bait – that indicate we are not completely there.

Temagami was rocked by a bomb blast yesterday. Well, that's the
way the radio news put it. Actually, there was a bomb on a bridge
on a logging road. We drive around a bit, not getting far enough
into the bush to see old growth, but we do find a small canoe
museum which has a 1905 Richardson canoe that closely resembles one my grandfather had. The town has the look of some towns
in B.C., the look of a jumping-off spot for eco-tourism, with
people on the main street dressed like they bought all their clothes
at Mountain Co-op.

As we near North Bay, where the premier lives, we see both
hills and construction on Highway 11. Right on the edge of the
city there is an actual runaway truck lane, our first one since B.C.
And we find out what runaway is in French – *hors de contrôle*.

We would really just like to push on, but we have to stop in
North Bay to see about our car insurance. It is a day out of date
now and we are Canadians, after all. North Bay is a big, by our

recent standards, city of 56,000. But we easily find the address given to us by our Ottawa agent, except that it turns out to be the former address. We are in a real estate office. The agent nicely copies the right address and phone number out for us and gives good directions. This is northern friendliness, I figure. And when we get to the right place, the agent easily does the paperwork for us in five minutes. Technology does have its moments.

On the way out, we hit a big intersection. It is where 17 meets 11, 17 being what we would have been on if we'd taken the Lake Superior route. Nancy was right, of course. This was a duller way. On the other hand, it was a different way. And now we know.

It is about here that I want to stop, at the Dionne Quints Museum, because – well, because why not? But the fork of the road we take to continue south is the wrong fork for the museum. I see it and I say the hell with it. Next time. Maybe tomorrow. There is a fancy-looking resort in Callander where we could stop for the night and catch the museum tomorrow. But the fancy-looking resort is closed up tight, forever. Onward.

Half an hour down the road is Sundridge, a faded resort town with a faded resort hotel, the Caswell Resort. I like it immediately. It has the lake (Bernard Lake), the beach and the lawn sweeping down to it, the shuffleboard court and the big lobby. When we were kids at Lake of the Woods the CPR had a resort nearby called Devil's Gap Lodge, a woody but rather elegant place. We used to walk around gawking at the place and at the rich (we thought) holidayers while our parents used the phone. This reminds me of that. An effort is being made to bring it back with renovation and redecoration and I hope it works. If there is anything we have learned it is that Canada needs more interesting roadside places. Not fancier ones, but places that have some roots. Whether Canada will support them is another question, since Canada seems to be at home, at the cottage, or sleeping in the camper.

The dining room is nice and the special is roast chicken. When the waitress tells us that, a European chap across the room says: "I cannot recommend it. The chicken was overcooked." Then a Canadian at the next table says: "I had it and I thought it was fine." It's like being back in Saskatchewan. As an act of affirmation, we order the chicken. It's perfectly fine, of course, a good Canadian chicken.

### Sort of the Last Day

Day 75 is, for all intents and purposes, the last day of the trip. Sort of: we will wind up at Mary and Stuart Parker's cottage on Stony Lake, spend a few days there, and then do the last three and a half hours back to Ottawa. And it is not exactly Day 75 either. Some days I didn't count, like the days at Lake of the Woods. Trips around the country are not that cut-and-dried. But this is more or less Day 75 and more or less the last day of the trip.

So we're feeling a combination of wistful and eager, eager to stop driving and flop for a while, wistful that the drive is nearly over. Nothing of much portent happens as we drive out of Sundridge. Typical of a lot of summer towns, it seems to have more businesses than people. You look at the population marked on the signs as you drive in and wonder how so few people could take up so many buildings.

This is the Friday of the Labour Day long weekend, a sunny and warm Friday, and we are on Highway 11, one of the main routes for the tension-filled fun-seekers from Toronto, but figure to be off it before the rush begins. We cross the Magnetawan River, another bridge we can't see off, and talk about being out of the North. There are still some lovely lakes and rock outcroppings, but it feels more civilized around here. You can get a good debate going in this country about what constitutes north. Torontonians talk about going up north when they go to Muskoka or Georgian Bay. Hardier souls would say that nowhere we have been on our trip even qualifies as north, not Prince Rupert, not Flin Flon. For me, there's a quality of Northern

Ontario that makes it different from the rest of the province, and I think it begins at North Bay.

As if to underline my point, more southern words appear on signs: Korean cuisine, waffle cones, Santa's Village, bistro, XXX. Then there are those big long complexes of gas station, souvenir shop, restaurant, and faux tepee that seem so typical of this quasi-north tourist area.

After half an hour we get passing lanes and more traffic. There are still signs warning of moose but who are we kidding? At Huntsville, just after the divided highway begins, we get off 11 and turn east on 60. One of the great things about driving in Ontario is the number of different roads, the possibility of never having to go the same way twice. Nancy notices that gasoline is fifteen cents a litre cheaper than in Kapuskasing.

These are busy cottage roads, an interesting mix. On 60, there are upscale resorts. These may be the nineties' equivalents of the Caswell. Instead of shuffleboard, roast chicken, and sandy beaches, we are offered golf courses, gourmet dining, and fax machines in the rooms.

South on 35, we pass Dorset, Lake of Bays. And when we get onto 118, travelling temporarily north because no road in this part of the province goes exactly east–west or north–south, we find ourselves driving through an area heavily populated with cottages. The cottages are modest and oldish; only the churches have fresh coats of paint. There is no traffic now. We are about due north of Stony Lake, maybe about an hour's drive.

At Haliburton we take another road, 121, to Tory Hill, then 503 to Gooderham, which looks like an ideal candidate for cottage country yuppification but seems to have escaped it. Some communities succumb easily to the city influences, becoming what the cottagers and hobby farmers want them to be. Others stubbornly hang on to their identities. You never know, when you drive into a town, which it will be.

Of course, I'd like mark this fateful day with an excellent lunch in a fish-on-the-wall restaurant. None is available, not even the trendy kind where fish is on the wall and blackened fish is on the menu. We find a Chinese–Canadian place along the road. A sign on the wall says "3 Beer Limit (with a meal)." Outside, a dog is chained to a truck and barks. I order a western sandwich.

Aside from getting lost at Buckhorn, less than ten minutes from our destination, the rest of the trip is fine. For this close to Labour Day, the countryside looks surprisingly lush and green. At 2:05, we hit the marina at Stony Lake. We are back.

# CONCLUSION

## *Canada's Next Century and*
## *Other Leftover Details*

This is September 5, the sixth hot, sunny day in a row. By my somewhat complicated calculations, this is Day 76 of the trip. Also staying at Mary's cottage with us are Karen and Kristhof, newly-weds from Switzerland. They have a rented car and are just starting out to see Canada. Karen has been here before and knows what she wants to see. They have already been in Montreal. Now they will go to Toronto, then up through Algonquin Park to Sudbury, then to Ottawa. Everybody has a certain Canada trip in mind.

We've been here six days, enjoying being in one place. The kids were out for a while. Mary told us about her play in Toronto, one we missed entirely. John's getting ready to do *Slam* in Ottawa. We talk, probably incessantly, about what we've seen, what we've learned, if anything. We tell our families about the conversation we had as we were heading down 507 the other day (from Gooderham to Buckhorn). I was trying to think summing-up thoughts, and was about as defeated by that as I was in trying to imagine a theme for the book at the outset. Can you sum up a country that takes weeks to drive across, has dozens of landscapes and just as many kinds of people? Isn't it the most supreme arrogance to think you can get a handle on it? Suddenly the spirit of Pollyanna of Green Gables came over me and I said to Nancy: "You know, I can count on the fingers of one hand the number of unpleasant people we met in seventy-five days." And we started through the exercise of trying to remember people we hadn't liked.

There was some institutional unpleasantness – disembodied voices on telephone lines, at 800 numbers; the front-desk people at the Algonquin who wouldn't tell me what room I was in; some anonymous vehicular unpleasantness – people in cars doing aggressive things, mostly guys with Alberta plates. But otherwise it was impossible to pinpoint people who had not been as nice as nice could be. From a distance we didn't like the guy in the restaurant in St. John's who insisted that his boys take their entire dinner from the salad bar. We didn't like all the parents who threatened their kids. We didn't like the guy in Sundridge who criticized the roast chicken. We disapproved of the people on the Inland Passage ferry who took up four seats each with their luggage and jackets. But if that was the full extent, we were going to have a tough time building a vacation horror story out of it.

So there's a summary: seventy-six days on the road in Canada and we saw maybe four people we didn't like. We always felt safe, always felt comfortable, always felt welcome, always felt surrounded by beauty, always felt at home. That says quite a bit about the country. If we felt less at home in Quebec, we know what to do about that – more French lessons, more practice. If we felt less at home in B.C., we'll just keep going back.

Betty wanted to know about our stay at Lake Louise and climbing to Lake Agnes. Mary Parker, the guest star for the Superior route, showed us her photographs of the Tobermory–Thessalon–Kenora leg. We told John about seeing his friends in Vancouver. One day I worked – if you can call it work sitting on a plastic rocking chair in the shade, with Stony Lake in the background and a young white pine, about three feet high, in the foreground, as I idly put stuff into a laptop computer. Beside me was a newspaper with some scrawling on the page with the weather map and some stories marked with an X. Those stories carried news about places we have been. It would be overstating the case to say we know those places now. But we've seen them, we know where they are, we know what they look like.

There was a cougar loose near the Metro Toronto Zoo, people thought. There was a fatal attack by a cougar near Princeton, B.C. The track of a hurricane was making huge waves on the East Coast, near Halifax. There was a picture of that, near Peggy's Cove, where we almost went, would have, if we hadn't been late for dinner in Halifax.

Familiar place names, different context. A story from La Baie said the terrible floods had washed away the tourist season in the Saguenay, as well as the bridges, roads, and houses. I wondered, in my plastic rocking chair, if that motel with the nice view of the lights across the river was still there. When you are a traveller you see only the bright side of places; it is hard to imagine that tragedy could happen there, or how anyone could want to move away.

The premiers of the provinces, all looking quite short, posed for a photograph at Jasper. High school students in Edmonton were being taught about the dangers of gambling. The weather for the Bruce Peninsula showed early morning fog, so we probably wouldn't see anything off the *Chi-Cheemaun* that day either. Too bad it's not nicer. It was 26°C in Winnipeg, 15°C in Banff. In Temagami, where we saw the canoe museum instead of the bombed bridge, protesters were setting up shop again, and a lodge owner said Why don't they stay in Toronto.

The Labour Day weekend was a little on the populated side on Stony Lake, with lots of boats and jetskis and other paraphernalia of the desperate funseeker. But we got to do something I've only done once before, stay at a cottage past Labour Day, after everyone has gone home. It is an experience worth rearranging your life for. You wait until the sun is setting and you go down to the dock and stand there, listening. Way in the distance you hear the quiet hum of traffic. And that's it. The rest is loon calls and whatever wind happens to be around. It is a quiet like no other.

We pack up the car for the last time, big suitcases in the back, the computer on top of the black suitcase. Then the small suit-cases in front, then, piled around them, the laundry, the books, the gin, the bag with all the disks and notebooks, jackets, the many maps we're not using. The cooler goes behind the front seat, no coffee in the Thermos this time, beside the almost unused picnic stuff from IKEA. The bag with the Ontario maps, the CAA books and accommodations books and all the spare pens, goes on the floor in front of the passenger seat, the notebook wedged between the seat and the centre compartment, a pen clipped onto the spirals. Then there's some other stuff just fired loose into the back seat, because who cares today.

And we're off at 11:40 a.m., taking our usual circuitous route (which we believe is shorter), taking back roads to Havelock and picking up 7 there. I try again to have a perspective on 7. If I had just arrived here from, say, Brandon, I would be admiring the trees and the lakes, trying to see over the bridges into the rivers and creeks.

We pick up the Ottawa CBC and the chatter is about more tele-vision channels. After Havelock is Marmora, where we turned south to go to Jim's farm back in July. We pass Madoc and Kaladar.

Then the hills with the boulders. We are behind a truck and the cars pile up behind it, but I am in no hurry.

The towns go by: Sharbot Lake, Wemyss, Perth, Carleton Place. Nancy drives, I take notes. Clouds. Red brick farmhouses. Very hot. Horses and fields. Split-rail fences. Deer warning signs. It looks like there is more activity along the highway than I remember. Maybe business is picking up.

I'm thinking that another way of getting a perspective on this trip is to plan the next one, a trip that will catch what we didn't see in three months – or at least catch some of it. Plotting that trip is one way of handling the enormity of the country, the enormity of the task of merely appreciating, never mind understanding, it.

Next time, we would drive through the Charlevoix, spend some time in Moncton, go over to Newfoundland and drive up the Viking Trail to St. Anthony's. In Nova Scotia we would see the western shore and maybe even Peggy's Cove. Maybe we would do the Cabot Trail again, because how could we not? And we would spend more time in New Brunswick, perhaps plan for high tide at the Reversing Falls. We would go to southwestern Ontario, see Stratford and Kitchener–Waterloo, visit the Lake Erie Shore and the southern part of Lake Huron. We would check out Niagara Falls and see how it compares to the West Edmonton Mall. We might stop again in Toronto, see the markets and even the SkyDome.

We would have to do Lake Superior again, making sure to see the Dionne Museum in North Bay on the way up, of course. In Manitoba we would see Lake Winnipeg and Gimli and the places where the Icelanders settled. We would try to get to Churchill, where the polar bears are, and Pine Falls, where my father worked as a missionary before he gave up religion and took up politics. In Saskatchewan, we would see the Gardiner Dam and Lake Diefenbaker and Prince Albert. In Alberta we would give Calgary a better shot, see Lethbridge and Waterton and Red Deer,

Kananaskis and the Icefields Parkway and try for the Peace River country up north. In B.C. we would drive the highway from Lilloet through Whistler and Squamish. We would see the Queen Charlottes. We would go back to Vancouver Island, take a week near Tofino, and do the Pacific Rim National Park.

Another trip would be simply to reverse what we did this time. Start on the Pacific in June and work our way back to the Atlantic in August. It would be a different perspective – on the trees, the crops, and especially the people. We might see Vancouver Island uncrowded; we might see gridlock at Green Gables. We would hit places at different times of day, when we had the time and the energy to look at them. The rhythm would change. A town at sunrise is very different from the same town at sunset. Doing the trip again, even in reverse, we'd know some extremely nice places to stay, and a few to avoid.

Near Carleton Place, a house with a big Canadian flag on it reminds me of a story I read recently about the government having a tough time keeping up with the demand for the flags it is giving away. I'm not surprised. Travelling through a country and living in it are not the same: we know that. Every town has its dark side, its unhappiness. But we didn't hear many people saying that they wanted to get away from where they were. We didn't hear many people apologizing for their homes, their home towns. And we certainly didn't hear anyone apologizing for Canada, despairing for its existence. We were warned that people, hearing we were from Ottawa, would be unfriendly. That was nonsense. People aren't like that in Canada. For them, politics takes place on one level; life takes place on another. But now I'm generalizing, something I promised I would not do.

We hit the Queensway, the expressway on the outskirts of Ottawa, at 2:47, passing Palladium Drive, which is still named that even though the new arena isn't called the Palladium any more. I love that. Given the way things work around here, it may be called

Palladium Drive forever. Decades from now, someone may want to rename the arena after it.

We go up the rise by Eagleson Road, the one where you can look ahead and see all of Ottawa spread out in front of you, and the Parliament Buildings if you look really hard past the downtown office towers and hotels. We hit the top of the rise and the whole downtown, including the Peace Tower, is obscured in haze. It is 31°C and not raining. We are in our driveway at 3:00 p.m., three months, two days, and 24,863 kilometres after we started. Not only are we still married, but we actually had fun. The car still runs beautifully, and, if we don't have huge insights into the country, we have at least fond memories of it.

I think we are going to miss the rhythm of the road, the idea of getting up in the morning, knowing you're driving but not sure what you're going to see, the possibility, always, of something unexpected and quite wonderful just around the next corner. And we're going to miss the focus the road gives to life, the feeling that what matters is not what's on the news but what's on the highway. In a way, we're in a bubble. But that's not a bad place to be, and I would argue that we get, from the road, a more balanced perspective on what's important than those who live each of their days reacting to headlines.

What does Canada need, you ask, to enter the twenty-first century? More passing lanes. More ferries. Reading lamps on both sides of the bed. Bridges you can see off. More animals beside the road. And more Canadians.

## ACKNOWLEDGEMENTS

Many people were extremely helpful in the planning and travelling that went into this book, although none of them should have to take any blame for it. The most helpful, before, during, and even after, was Nancy, without whom it would have been absolutely impossible to do this, and not much fun either. It was her lot in life each day to pore over the guide books, the maps and accommodation guides, then spend what must have seemed like hours on the phone, and sometimes was, trying to get us a place to stay or a seat on a ferry or our automobile insurance renewed. She did all the accounting, the faster half of the driving, and all of the picture-taking. The pictures don't show here, but they were great to have in front of me when I sat down to write, trying to recall what a certain place looked like. They also helped me to reconstruct the mood of the trip, which was always good, and she can take credit for that too. Nancy also did all of the laundry (I helped fold a couple of times; the rest of the time I claimed I needed to work on my notes) and 98 per cent of the postcards. She listened patiently to theories and produced some of her own, which I have occasionally pilfered. Most important, she endured every single one of the moods I am capable of producing over a three-month period in a car. I have invited her on the next trip and hope she will accept.

My publisher, editor, and fellow Scot, Doug Gibson, was as encouraging as always on this, our fourth project together. In his editing, Doug consistently amazed me with his knowledge of what is where in Canada. Many times he was able to tell me that I could not have been looking at what I thought I was looking at from a given spot – a sunset, a mountain, an ocean – because I was facing the wrong way. This invariably sent me back to my map collection and invariably forced me to conclude he was right – except maybe for once in Saskatoon.

I owe a debt to my editors at the *Ottawa Citizen*, particularly Jim Travers, Sharon Burnside, and Don Butler, for letting me loose on the project. At *Maclean's*, where some columns written in progress were published, I am grateful to Bob Lewis, Michael Benedict, and Carl Mollins.

Many of the people who were nice to us on the road have been mentioned in the text, but deserve to be thanked again. Others, whom we either left behind or somehow missed on our travels, offered advice, analysis, and travel tips that were valuable. Here they all are, east to west:

In Atlantic Canada: Peter Pickersgill, Ken Harvey, and Jan Power (also Emma, Jordan, and Katherine), Sonia Harvey, Dick Cook, Dirk van Loon, Penny and Kate Carver, Stephanie Carver and Bill Greenlaw, Debby Carver and Tim Matthews, Tracy Westell and Avy Dolgoy, Andy Moir and Chris Callahan, Rose Potvin and Carmen Thompson.

In Central Canada: Steve Stafford, Dr. Wallace MacKinnon, Ruth Gordon (who, had she lived, would have caught many misspellings and blocked some metaphors), John Gordon, Brian Doyle, Randall Ware and Micheline Rochette, Doug and Brenda Small, Enid Delgatty Rutland, Gerry and Karen Zypchen, Simon Caters, John Watson, Ken Rockburn, Jerry Heath, Jim and Gwelda Thain, Tim and Joan Murray, Sally Lewis, Mary Gordon, Alison Gordon, Betty Thain, Mary and Stuart Parker, Ted and Cheryl

Lake, Ned and Shelagh Basher, Sharon Robinson, Susan Greer, John Macdonald, Elizabeth Campbell and Peter Carver.

In the West: Bill Millar, Michael and Sandra Cox, my terrific aunts, Lois and Ruth Gordon, Ewan Pow, Jack Gibson, Don Gardner, Brian Marshall, Terry and Colleen Mitchell, Harvey and Ginger Young, Boom and Ellie Cristall, Lyle and Bev Macson, Bruce and Barb Penton, Vern and Nettie Small, Peter and Sharon Butala, Guy and Margaret Vanderhaeghe, Gordon Morash, Rick Laiken, Peter and Kathy Maser, Bob and Mary Smith, Evelyn Kipp, Paul Conder, Jon Teague, Jill and Patrick Nagle, Iain Hunter and Louise Dickson.

All of you: thanks again. When you're ready for your Canada trip, we're ready to return the favour.

*Ottawa,*
*January, 1997*

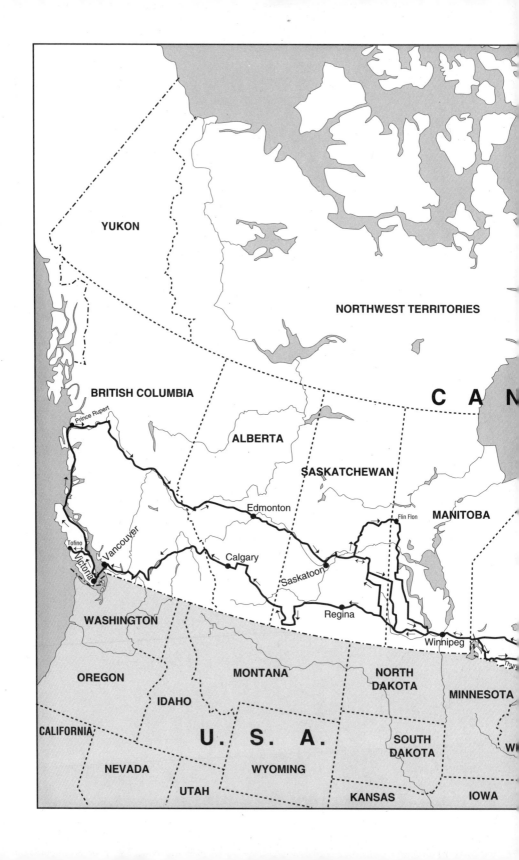